Machine Learning, Natural Language Processing, and Psychometrics

A volume in
The MARCES Book Series
Hong Jiao and Robert W. Lisstiz, *Series Editors*

The MARCES Book Series

Hong Jiao and Robert W. Lissitz, *Series Editors*

Machine Learning, Natural Language Processing, and Psychometrics

edited by

Hong Jiao
University of Maryland

Robert W. Lissitz
University of Maryland

≡IAP

INFORMATION AGE PUBLISHING, INC.
Charlotte, NC • www.infoagepub.com

Library of Congress Cataloging-in-Publication Data

A CIP record for this book is available from the Library of Congress
http://www.loc.gov

ISBN: 979-8-88730-604-9 (Paperback)
      979-8-88730-605-6 (Hardcover)
      979-8-88730-606-3 (E-Book)

CONTENTS

CHAPTER 1

THE ITEM FACTORY

Intelligent Automation in Support of Test Development at Scale

Alina A. von Davier[1]
Duolingo

Yigal Attali
Duolingo

Andrew Runge
Duolingo

Jacqueline Church
Duolingo

Yena Park
Duolingo

Geoff LaFlair
Duolingo

ABSTRACT

Test development for a high-volume, high-stakes test is a highly complex process. In this chapter, we are proposing a new framework for managing test development at scale, *the item factory*, based on the concept of intelligent automation used in manufacturing. This framework leverages automation for item generation and quality review processes, human expert review processes (including training and quality assurance), crowdsourcing (including pilot research studies, A/B testing, and large-sample pilots), and statistical quality assurance.

Machine Learning, Natural Language Processing, and Psychometrics, pages 1–25
Copyright © 2024 by Information Age Publishing
www.infoagepub.com

An educational assessment is an efficient way to evaluate individuals' skills. The test may be used for a variety of purposes, including university admissions, job applications, and immigration. As such, it is important that the test items are of high quality and that they accurately elicit and measure abilities being tested. Developing content for a test (i.e., designing, writing test items that are aligned with a theoretical framework and have good psychometric properties) can be a complex and time-consuming process, but it is essential for ensuring the reliability and validity of the test.

The first step in developing test items in a traditional assessment is to determine the purpose of the test, including the skills and constructs that it will assess. This is important because the evidence collected from test takers responses to these items needs to support the score users' interpretation of the test scores based on the stated purpose of the test, such as "test takers above this cut score are prepared for university study." See the work of Mislevy et al. (2003) on Evidence-Centered Design (ECD) and of Arieli-Attali et al. (2019) on the Extended Evidence-Centered Design (x-ECD) and examples of how human-centered values and ethical principles can be incorporated in test design. The purpose of the test informs the test design through means such as the review of existing published papers and materials, research on current trends in the domain of testing, and expert-led brainstorming sessions. These theoretical considerations will help create the task design, item specifications, guide the development of the items, and ensure that the items are aligned with the test's goals. Once the purpose and goals of the test have been established and the items and tasks designed, the next step is to create a pool of potential items and to decide on the design of test delivery, be it a linear test, an item-level adaptive test, a multistage adaptive test, or combinations of these designs. Traditionally, subject-matter experts (SME) write the items according to the item specifications defined in the previous stage. These items are then piloted through administration to samples of potential test takers that are representative of the testing populations for the purpose of ensuring the quality of items and estimating their difficulty and other item parameters. Both activities (item writing and pilot testing) are extremely time consuming, expensive, and difficult to manage efficiently and thus inherently result in a relatively smaller item pool, which in turn exposes the test to security concerns. In addition, the pilot samples are small and rarely representative of the testing population leading to concerns about the accuracy of their estimated parameters.

In this chapter, we are proposing a new framework for managing the item development stage for a high volume, high-stakes test which we refer to as *an item factory*, based on the concept of intelligent automation used in manufacturing. We integrate subsequent piloting activities into this framework and discuss how these activities could be made more efficient.

The items factory framework relies on automation, AI, and engineering principles to make the item development process scalable for high-volume, high-stakes testing in the digital era

The item factory relies on automation, namely automatic item generation methods (see Attali et al., 2022), automatic filtering of content for quality control, and automatic quality assurance systems for the individual items and for the item pool. The role of automation is to achieve efficiency, scalability, comparability, and standardization of the items, in order to support the quality and integrity of a large-scale high-stakes assessment program.

The item factory also relies on the use of AI. As AI systems become increasingly integrated into educational contexts, it is essential to consider the concept of human-centered AI and the role of trust in these systems. Human-centered AI refers to the design and implementation of AI technologies that prioritize human values, needs, and goals. In the context of educational testing, this means creating AI systems that align with pedagogical principles, ethical considerations of educators and learners, and test takers' experience and access. Trust in AI systems is crucial for the widespread adoption of these technologies, as users must feel confident in the reliability, fairness, and accuracy of the AI-driven recommendations and assessments. In this chapter we discuss human-centered AI in testing, addressing the design principles and ethical considerations that must be taken into account when collaborating with AI-driven tools. We emphasize the features of human-in-the-loop AI as one approach to support human-centered AI processes and decisions in the item factory. Furthermore, we refer to the notion of trust in AI systems, examining factors that influence user trust, such as transparency, explainability, and accountability. These principles are well captured by the Duolingo English Test Responsible AI Standards of Burstein (2023) and will be addressed throughout the chapter.

From a development perspective, we discuss the application of engineering principles for the design of an efficient item production process. The discussion will build on ideas from previous work on assessment engineering (Luecht, 2008), learning engineering (Dede, Richards, & Saxberg, 2019), and computational psychometrics (von Davier, 2017; von Davier et al, 2021).

BACKGROUND

The closest match for the item factory is the framework proposed by Luecht (2008) as assessment engineering. Like us, Luecht promotes the use of manufacturing principles to design, score and monitor the quality of online tests. Similarly, learning engineering (Dede et al, 2019) posits that the teaching and learning processes can be engineered in the sense of including evidence-based approaches, measurable outcomes, and iterative processes and can utilize student data from online platforms to provide feedback, and create better and more engaging learning experiences. The principles of learning engineering are similar to those used for item design and item field testing in an item factory. On the other hand, the computational psychometrics which is a framework (von Davier, 2017; von Davier et al., 2021) that emphasizes the need for the incorporation of data-driven algorithms in the psychometrics analyzes in order to address the expansion of the data size and data types in educational tests. These approaches informed the design and development of the Duolingo English Test item factory, and led to the extrapolation of the general principles for an item factory as described in this chapter.

THE ECOSYSTEM OF THE ITEM FACTORY

An item factory is a system that automates the production of test items for educational tests, using principles of architecture for smart manufacturing as described, for example, in NIST Advanced Manufacturing Series 300-1 (Barkmeyer & Wallace, 2016), in addition to the traditional assessment science principles. These principles are described in the next section.

The ecosystem of an item factory for a high-stakes test consists of several components, including subject-matter experts (SMEs), item and test creation following ECD, eECD, and human-centered values and ethical principles, automatic tools for scalability and item generation, and a human review process as part of the human-in-the-loop approach by using a flexible platform. The item factory ecosystem includes both a machine-centered component (automatic tools for generating and reviewing items) and a human-centered component (SMEs who are involved in the design, review, and editing of the items, and managers that oversee the whole process). Hence the item factory is an example of the human-in-the-loop-AI ecosystem, where human experts are involved in the system's decisions. This supports the factors that influence user trust, such as transparency, explainability, and accountability.

In the next section, we will discuss the principles of architecture for smart manufacturing and how they can be applied to the development of an item factory for an assessment.

PRINCIPLES OF ARCHITECTURE
FOR SMART MANUFACTURING

The principles of architecture for smart manufacturing as described in NIST Advanced Manufacturing Series 300-1 include:

1. *Modularity*: This principle involves breaking down the manufacturing process into smaller, more manageable components that can be easily rearranged or replaced.
2. *Interoperability*: This principle involves the ability of different systems and components to work together seamlessly.
3. *Reusability*: This principle involves the ability to reuse components or systems in different contexts or applications.
4. *Flexibility*: This principle involves the ability to adapt to changing requirements or conditions.
5. *Scalability*: This principle involves the ability to expand or contract the system as needed.
6. *Maintainability*: This principle involves the ability to easily maintain and repair the system.

These principles can be applied to the development of an item factory for an assessment in several ways. First, modularity allows for the creation of different modules or components that can be easily reused, or rearranged, or replaced. For example, an item factory may include modules for and within item generation, item review, and item editing. This allows for flexibility in the production process, as different modules can be added or removed as needed. In a hybrid-digital system, some item types may be developed by human experts only, and therefore, this process may constitute a separate module within the item generation component.

Interoperability requires that the many components of the system, such as the automatic tools for item generation and the platform for review and editing, work together seamlessly in order to produce high-quality test items.

Reusability is another key principle in the development of an item factory. By using reusable components or systems, the production process can be more efficient and cost-effective. For example, an item factory may use a database of previously generated items that can be modified and reused for different tests, such as the Practice Test, a free opportunity to experience the testing process.

Flexibility requires that the item factory is able to adapt and produce items that reflect the changes in test design as skills and testing needs change over time. This may involve updating the automatic tools or modifying the review process.

Scalability is critical for an item factory, as the demand for test items is high since having a large item pool protects the integrity and validity of the test scores in case items are harvested through nefarious methods. On a practice test, the need for scalability is lower than on a certified test; hence, the system needs to be able to expand or contract as needed in order to meet these changing demands.

Finally, maintainability is crucial for the long-term success of an item factory. By designing the system with easy maintenance and repair in mind, the production process can be more efficient and cost-effective. In the case of the item factory this means that we need to identify the relevant metrics for the success of the system and build a quality control system for monitoring these metrics. See Liao et al. (2022) for an example of such a system for monitoring test scores. A similar system is needed for monitoring the item development process.

One of the advantages of following these six principles in designing the item factory is that one can develop metrics to monitor and improve the system's performance for each of these levels, as well as aggregated metrics. This will be discussed later in the chapter.

ITEM GENERATION

In this section we describe the first part of the item factory process: item generation.

Item Design

The first step in generating items is item design. Researchers and test developers design item prototypes according to a particular theoretical framework and the test design principles. More importantly, for the item factory proposed here, the item design must include considerations for automatic item generation (AIG), automatic scoring, and for ensuring test integrity (see Burstein et al., 2022). Then, these prototypes are piloted in research settings and iteratively revised and improved. Once they are satisfied with the items, test developers finalize item specifications that describe the constructs and subconstructs the item type is intended to measure, the intended difficulty of the item, user interaction details, grading mechanisms, instructions, etc. The design step is similar to the first steps in a traditional test design. An item factory is by definition geared to create items for existing item types, and less so to develop a new item type, but since the factory is modular and has a systematic approach to test development, many features can be used or reused to design new and complex item types. See Attali et al (2022).

Most of this work is manual and requires a high level of expertise, although processes can be created to follow the six principles of smart manufacturing here as well.

As mentioned before, the item factory relies on automation. Hence, once the potential item types, specifications, and examples of items for each item type have been designed, the next step is to use automatic tools to generate items following these specifications, format, and style. These tools can include computer programs, algorithms, and other automated processes that can quickly generate a large number of items based on certain criteria. These tools can be used to generate items that are grammatically correct, assess specific skills or abilities, and meet other criteria that have been established for the test. In principle, the items could be generated at scale by human experts, and this effort would require a large operational unit, and a large number of staff involved in the quality control. This is how the traditional assessments have operated over the past 60 years. Moreover, the cornerstone of a modern item factory is that it has the potential to integrate AIG into the test development process instead of an extremely complex, expensive and insular human item generation.

Item Generation at Scale

The development of an item factory for a global high-stakes test is a complex task that requires the integration of various tools and processes. Although automatic item generation has been used for a while now (see Gierl et al., 2012), the way one can generate items at scale nowadays takes advantage of the rapid progress in artificial intelligence (AI). Attali et al. (2022) present a significant advance in item generation that allows test developers to use AIG for complex item types, in contrast to the approaches in Gierl that are extremely limited in application. This application, however, is anything but simple. It requires multiple considerations and iterations that are described below. It is possible that in the future, AIG will become simpler and more standardized. At the core of this ecosystem is the use of natural language processing (NLP) models, such as large language models (LLMs; GPT-3, GPT-4, BERT, etc), to generate test items. These models are trained on large datasets of text-based content and are able to generate complex items that mimic human-generated questions and responses (see Brown et al., 2020, and Khan et al., 2020). Sphinx (Khan et al., 2020), for instance, is a hybrid system that automatically generates reading texts using advanced language modeling techniques, but relies on human experts to generate reading comprehension questions, and item models to generate simple grammatical questions, such as sentence fragment correction questions.

GPT-4 is a powerful model that can generate a wide range of test items, including multiple-choice questions, short-answer questions, and free-response questions. Other generative models may be considered and combined with the LLMs, depending on the availability and on the needs. For example, *Stable Diffusion* (Rombach et al., 2022) is a large computational model for generating images that may be suitable for test items making use of images.

Once the LLM has been selected, it is important to fine-tune the model and the prompt to ensure that high-quality items are generated. Fine-tuning the model involves training the model on a specific dataset of the content of interest, adjusting the model's parameters, and evaluating the results. It is also important to consider the specifications, format and content of the test items, as different test formats may require different types of items. Fine-tuning the prompt involves design improvements and engineering efforts for developing better scripts for more efficient prompts.

Once the model is trained and fine-tuned, the next step is to use it to generate a large number of test items. The process of designing an item type with AIG in mind is extremely complex, and until very recently it was intractable for almost any complex item type. Attali et al. (2022) showed how AIG was possible for an interactive reading task and LaFlair et al (2023) showed how to use AIG for an interactive listening task that includes virtual agents. The model can be used in conjunction with additional automated tools to generate hundreds or even thousands of items in a short period of time. However, it is important to note that not all of these items will be suitable for use on the test. In order to ensure that only high-quality items are included, the item factory must include a series of (automatic) filters to remove biased and inappropriate content and a set of human reviews (at least at this stage of development, in 2023) to identify problematic content that the automated filters miss. This is described next.

ITEM REVIEW

In this section we discuss how the item factory supports the item review and how the item review follows the human-centered values of fairness and ethics. This discussion is contextualized in the argument-based fairness approach developed for AI-enhanced assessments (Huggings-Manley, 2022) and incorporates diversity and inclusion considerations from test design and content generation, to administration and post-administration quality control, all within the paradigm of the digital-first testing (see Burstein et al, 2022). In particular, we will describe automatic tools, human review, and principles for the sensitivity review process.

The process of item review involves both automatic filters and SMEs reviews. Both activities are facilitated by a flexible platform and a human management system that allow for real time transitions from one phase to the next and for the SMEs collaboration. We will describe these in the rest of the section.

Automatic Item Review

One important aspect of the item factory ecosystem is the use of automatic filters for quality control. These filters also use language models to check both the prompts and the items for quality and for biases. These models are trained to detect patterns of language that may be biased or discriminatory, and can be used to flag items that may be inappropriate for use on the test. This is especially important for global tests, as different cultures and languages may have different views on what is customary and acceptable.

In addition to automated filters on the items' text, the item factory may also include other tools to check for biases. For example, the factory may include a tool that checks for images or graphics that may be inappropriate or offensive. Given that many tests include images or graphics as part of the test items, this may be particularly important. The automated item review with automatic filters also follows the principles of smart manufacturing, as all six principles can be implemented and followed. As mentioned above, metrics can be developed to help improve or monitor the processes of item quality.

Last but not least, the item factory includes a platform that facilitates human review. This is described in detail in the next subsection.

Subject-Matter Expert Item Review

The item factory relies on the human-in-the-loop approach to support transparency, explainability, and accountability of the testing program. Several types of reviews are considered as part of the item factory. For example, the Fairness and Bias (FAB) review is a key step in the content review process, where two to three reviewers separately judge each stimulus and award a fail or pass decision based on internal FAB guidelines adapted from Zieky (2016). These reviews are described in more detail next.

Once the items have been generated and screened automatically for quality and biases, the next step is for the SMEs to review and edit the items to ensure that they (a) are of high quality and (b) meet the standards of the test. This may involve editing the wording of the items to make them clearer or more concise, or adding additional information or context to the items.

For new item types, it is customary to conduct focus groups and test the items with a group of potential test takers to ensure that the new items are effective at measuring the desired skills and abilities. This step is not directly part of the item factory, because the factory is most appropriate for existing item types, but it is an essential part of the item development process, it requires human input, and it supports the introduction of new item types both in traditional and modern item development.

During the review process, the reviewers should also consider factors such as the difficulty of the items, the clarity of the instructions, and the appropriateness of the content. If any items are deemed inappropriate or do not meet the test's criteria, they should be removed from the pool of potential items.

This part of the item factory has two major systems: (a) a flexible platform that facilitates an asynchronous online human review, (b) and a human management component to monitor the quality of the reviews.

Item Review Platform

After the items have been generated, they are reviewed and edited (if applicable) by a team of expert reviewers who are knowledgeable about the test's goals, constructs, and subconstructs on an item review platform to ensure that the items are accurate, relevant, and appropriate for the test. The platform needs to be flexible and allow for real-time editorial work and collaboration.

An item review platform is a tool designed to facilitate the review of item content by SMEs. This type of platform typically includes a collaborative space where reviewers can incorporate their suggestions into the items and receive feedback, as well as a system for tracking editorial suggestions, delivering and displaying feedback on editorial suggestions, and managing the review process.

One key feature of an item review platform is the ability to manage the tasks and results of human reviews. This includes assigning specific items to be reviewed, setting deadlines for reviews, and tracking the review progress. The platform may also include tools for collaborating with other reviewers, such as discussion forums or document sharing capabilities. This feature of the platform is the core of the system and it is what makes it a factory, where automation and human expertise come together to produce quality content efficiently and elegantly.

Item Reviewers

Item reviewers are SMEs in the constructs being measured by the test. The manager of the reviewers ensures that the reviewers are trained on the item specifications and scoring rubrics, and calibrated according to the standards of the assessment program. The manager develops the necessary training materials and sets up the training and calibration sessions. This work is similar to traditional item development, particularly in parallel with the training of the graders for constructed response items—see Wang & von Davier (2014). The reviewers are also monitored for the quality of their work.

Quality Control

The platform follows the six principles of smart manufacturing and includes metrics for monitoring reviewers' work (e.g., score distribution, time distribution, attempts, etc.) and item quality (e.g., the number of edits, the number of reviewers per item, and the rate of agreement among the reviewers, if applicable). The overall quality of the items can be tracked following the metrics recommended in Allaouf (2007), the statistical quality control methods described in Lee and von Davier (2013), and the architecture and visualization described in Liao et al. (2022).

EXAMPLE OF AN ITEM FACTORY

In this section we describe the item factory developed for the Duolingo English Test (DET; Cardwell et. al., 2022). The Duolingo English Test is a high-stakes English language test that can be taken any time, anywhere in the world, as long as one has access to a decent internet connection and a quiet space. It is a digital-first assessment, meaning that it was designed to be digital from the beginning, allowing it to easily incorporate automatic tools and AI models as needed. As a high-stakes test it is essential that its items are of high quality, fair towards all test takers, and culturally appropriate for a diverse range of individuals. To ensure that these standards are met, the DET item factory utilizes human-in-the-loop-approach to AI: a combination of automatic tools and human design and review to generate and edit items as described above. Figure 1.1 describes the stages and the iterations of the whole process for generating items. The item factory for the DET includes an A/B testing platform for item design that is described next.

Item Design

In the DET setting, the item design process for new item types is theory-based. Researchers create several variants of the new item types according to the x-ECD (Arieli-Attali et al., 2019), the theoretical ecosystem framework for digital-first assessments (see Burstein et al., 2022; Langenfeld et al., 2022), and the Common European Framework (CEFR; Council of Europe, 2020). The first draft of the item specifications are also created at this stage. After several item variants are designed, they are field tested.

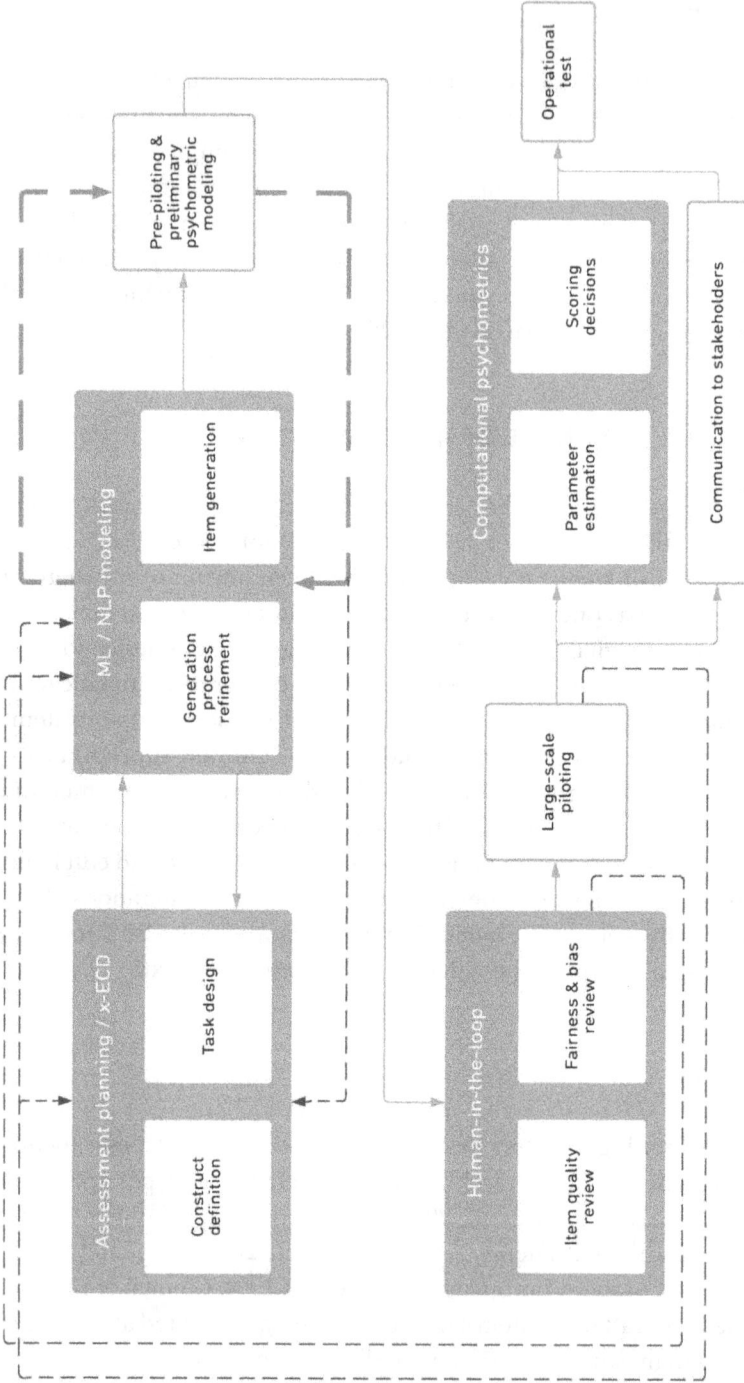

Figure 1.1 The item development process of the Duolingo English test.

A/B Testing

A traditional approach in assessment has been that of field testing. Field testing can be done by administering the items to a group of test takers and collecting data on their responses. This data can then be analyzed to determine the reliability and validity of the items. In traditional test development, this procedure is time consuming and expensive. In a digital-first assessment, this process can be shortened and improved by leveraging the available online platforms. In the DET setting a pre-pilot platform is used for field testing (a testing bed for research questions where potential test takers opt in to participate and try out new item types as part of their practice efforts).

This is the high-stakes test equivalent of the A/B testing platform for which the Duolingo learning app is known. This alternative approach to A/B testing is necessary in the context of a high-stakes test, as experimentation in the certified test would jeopardize the comparability and standardization of test sessions. This large-sample, iterative, alternative A/B testing of different item features on potential test takers is key for the quality of the items. The data gleaned from the pre-pilot platform is used to evaluate the interaction of test takers with the questions, estimate the difficulty level, receive feedback on the item design, and iterate on the design of items. It takes several iterations and field testing to achieve the desired item format.

Item Generation

The next component of the DET item factory is the generation of items at scale; this is accomplished by the use of LLMs to generate items in order to scale up the test development process. These tools use algorithms to create questions and tasks that are designed by researchers in a way that matches the format and content of the existing items on the test. This helps to ensure that the items produced are consistent with the test format and relevant to the skills being measured. See Figure 1.2 for an illustration of how we used GPT-3 in 2021 to generate passages for an academically oriented interactive reading task. With only three examples from sociology, business, and biology, GPT-3 is able to create as many passages as needed from any domain and any topic (for example, medical technologies). For a detailed description of the use of AI for item generation at Duolingo, see Attali et al (2022).

Item Review

While automatic tools are helpful in generating items, they are not perfect. That is why the next step in the process is a review of the items. The

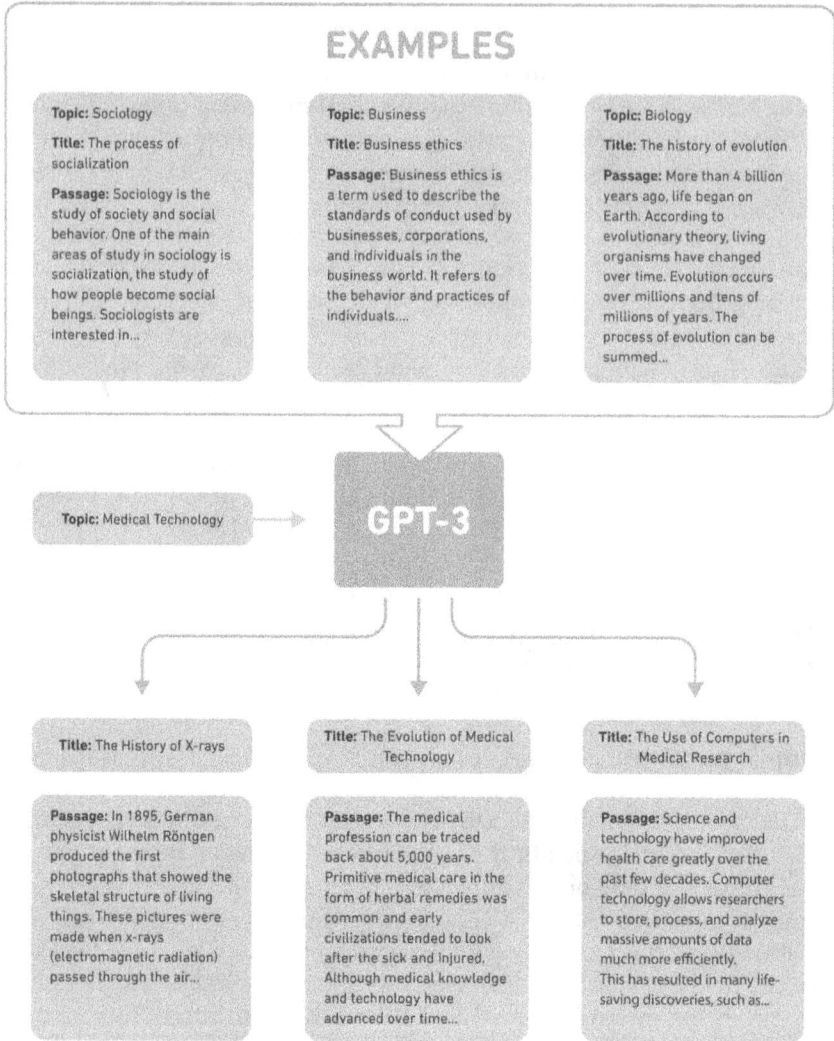

Figure 1.2 Passage generation for an interactive reading task on the Duolingo English test.

first review is automatic, using LLMs to filter content that is inappropriate and insufficient for high-stakes tests. This automatic filter is helpful, though not sufficient.

After the automatic review, the items go to humans for review. This review includes several components, such as an item quality review, a fairness and bias review, and a fact check.

The quality review is designed to ensure that the items are clear and easy to understand, and that they are relevant to the DET and language skills being measured. This review is conducted by a team of expert test developers and item writers who are familiar with the test format and content.

The fairness and bias review is a crucial component of the human review process, ensuring that all test takers have an equal opportunity to accurately demonstrate their language skills regardless of their gender, country, language, and culture of origin. This review ensures that the items do not unfairly advantage or disadvantage any particular group of test takers, and that they are appropriate for a diverse range of individuals. Items are examined to guarantee that they do not contain cultural and linguistic biases, offensive content, or content too specific to a culture that could unfairly impact certain test takers.

Finally, the fact check is carried out to ensure the factual accuracy of the items. This review is conducted by a team that verifies the accuracy of the content and makes sure that all information contained in the items is up-to-date and accurate. This new type of review was introduced in response to the fact that LLMs tend to "hallucinate" and confidently create misinformation. Inaccurate claims may potentially distract or confuse test takers in a way that impacts their performance, leading to construct-irrelevant variance. Fact checking is thus considered necessary to prevent any potential interference from sociocognitive factors on test performance (Burstein et al., 2022).

Overall, the combination of automatic tools and human review helps to ensure that the items produced for an international English language test are of high quality, fair towards all test takers, and culturally appropriate for a diverse range of individuals. This is not only essential for ensuring the validity and reliability of the test, but also for building trust with test takers and stakeholders.

In addition to the review process described above, our item factory also has a number of other quality control measures in place. For example, all items are subject to statistical analyses to ensure that they are measuring the skills they are intended to measure. Items that do not meet the required standards are either revised or discarded.

Furthermore, our item factory has a human management system that includes a number of activities to ensure that the review process is consistent and reliable. Reviewers are trained on the review criteria and are provided with detailed guidelines to follow. Reviewers also have access to a range of resources, including research materials and expert guidance, to help them in their work. Additionally, fairness reviewers receive random training items interspersed among the assigned items that help them stay aligned on the guidelines. The training items, on the surface, look exactly the same as regular items that they are asked to review. Once they submit a decision for a training item, they receive immediate feedback on (a) the true decision for the item and (b) the category within the guidelines that the item violates.

The Item Review Platform

To facilitate efficient item review processes, machine learning engineers, software engineers, and researchers developed an item review platform for the DET to support the review of item content by SMEs. As mentioned above, this type of platform typically includes a collaborative space but also an administrative space for managing the review process and the reviewers. The ability to manage the tasks and results of human reviewers is an important characteristic of the platform for scalability. See Figure 1.3 for an example from the administrator view.

As mentioned in the first part of the chapter, the main purpose of an item review platform is to efficiently facilitate the quality, fairness, and accuracy of the item content being reviewed. In the DET setting, this platform has been adapted to the DET needs, as an international language test. This includes the specific way in which the DET program manages reviewers, which is online and asynchronous, and the types of reviews needed such as checking for cultural bias and fact-checking the information contained within the item. The platform provides an administrator portal and a reviewer portal. The metrics evaluated pertain to both content review and reviewers' performance. See Figure 1.4 for an example from a training session from the reviewer portal.

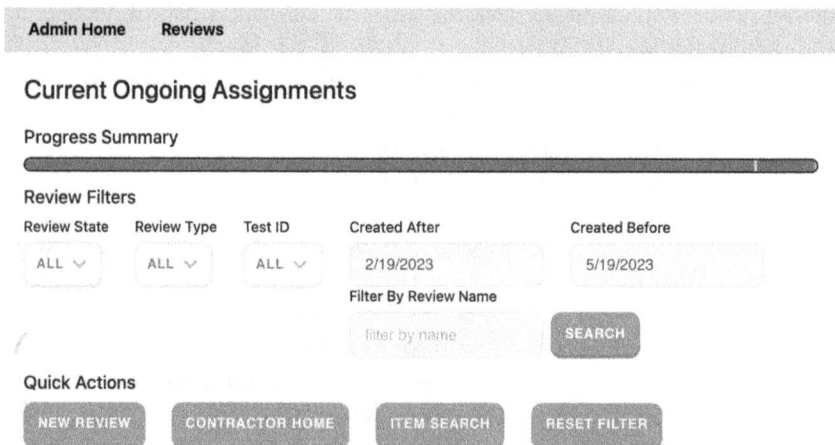

Figure 1.3   The DET Item Factory: A screenshot from the administrator view.

Training Feedback

Text	Your Label	Our Label	Your Codes	Our Codes	Your Comment	Explanation
Economic growth and urbanization are two closely related concepts that have helped shape North America. Economic growth refers to the increase in the production of goods and services within an economy over time. This growth can be measured through factors such as the Gross Domestic Product (GDP), which represents the total value of all goods and services produced in a country in a given year. North America, being one of the wealthiest and most prosperous regions in the world, has experienced significant ~~economic growth over the past few centuries~~	Fail	Pass	Global Relevance	N/A	Global relevance	This passage is a pass. I would suggest an edit to delete the judgment from the part of the sentence "North America, being one of the wealthiest and most prosperous regions in the world, has experienced significant economic growth over the past few centuries."

Figure 1.4 The DET Item Factory: A screenshot from the reviewer portal. The training feedback.

One potential benefit of using an item review platform is the ability to streamline the review process. Other benefits include allowing reviewers to see the items as they would appear on the test which is important for a digital-first test with dynamic content, allowing items to move smoothly between different stages of the review (item quality and fact check review, fairness and bias review, etc) with feedback from previous stages; the platform facilitates the managers' oversight in terms of progression of the reviewed content, reviewers' agreement and the opportunity to provide feedback at each stage. By centralizing the review process and providing a clear set of guidelines and instructions, reviewers can more easily focus on their specific tasks and provide more efficient feedback. This can also help to reduce the time and effort required to review content, allowing reviewers to focus on other tasks or projects. In addition, the platform includes metrics and visualizations to make sure that the items are aligned with the item/task specifications.

Another potential benefit of an item review platform is the ability to improve the quality of the content being reviewed. By providing a collaborative space for reviewers to share their editorial suggestions, the platform can help identify potential issues or areas for improvement that may not have been identified through individual review. Additionally, in a bespoke platform, it is possible to design reviewer calibration processes that fit the needs of the assessment development program. This can help to ensure that the content being reviewed is of the highest possible quality and free of any errors or biases. The item review process follows recommendations from Zieky (2006, 2016). Overall, an item review platform is a valuable tool for facilitating the review of item content by SMEs.

Piloting

After the items have been reviewed, they are administered to potential test takers as part of their practice efforts or directly on the certified test as unscored items, depending on the item type and situation. If any of the items do not perform well during the field testing, they are removed from the pool of potential items. The remaining items can then be included in the operational item bank. At Duolingo we introduced a computational psychometrics framework (von Davier, 2015; von Davier et al., 2021) for item piloting, where the LLMs and psychometric models such as IRT models are combined to estimate the item parameters (see McCarthy et al., 2021). In Settles et al. (2020), item difficulty is estimated by training supervised learning models on content rated according to the Common European Framework of References (CEFR) guidelines and labeled by human experts. For instance, for real vocabulary items in a yes/no vocabulary task, features like word length, frequency, and character-level attributes are used to estimate difficulty; for pseudowords, a character-level language model trained on a spoken English corpus can be a substitute for word frequency. For passages, both engineered features (such as sentence length, average log word frequency, token-type-ratio, and tf-idf) and neural network language model embeddings like BERT (Devlin et al., 2018) are used to estimate item difficulty. More recently, it has been demonstrated that these supervised learning models can be improved by incorporating operational data through fitting item response theory (IRT) models using a generalized linear mixed model (GLMM) (De Boeck & Wilson, 2004) within a multi-task supervised machine learning framework. The resulting models can achieve similar accuracy to a standard two-parameter IRT model while requiring significantly less test-taker response data (McCarthy et al., 2021). We are continuing to experiment and improve on this method for all item types.

Microservices

Microservices are an architectural and organizational approach to software development where software is composed of small independent services that communicate over well-defined APIs. They allow for a faster and modular development. In the case of the item factory, the item microservice keeps track of the development of an item (e.g., its metadata and editorial journey). It works together with other microservices to help manage the lifecycle of items from development and piloting, to adding them to item banks and administering them to test takers.

Quality Control

A monitoring system called AQuAP, Analytics for Quality Assurance of the Pool, is being developed to maintain the quality and health of the item bank through continuous evaluation of various metrics. This system is designed to keep experts informed with alerts and regular updates sent directly to their preferred communication channels, such as Slack or email. The monitoring system also incorporates visualizations to better identify patterns and trends within the item bank.

Metrics used to assess the item bank's performance can be applied at the individual item level or as aggregates. In order to maintain the quality of the item pool, we identified different metrics throughout the item development process, such as the exposure rate, item deterioration, empirical

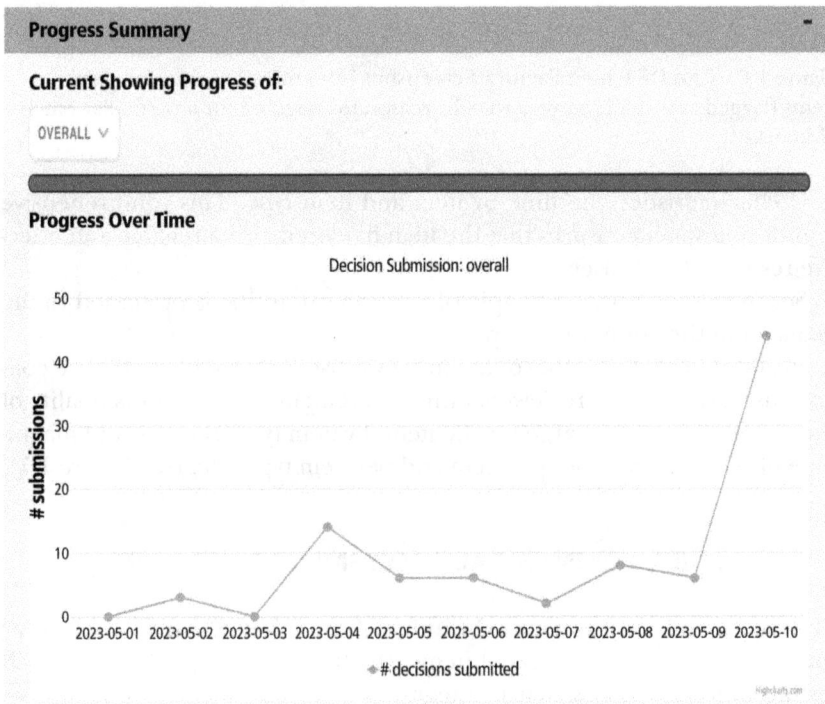

Figure 1.5 The DET Item Factory. Screenshot from the administrator portal. Example of the decisions submitted during a specific time window.

Review Summary   ▬

Flag Received from Any Reviewer

Number of Items with Flags
(From Any Reviewer)

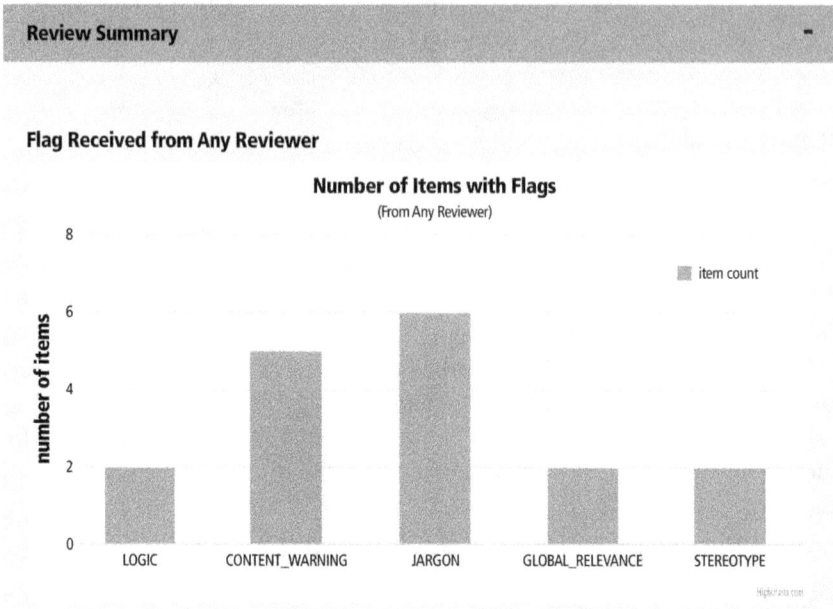

Figure 1.6 The DET Item Factory. Screenshot from the administrator portal. Items flagged across all the reviewers by reason for flagging for a particular batch of items.

item characteristics, the time by item and item type. This comprehensive monitoring system ensures that the item bank remains a reliable and effective resource for its users.

See Figure 1.6 for an example of a visualization that is presented to the manager in the administrator portal.

In addition to the quality of the items we also evaluate the SMEs: we continuously evaluate the reviewers rating agreement, the reviewers quality of review, the rate of discharge for the items by item type, the rate and magnitude of the editorial work per item and per item type, etc. (see Figure 1.7).

OTHER COMMERCIAL ASSESSMENT PLATFORMS

The DET Item Factory seems to be unique from other assessment platforms for (a) automatically generated items, (b) the pre-pilot platform for A/B testing of item features that is integrated with the other parts of the system, and c) the platform that is focused on the human review of items. Other commercial platforms do not have robust review workflows; often the item writing and review would occur in word processing documents or

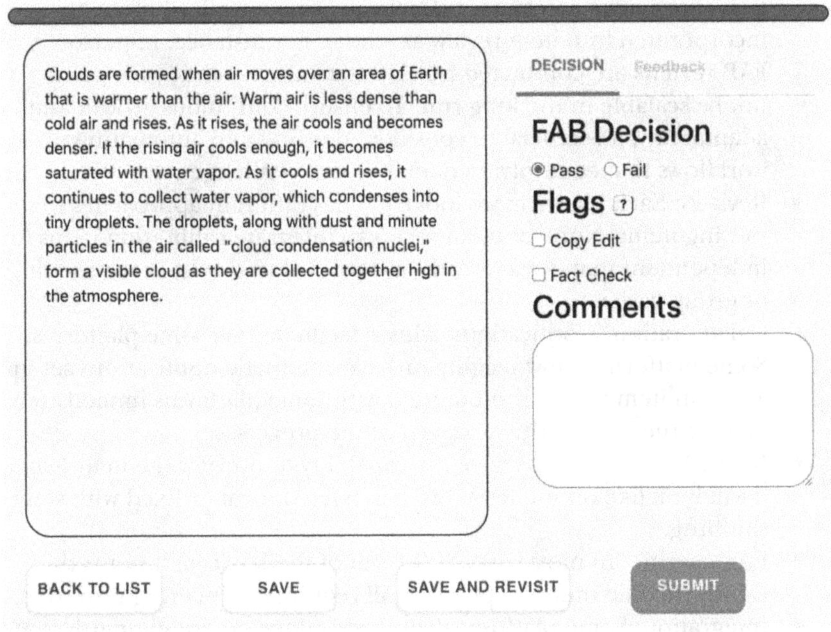

Figure 1.7   The DET Item Factory. Screenshot from the reviewer portal. Fairness and bias review for a specific item.

spreadsheet programs that would then be either uploaded via QTI (see also IMS Global Learning Consortium, downloaded July 7th, 2023) or manually added to the platform once finalized.

The table labeled Applications with IMS QTI support (https://en.wikipedia .org/wiki/QTI#Applications_with_IMS_QTI_support) provides a useful list of assessment platforms. Here we list a recommendation for considerations for choosing a platform.

Considerations on Evaluating Commercial Platforms

- Managing process/workflows: In today's fast-paced world, established workflows are essential for efficient and effective operations. However, there is always room for improvement and innovation. One key area to explore is the possibility of adjusting and automating these workflows. Several platforms still depend on manual processes, utilizing metadata and tagging to indicate the current step in the process. This can lead to inefficiencies and limitations in scalability. Furthermore, some platform processes lack an explicit

FAB (Formative Assessment Blueprint) step, with FAB often being incorporated into item review as a note. For instance, in-person FAB reviews are conducted for K12 state assessments, which may not be scalable in the long run. To ensure continuous growth and adaptability, it is crucial to consider adjusting and automating these workflows to meet evolving demands and challenges.

- Reviews: Each platform we looked at has different approaches to reviewing items. None of them seems to integrate calibration items for independent item review work (as opposed to synchronous training or group review).
- Collaboration/Notifications: This is facilitated on some platforms. Some platforms allow tagging or have automatic notifications set up when an item review is submitted, with some platforms immediately moving the item to the next part of the process.
- Items: Many platforms have the capability to preview the item (what it will look like on the test), often as a fixed form or fixed with some shuffling.
- Engineering: In most cases, if the out of the box tool is not sufficiently flexible then the process will require engineering resources.
- Integration: Some platforms have restrictions on the standards that they follow, say QTI, and have, therefore, a limited flexibility on what elements are customizable.
- Security: Many platforms have different levels of access by role (contractors, test developers, platform administrators).
- Accessibility: The idea is to have all intended users interact with the tool for example, some platforms integrate with a screen reader.
- Company support: Most platforms are set up to provide assessment and/or psychometric support (cost included in contract). They may impose their processes on the organization and one may not have a choice in using these services even if one doesn't need their support or if one needs more flexibility.

CONCLUSION

In this chapter we described the general principles of an item factory, a system that follows the six principles of smart manufacturing. We also provided more details on how such an item factory was developed for the Duolingo English Test, a digital-first high-stakes English language test. This item factory uses a combination of automatic tools and human review to generate and edit items for our global English language test. This process ensures that the items produced are of high quality, fair towards all test takers, and culturally appropriate for a diverse range of individuals. The use of automatic tools helps to ensure consistency and efficiency, while the human review process adds an extra level of quality control and ensures that the items meet the required standards. By combining these two approaches, we are able to produce items that are valid, reliable, and of the highest quality. Finally, once the items have been edited, reviewed, and piloted, they can be added to the test item bank, where they can be used to create new test versions. This process allows the item factory to continuously generate new items for the test, ensuring that the test remains up-to-date and relevant.

Overall, the development of an item factory for a global English language test is a complex and multifaceted process that requires the integration of various tools and processes. By using large language models to generate test items, and using filters to remove biased and inappropriate content, the item factory can ensure that the test remains high-quality and fair for all students. At Duolingo we also launched the Responsible AI Standards (Burstein, 2023) to guide our work and our own auditing processes. These standards, similarly to the item factory, are generalizable to other assessment programs. It is our hope that these tools and processes can help testing organizations adopt new technologies in responsible ways, so that we all together can better support all learners.

NOTE

1. In the first draft of the chapter the authors used the ChatGPT (open.ai) to generate passages of 200–300 words on specific parts of the chapter. These passages have been heavily edited by the authors and integrated with the authors' writing. The use of this technology in writing a chapter on an Item Factory is an intended pun.

REFERENCES

Allalouf, A. (2007). Quality control procedures in the scoring, equating, and reporting of test scores. *Educational Measurement: Issues and Practice, 26*(1), 36–46.

Barkmeyer, E., & Wallace, E. K. (2016). Reference architecture for smart manufacturing. Part I: Functional models. In *NIST Advanced Manufacturing Series 300-1*. http://dx.doi.org/10.6028/NIST.AMS.300-1

Burstein, J. (2023). *Responsible AI standards.* Duolingo. https://go.duolingo.com/ResponsibleAI

Burstein, J., LaFlair, G. T., Kunnan, A. J., & von Davier, A. A. (2021). *A theoretical assessment ecosystem for a digital-first assessment—The Duolingo English Test.* https://duolingo-papers.s3.amazonaws.com/other/det-assessment-ecosystem.pdf

Cardwell, R., Naismith, B., LaFlair, G. T., and Nydick, S. (2023). *Duolingo English Test: Technical manual.* Available online at: https://duolingo-testcenter.s3.amazonaws.com/media/resources/technical_manual.pdf

Council of Europe. (2020). *Common European framework of reference for languages: Learning, teaching, assessment—Companion volume.* Council of Europe Publishing. https://www.coe.int/lang-cefr

De Boeck, P., & Wilson, M. (Eds.). (2004). *Explanatory item response models: A generalized linear and nonlinear approach.* Springer.

Dede, C., Richards, J., & Saxberg, B. (2019). *Learning engineering for online education: Theoretical contexts and design-based examples.* Routledge.

Devlin, J., Chang, M. W., Lee, K., & Toutanova, K. (2018). *BERT: Pre-training of deep bidirectional transformers for language understanding.* arXiv preprint arXiv:1810.04805.

Gierl, M. J., Lai, H., & Turner, S. R. (2012). Using automatic item generation to create multiple-choice test items. *Medical Education, 46*(8), 757–765.

Huggins-Manley, C., Booth, B. M., & D'Mello, S. K. (2022). Toward argument-based fairness with an application to AI-enhanced educational assessments. *Journal of Educational Measurement, 59*(3), 362–388. https://doi.org/10.1111/jedm.12334

IMS Global Learning Consortium, Inc. (n.d.). Specification document license. IMS Global Learning Consortium. Retrieved July 7, 2023 from http://www.imsglobal.org/speclicense.html

Khan, S., Huang, Y., Pu, S., Tarasov, V., Andrade, A., Meisner, R., et al. (2020). *Sphinx: An automated generation system for English reading comprehension assessment.* Presentation at the International Conference on Learning Analytics and Knowledge, LAK20.

Mislevy, R. J., Almond, R. G., & Lukas, L. A. (2003). *A brief introduction to evidence-centered design.* ETS Research Report, RR 03-16. ETS.

LaFlair, G. T., Runge, A., Attali, Y., Park, Y., Church, J., & Goodwin, S. (2023). *Interactive listening—The Duolingo English Test* (DRR-23-01). Duolingo.

Lee, Y-H., & von Davier, A. A. (2013). Monitoring scale scores over time via quality control charts, model-based approaches, and time series techniques. *Psychometrika, 78,* 557–575.

Luecht, R. M. (2008). Assessment engineering in test design, development, assembly, and scoring. Invited keynote address at the Annual Meeting of the East Coast Organization of Language Testers (ECOLT), Washington, D.C.

McCarthy, A. D., Yancey, K. P., LaFlair, G. T., Egbert, J., Liao, M., & Settles, B. (2021). Jump-starting item parameters for adaptive language tests. In *Proceedings of the 2021 Conference on Empirical Methods in Natural Language Processing* (pp. 883–899).

Rombach, R., Blattmann, A., Lorenz, D., Esser, P., & Ommer, B. (2022, June). High-resolution image synthesis with latent diffusion models. In *2022 IEEE/CVF Conference on Computer Vision and Pattern Recognition* (CVPR) (pp. 10674–10685). IEEE.

Settles, B., LaFlair, G. T., & Hagiwara, M. (2020). Machine-learning driven language assessment. *Transactions of the Association of Computational Linguistics, 8,* 247–263.

von Davier, A.A. (2017). Computational psychometrics in support of collaborative educational assessments. *Journal of Educational Measurement, 54*(1), 3–11.

von Davier, A. A., Mislevy, R. J., & Hao, J. (2021). *Computational psychometrics: New methodologies for a new generation of digital learning and assessment. With examples in R and Python.* Springer Verlag.

Wang, Z., & von Davier, A.A. (2014). *Monitoring of scoring using the e-rater automated scoring system and human raters on a writing test.* ETS Research Report, RR-14-04. https://www.ets.org/research/policy_research_reports/publications/report/2014/jsek.html

Zieky, M. (2006). Fairness reviews in assessment. In S. M. Downing & T. M. Haladyna (Eds.), *Handbook of test development* (pp. 359–376). Routledge.

Zieky, M. J. (2016). Developing fair tests. In S. Lane, M. R. Raymond & T. M. Haladyna (Eds.), *Handbook of test development* (2nd ed.) (pp. 359–376). Routledge.

CHAPTER 2

APPLICATIONS OF TRANSFORMER NEURAL NETWORKS IN PROCESSING EXAMINEE RESPONSES

Susan Lottridge
Cambium Assessment, Inc.

ABSTRACT

Cambium Assessment, Inc.'s (CAI) has adopted transformer neural network models in all of its deployed engines for automated scoring of essays, constructed response items and speech items, for the detection of crisis text in student responses, and for providing feedback to students beyond rubric scores. In this chapter, we provide an overview of the transformer model architecture, the notion of pretraining and fine-tuning, subword tokenization, and the contextual and positional embeddings used to represent text. We then provide examples of performance of these models in the scoring of text and speech, crisis paper detection, and in feedback. We wrap up the chapter discussing key issues in transformers that complicate their use in assessment, including the lack of explainability, potential misalignment of data used to train transformers and examinee responses, limitations on length of respons-

Machine Learning, Natural Language Processing, and Psychometrics, pages 27–56
Copyright © 2024 by Information Age Publishing
www.infoagepub.com

es, and the technical requirements to support transformers for large-scale assessment. We hope that the chapter provides the measurement community with an understanding of the functioning of these powerful architectures and encourages measurement professionals to conduct research on these tools in support of new and better ways to measure what students know and can do.

Automated scoring (AS) is the use of statistical and computational linguistic methods to model scores produced by human raters to unconstrained open-ended test items such as essays. AS is used to produce scores more quickly, reduce scoring costs, ensure consistent scores within and across test administrations, and potentially produce higher-quality scores when combined with human scores (Foltz et al., 2020). AS engines and models are typically expected to produce scores that are interchangeable with human scores—that is, they are trained to emulate human scoring. While they may not use the same methods in score production (i.e., they do not understand language), the expectation is that the engine scores behave similarly to human scores and that they use features which generally reflect the rubric—and construct—measured by an item (Yan & Bridgeman, 2020).

Cambium Assessment, Inc. (CAI) has embraced deep learning, or multilayered neural networks, in its automated scoring engines since 2018. These approaches, particularly using transformer neural networks, have allowed CAI to score responses and items that we could not otherwise score or allows us to score them more accurately. In other words, they have enabled us to meet or exceed human scoring performance on many item types. Because they tend to work so well across classes of item types, CAI uses a consistent engine design across items. They also have demonstrated the capability to provide more fine-grained feedback beyond rubric scores, either in the form of annotations or checklist-type scores.

CAI's original scoring engine, Autoscore 1.0, used a classical engine architecture (Cahill & Evanini, 2020) that used a combination of expert-derived features and latent semantic features (LSA; Deerwester, Dumais, & Landauer, 1990) which were then entered into a statistical model (ordered probit regression). The expert-derived features included the identification of spelling and grammar errors, as well as computation of text complexity, sentence variety, and paragraphing. Considerable preprocessing was conducted—including text cleansing, spell correction, lemmatization, and vocabulary size restrictions—prior to submitting responses to the LSA model. While this engine met industry standards on most essay scoring items, it did not meet or exceed human benchmarks on some rubrics and item traits and it did not perform well on short constructed response items. It was our view that the short-comings of LSA were in part the issue; namely, LSA is a bag-of-words methodology that ignores word order and instead relies on global patterns of word occurrence. Additionally, even with the careful attention paid to text cleansing to create the LSA vocabulary, words not appearing in the vocabulary, such as mis-spelled words or rare words, were simply ignored during modeling. While LSA is a very powerful tool in modeling text, we felt that the emerging neural network language modeling capabilities were better suited for scoring responses.

CAI sought to complement the classical model with deep learning models, first with 1-dimensional convolutional (LeCun, 1989; Kim, 2014) and recurrent neural networks (Rumelhart, 1985; Hochreiter & Schmidhuber, 1997; Chung et al., 2014) and later with transformer networks (Vaswani et al., 2017). The inclusion of these approaches was intended to better model examinee language by first taking in consideration word order—locally in 1-D CNNs, and globally in recurrent neural networks. However, while these networks, when combined with word embeddings such as GLOVE (Pennington, 2014) and Google (Milokov et al., 2013), performed very well on ELA and math short constructed items (Ormerod et al., 2023) and in crisis alert detection (Ormerod & Harris, 2018; Burkhardt, Lottridge, & Woolf, 2021), they did not perform consistently well on essays. The creation of transformer models and their success in modeling natural language understanding tasks (Wang et al., 2018; Wang et al., 2020), coupled with their release of models in platforms such as huggingface,[1] allowed the team to examine their potential to model essay scoring and other tasks. Initial experimental results demonstrated that the application of the transformer, fine-tuned on the scoring tasks, produced generally better results than the classical model for essays, and supported similar or better performance on other tasks (Lottridge et al., 2023; Rodriguez, Jafari, & Ormerod, 2019). The evolution of the modeling approaches is described, by operational implementation, across six classes of CAI modeling tasks in Figure 2.1.

Of note, CAI operationally deployed models that included the transformer architecture in 2020 for crisis paper detection, essay scoring, and short answer scoring. CAI deployed a fully-transformer based engine for speech scoring in 2022 and is in the process of modeling writing feedback features for deployment in 2023. In this chapter, we will provide an overview of transformers, discuss in more detail their application at CAI, and end with a discussion on issues with transformers and future directions in their use in assessment.

OVERVIEW OF TRANSFORMERS

As suggested by their name, transformer networks have their roots in language translation because they transform text from one language into another. Their approach and architecture rely on five key concepts. These concepts are presented in Table 2.1 and are described in more detail in

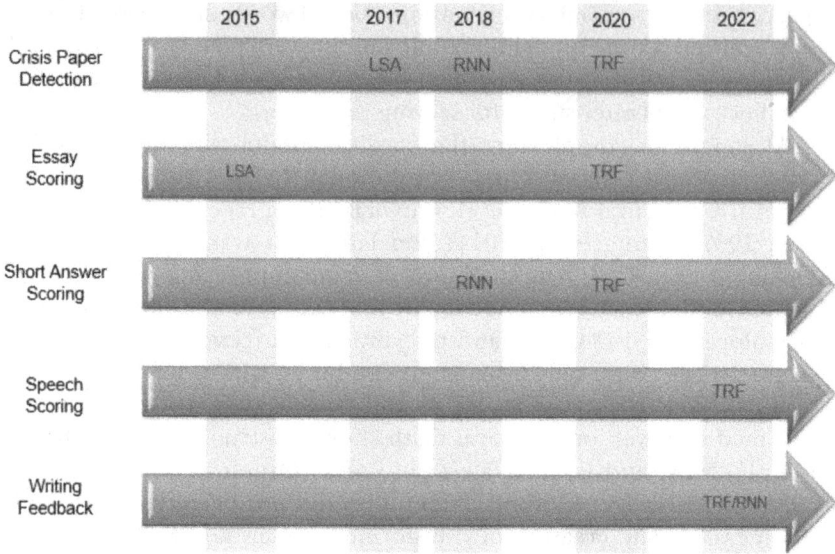

Figure 2.1 Evolution of modeling approaches across CAI engines from 2015–2022. *Note:* LSA refers to a classical framework with expert-derived features and LSA. RNN refers to the use of recurrent networks as stand-alone model (crisis paper detection) or combined with a classical method (short answer scoring). TRF refers to the use of transformer networks as stand-alone model (crisis paper detection and speech scoring) or combined with a classical method (essay and short answer scoring, writing feedback).

TABLE 2.1 Key Concepts of the Transformer	
Concept	**Description**
Architectural Elements	Feed-Forward networks and self-attention support back-propagation and batch gradient descent and the learning of relationships among words to optimize prediction task
Pretraining and Fine-tuning	Language model pretrained on one task and then fine-tuned on new task
Subword Tokenization	Vocabulary is mix of words, subwords, and characters
Contextual Embeddings	Token modeling uses full sentence versus small window of words
Positional Embeddings	Assign numeric value to word in each position and use in modeling task

the proceeding text. Because automated scoring focuses on prediction of scores, the discussion of transformers focuses on one part of their architecture (called an encoding); the second part of the transformer architecture (called a decoding) is not discussed as it is typically used for sequence-to-sequence tasks such as language translation.

Architectural Elements

The key architectural elements of the transformer are four-fold: (a) the preservation of words and word order throughout the model; (b) the use of feed forward networks, (c) the concept of attention; and (d) the use of multiple heads. These methods are described in the Vaswani (2017) paper and in Jay Alammar's excellent post, "The Illustrated Transformer."[2] Each transformer layer consists of a self-attention layer and a feed-forward network, and the transformer architecture consists of multiple layers (often 12 or 24). The use of feed forward networks throughout the transformer helped to solve the exploding or vanishing gradient problems that occurred for recurrent neural networks for long sequences (Vaswani, 2017). As noted in Figure 2.2, words, represented as high-dimensional embedding vectors, are inputs to the model and are represented throughout each transformer layer. Embedding vectors can be thought of as numerical representations of words whose purpose is to represent their semantic meaning.

The original transformer used self-attention, which can be thought of as a way for the model to ask itself which input words are most important in the predictive task. It is the self-attention mechanism that allows the transformer to model the relationship of words to one another in the predictive

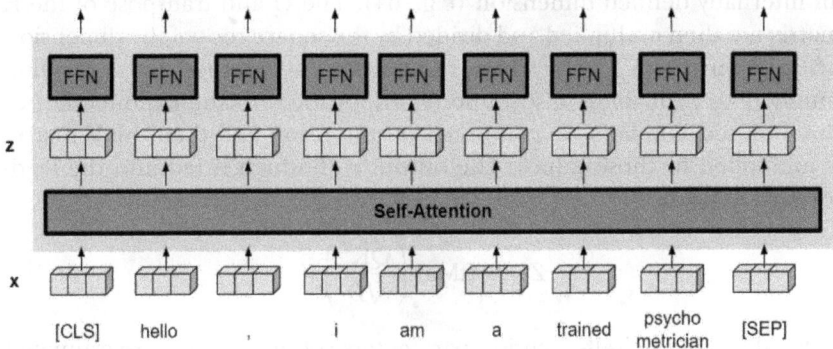

Figure 2.2 Visualization of a transformer layer. *Note:* FFN refers to a feed forward network. The [CLS] and [SEP] tokens refer to start and end of sentence tokens, respectively. Each token is associated with an embedding (x) in a high-dimensional embedding space. After self-attention is applied, the output embeddings (z) for each token are mapped to the feed forward network. Note that in many embeddings the word "psychometrician" would be divided into subwords; that is ignored for simplicity in this and later diagrams.

| [CLS] | hello | , | i | am | a | trained | psycho metrician | [SEP] |

| [CLS] | hello | , | i | am | a | trained | psycho metrician | [SEP] |

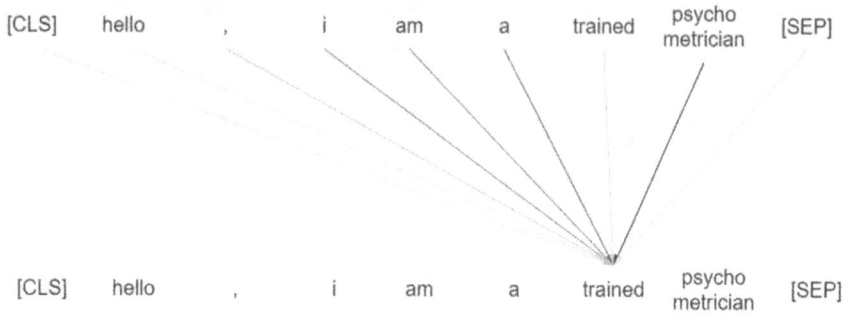

Figure 2.3 Visualization of a self-attention focusing on the prediction of the word "trained." *Note:* The shading of the arrows reflects the SoftMax probabilities, with darker lines associated with larger Softmax probabilities. The SoftMax probabilities would be computed for each output word in the sentence.

task. Figure 2.3 illustrates this relationship for the example in which the words 'I', 'am', 'a', and 'psychometrician' are all likely strongly associated with the word 'trained.' Later transformers used variations of self-attention to either improve its performance or to reduce its size.

Self-attention is implemented by using three matrices (Queries, Keys, Values). In self-attention, the input matrix (**X**), which is a NxE representing the number of words (*N*) by the embedding dimension (*E*) is multiplied by each of the Query, Key, and Value weights to produce **Q**, **K**, and **V** matrices. The Query, Key, and Value matrices are of the form ExD, where *D* is an internally defined dimension (e.g., 64). The **Q** and transpose of the **K** matrix are then multiplied and divided by the square root of the dimension of the matrices (e.g., 64). Then, the SoftMax—a method for converting numbers to probability distributions proportional to the exponentials of the inputted numbers—is computed on the result and then the **V** matrix is multiplied by those values. The output is *Z*, which is fed into the feed-forward network.

$$Z = \text{SoftMax}\left(\frac{QK^T}{\sqrt{D}}\right)V$$

Finally, multiple self-attention parameters (often, 8 or 12) are estimated in parallel to allow the model to 'learn' different aspects of the text. These parallel networks reflect different representations of the response that are then later combined for the predictive task and put output of the formula above back into the embedding dimension size, E. The notion of multiple 'heads' is common in neural nets and is thought to allow the model to leverage the use of different initializations and subsequent estimated weights that can capture different components of a complex input, akin to the brain having many neurons to represent a thought, action, or sensation (Goodfellow, Bengio, & Courville, 2016).

The feed-forward network appearing in Figure 2.2 takes as input the embedding for each word and produces an output for that word in the same dimension as the input. The parameter weights are the same for each word—that is, the same network is applied for each word. In Vaswani (2017), this network has one hidden layer. Besides these architectural details, other layers in the transformer manage details that support optimal calibration of parameters (e.g., normalization) and parameter management.

As an example of the size of one transformer layer, the Bidirectional Encoder Representations from Transformers or BERT model—which has an embedding dimension of 768, 64-dimension key-value-pairs and 12 attention heads—has 2,362,368 self-attention parameters. The two-layer feed forward network has many more parameters than the self-attention layer, because the hidden layer is four times the size of the input and output layers (4,722,432). Combined with the various other layers (3,072), BERT has a total of 7,087,872 parameters in one transformer layer. For the 12 transformer layers, the internal architecture has 85,054,464 parameters. When input embedding parameters and the output parameters are added into the model, the total number of parameters is approximately 110 million for the 12-layer BERT (i.e., BERT-Base) model.

Pretraining and Fine-Tuning

Transformers use the concepts of pretraining and fine-tuning, which can be thought of as an implementation of transfer learning whereby a model is trained for one task and is used for another task. Here, the model is pretrained on one task, and then fine-tuned to a target task. In the case of automated scoring, the target task is the score prediction. Model pretraining typically focuses on building a language model—that is, a model which can predict the next word in a sequence or a masked work in a sequence. As an example of this task, Figure 2.4 illustrates the results of a model trained to predict a masked word in a sentence. In this example, the model is tasked with prediction the masked word, identified by "[MASK]," using the surrounding words in the sentence. The model outputs reflect the SoftMax probabilities ('score'), the token id associated with the word, the word itself, and the sentence with the masked word replaced by the chosen word. The top choice, with a SoftMax probability of .083, was "professional," followed by "certified." The SoftMax probability is computed across all tokens in the model vocabulary (30,522, for BERT-Base).

Many pretrained models are publicly available. Researchers have the option of using the pre-existing models or training their own model. Pretraining

```
1  string = "Hello, I am a [MASK] psychometrician"
2  unmasker(string)

[{'score': 0.08286736905574799,
  'token': 2658,
  'token_str': 'professional',
  'sequence': 'hello, i am a professional psychometrician'},
 {'score': 0.08180428296327591,
  'token': 7378,
  'token_str': 'certified',
  'sequence': 'hello, i am a certified psychometrician'},
 {'score': 0.05984888970851898,
  'token': 4738,
  'token_str': 'trained',
  'sequence': 'hello, i am a trained psychometrician'},
 {'score': 0.04073508083820343,
  'token': 4591,
  'token_str': 'qualified',
  'sequence': 'hello, i am a qualified psychometrician'},
 {'score': 0.040260639041662216,
  'token': 12560,
  'token_str': 'practicing',
  'sequence': 'hello, i am a practicing psychometrician'}]
```

Figure 2.4 Top five masked word predictions for inputted sentence using the BERT pretrained model from Huggingface.

is expensive, requiring specialized hardware, large datasets, and technical expertise. Because of this, language models are typically trained once and effort is placed on downstream fine-tuning tasks. Table 2.2 presents examples of pretrained models, the data on which they were trained, the attention model, and the prediction task. Pretrained models typically come in different sizes. For example, BERT-Large has 330 million parameters, while BERT-Base has 110 million parameters (Devlin et al., 2018). Models can have both cased (i.e., have upper- and lower-case letters) or uncased versions (i.e., have only lower-case letters). As can be observed in the table, the models vary in the data used in training, the attention model, and the pretraining task. BERT was among first transformers and BERT-Base was used in the first deployment in CAI's essay scoring engine. We have found that the available models tend to perform similarly to one another across scoring tasks and have recently focused on using memory-efficient (i.e., small) pretrained transformer models (Ormerod, Malhotra, & Jafari, 2021). As an example, the first BERT-Base models deployed were 425MB and the current deployed models (ELECTRA-small) are 55MB (12 million parameters).

Pretraining one's own model requires six steps, including identifying the dataset on which to train, determining the training task (i.e., masked word prediction), preparing the data, building a tokenization scheme, choosing

TABLE 2.2   Example Pretrained Models

Type	Data	Model	Task
BERT (Devlin et al., 2018)	Wikipedia, BooksCorpus (3,200M words)	Self-attention	Predict masked word and next sentence
ELECTRA (Clark et al., 2020)	Wikipedia, BooksCorpus (3.3M words)	Self-attention plus adversarial training	Predict which tokens are replaced by a masked language model
ConvBERT (Jiang et al., 2020)	OpenWebText (32G)	Convolutional heads as self-attention	Predict which tokens were replaced by a masked language model
XLNet (Yang et al., 2020)	Wikipedia, BooksCorpus, Giga5, ClueWeb, Common Crawl (33B words)	Variant of autoregression + self-attention	Predict masked word
DeBERTa (He et al., 2021)	Wikipedia, BooksCorpus, OpenWebText, Stories (78G)	Separating out position and word embeddings in prediction	Predict masked word

the transformer model, and training the model (Figure 2.5). As noted earlier, most models use publicly available datasets, but other data could be used, such as examinee responses. The dataset, however, does need to be

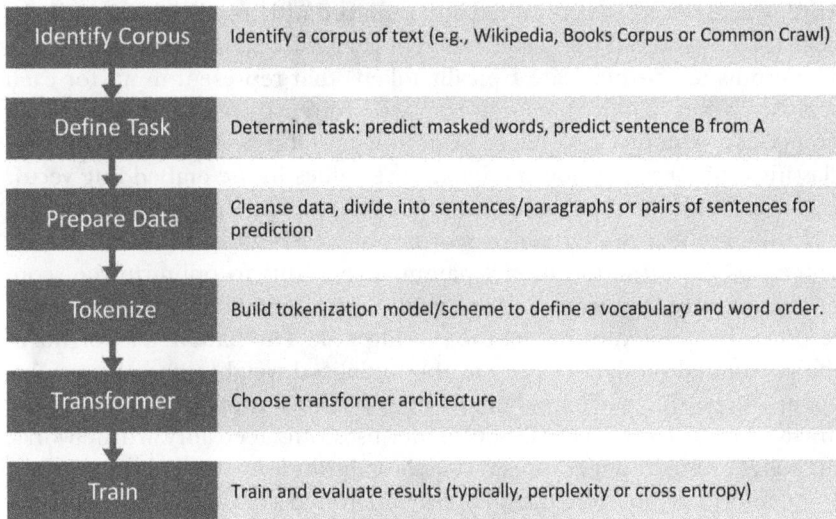

Identify Corpus	Identify a corpus of text (e.g., Wikipedia, Books Corpus or Common Crawl)
Define Task	Determine task: predict masked words, predict sentence B from A
Prepare Data	Cleanse data, divide into sentences/paragraphs or pairs of sentences for prediction
Tokenize	Build tokenization model/scheme to define a vocabulary and word order.
Transformer	Choose transformer architecture
Train	Train and evaluate results (typically, perplexity or cross entropy)

Figure 2.5   Steps for pretraining a transformer model.

quite large (at least a few gigabytes of text) to generate a robust model of the language because language use is complex. As noted earlier, the task is typically either predicting the next word from prior words or predicting masked words from those words surrounding the masked word. Training data are typically at the sentence or paragraph level. Example training data might be a set of tuples of sentences with masks and without masks ("Hello, I am a [MASK] psychometrician," "Hello, I am a professional psychometrician"; "I'm a trained psychometrician"). Most training examples will not include masking to maximize the data used to model language. In the case of BERT, approximately 15% of words were masked, and for some percentage of those the corrected versions were randomly chosen to be incorrect to address the potential for overfitting. In the case of next word prediction, the masked word always appears at the end of the phrase or sentence. Once the data are prepared, the vocabulary is created using the words appearing in the training data. Models such as BERT and DeBERTa that do not use adversarial methods are easier to train. Others, such as ELECTRA, are more complex as they are estimating two models: one to predict the masked words and another to detect which word was masked (if any). After these steps, one can train the model; this work is typically done on Tensor Processing Units (TPUs) or large Graphics Processing Units (GPUs). Model performance is evaluated using cross entropy or perplexity[3] on a held-out test set. A development set is also used to monitor training as well, and to determine when to end training.

Once a model is pretrained, it can then be fine-tuned for a specific task. In fine-tuning, the layer used during pretraining to predict the next word or masked word is removed and replaced with another layer (called a head). This head can use classification or regression as the statistical model. The inputs to this head are typically tokens that represent input for each representation of the examinee response (often the "[CLS]" token that prepends a sentence to signal its beginning). In this case, the input into the classification or regression model are the values in the embedding vector associated with the representation ("[CLS]" token in Figure 2.6).

In the context of automated scoring, one can think of the fine-tuning process as adjusting the model parameter weights to optimize the score prediction; in other words, the semantic representation of the examinee response is updated to reflect the scoring task. The parameter weights of the pretrained model are used as the initialized weights, and the weights are updated using batch gradient descent and back-propagation during the fine-tuning process. Because the model uses only feed forward networks, the weight updating mechanism is well-established.

As one final note on the value of fine-tuned transformers, Figure 2.7 illustrates the predictive quality on the Generalized Language Understanding Evaluation (GLUE) tasks (Table 2.3). As noted in the figure, the

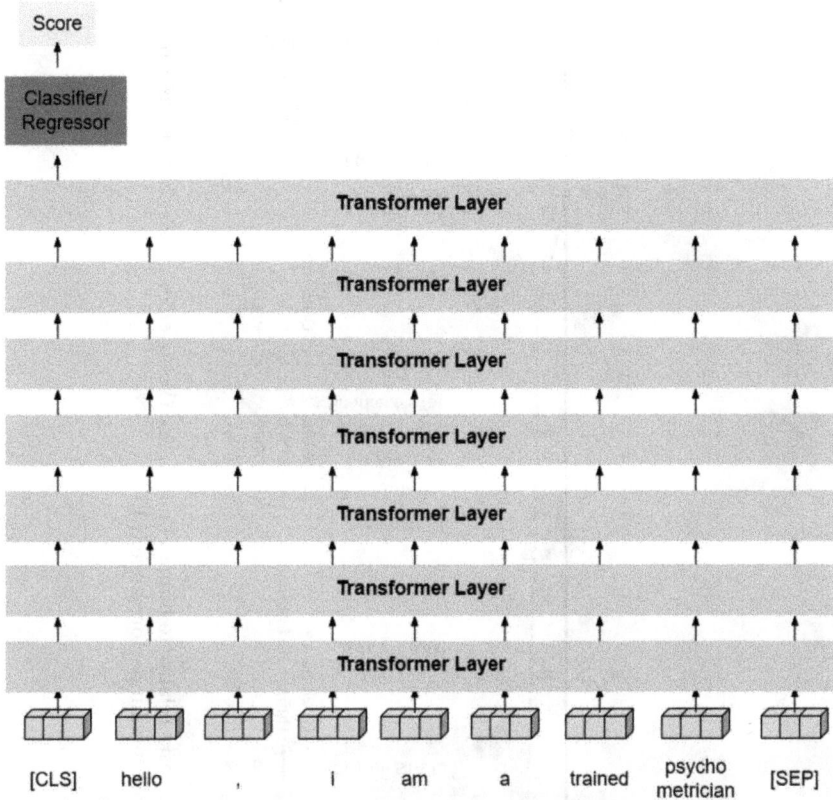

Figure 2.6 Fine-tuning design (using seven transformer layers). *Note:* Often 12 to 24 layers are used, but the number of layers is configurable.

OpenAI GPT model[4] represents one the first transformer attempts at modeling these tasks, and the improvement of the various transformer models (BERT, XLNet) illustrate the ability of transformers (or ensembles of transformers) to approximate or exceed the human performance benchmark (black line in the figure).

Subword Tokenization

As with all automated scoring engines, examinee responses are tokenized, or mapped into defined units. Tokens can be words, characters, or subwords. Tokens are represented in both contextual embeddings and positional embeddings (which are discussed in the next section). Embeddings that use character-level tokenization have relatively small vocabularies

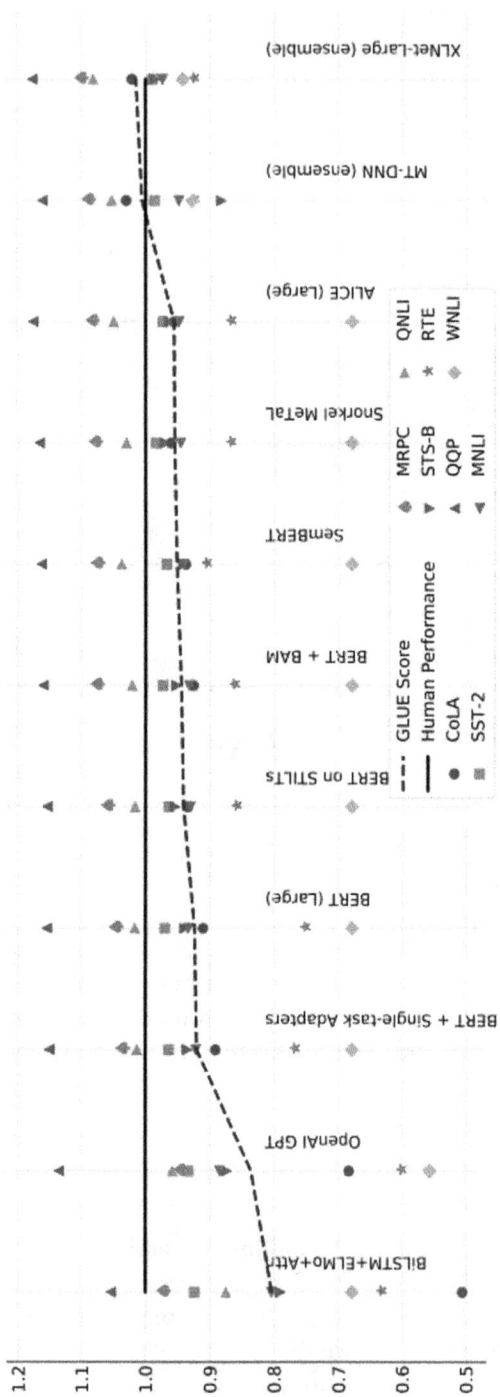

Figure 2.7 Deep neural network performance on GLUE tasks relative to human benchmark (Wang et al., 2020). *Note:* y-axis is rescaled agreement performance across all tasks, set such that human performance is 1.

TABLE 2.3 Generalized Language Understanding Evaluation (GLUE) Tasks

Type	Dataset Name	Task Description
Single—Sentence	CoLA	Is sentence grammatical?
Single—Sentence	SST-2	What is sentiment of sentence?
Sentence Similarity	MRPC	Is this a paraphrase of this sentence?
Sentence Similarity	QQP	Is this pair of questions semantically similar?
Sentence Similarity	STS-B	How similar are these pairs of sentences on a scale from 1 to 5?
Sentence Inference	MNLI	Does that sentence follow this sentence?
Sentence Inference	QNLI	Does this paragraph contain the answer to this question?
Sentence Inference	RTE	Is the relationship between sentence 2 and sentence 1 one of entailment, contradiction, or neutrality?
Sentence Inference	WNLI	Is this the referent for the pronoun in this sentence?

and are often robust to spelling errors; however, they can be difficult to interpret because letters do not carry semantic level information in the way that words do in language. Embeddings that use word tokenization retain semantic information but can require large vocabularies and thereby suffer from the effects of word sparsity (Guthrie et al., 2006). Subword embeddings offer a balance between character and word embeddings, by allowing the vocabulary to contain common words, common subwords, and all relevant characters. This approach supports the ability to model semantics without the drawbacks of sparsity (Sennrich et al., 2015). As an example, if the word 'psychometrician' is not a word in the vocabulary, it can be divided into three subword tokens: 'psycho', 'metric', and 'ian'.

Many transformers build vocabularies using a method called byte pair encoding (BPE; Gage, 1994). This approach iteratively and recursively builds a vocabulary of words and subwords based upon the frequency of their occurrence. Note that BPE does not build the vocabulary based upon the morphology of the words. This method follows the procedure in Figure 2.8. Once N iterations have been completed, then the vocabulary is created from the top K most frequent tokens, often while also ensuring to include all important characters if not in the top K tokens.

To illustrate the application of the BPE method on Abraham Lincoln's Gettysburg Address, the BPE was run for 200 iterations and the most frequent 87 words, subwords, and characters were selected. Figure 2.9 presents the results ordered by length. Note that this vocabulary is a mix of characters, words, and subwords, and that the subwords do not necessary have meaning. Additionally, note that the vocabulary is tied language of the speech itself—that is, the vocabulary tokens rely heavily on the text used to train it.

For j from 1 to N
- Tokenize text into words
- Divide each word into characters
- Get counts of all pairs of consecutive characters
- Pick top pair and rebuild vocab using that pair

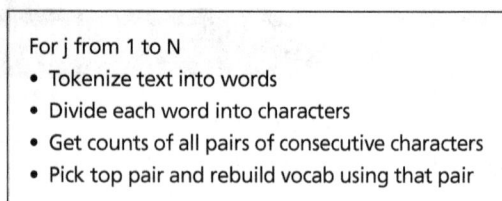

Figure 2.8   Byte-pair encoding procedure.

'-', '—', ',', '.', 'a', 'b', 'c', 'd', 'e', 'g', 'i', 'l', 't', 'w', 'y', 'an', 'at', 'be', 'ed', 'en', 'ga', 'he', 'in',
'is', 'it', 'iv', 'me', 'no', 'of', 'on', 'or', 'so', 'to', 'us', 'we', 'ago', 'all', 'and', 'are', 'can', 'far',
'for', 'men', 'new', 'not', 'our', 'the', 'ure', 'war', 'who', 'dead', 'four', 'from', 'gave',
'have', 'here', 'long', 'that', 'ther', 'they', 'this', 'what', 'equal', 'field', 'forth', 'great',
'score', 'seven', 'shall', 'sting', 'these', 'which', 'years', 'living', 'nation', 'people', 'rather',
'brought', 'created', 'fathers', 'liberty', 'dedicate', 'devotion', 'conceived', 'continent',
'dedicated', 'proposition',

Figure 2.9   Vocabulary of the "Gettysburg Address" after 200 iterations and choosing the top 87 tokens.

Contextual Embeddings

As noted earlier, word embeddings are vector representations of words and/or subwords (Milokov et al., 2013) and are a more efficient (i.e., re-duced-dimensionality) method to represent words than a dummy-coded (i.e., 1 if word exists and 0 otherwise) representation of a vocabulary. Anec-dotally, word embeddings are thought to represent semantic information, although this has not been systematically verified via empirical methods and is itself a difficult problem (Schnable et al., 2015). The idea underlying word embeddings is that words which appear in similar contexts should have high cosine-similarity (i.e., normalized dot product) values with one another, and those that do not appear in similar contexts should have low cosine-similarity.

Prior to transformers, word embeddings were trained using small con-text windows of approximately 5–10 words and the order of words in the window was not modeled. In these embeddings, words with multiple mean-ings would have one embedding value. For instance, the word "bank" in the phrase "steep bank" and the word "bank" in the phrase "bank account" have the same embedding vector. Transformers extended the embedding concept to include the entire context of the word and included word order in the modeling via the positional embedding (described next). In the later layers of a transformer model, the word "bank" would have different embeddings depending upon the context of use. As a result, transformer word embeddings are considered contextual embeddings.

Positional Embeddings

Transformer models include word order as inputs to the model by representing word order in a positional embedding. Word order can be represented using a function (i.e., fixed) or can be modeled as part of the pretraining process. In the original Vaswani transformer paper, the word order is represented using alternating sine and cosine functions. In many of the transformer models (e.g., BERT, ELECTRA), the positional embedding is summed with the contextual embeddings. In some, like DeBERTa, the positional embeddings are included as separate inputs in the prediction.

In the Vaswani paper (and many subsequent transformers including BERT), the positional embeddings are applied to each embedding dimension and each word using the following functions:

$$PE_{(pos,2i)} = \sin\left(\frac{pos}{10,000^{\frac{2i}{d}}}\right)$$

$$PE_{(pos,2i+1)} = \cos\left(\frac{pos}{10,000^{\frac{2i}{d}}}\right)$$

where *pos* refers to the order of the word in the response, i refers to the ith dimension in the embedding, and d refers to the size of the embedding. Note that for even embedding dimensions (e.g., $0, 2, 4$) the sine function is used, and for odd embedding dimensions, the cosine function is used. The perceived benefit of using the functional representation of order is that it can be used for text of any length, whereas a learned representation would not be able to represent order if a new piece of text exceeded the length of the learned model. Table 2.4 presents an illustration of the first eight positional embedding values for a 10-word piece of text.

CAI has investigated whether randomly shuffling words would impact the quality of score prediction for a Conventions trait and for semantically based traits such as making a claim and sustaining argument for the claim (Lottridge, et al., 2020). For half of the items studied, the transformer model (BERT) predicted the expected lowest rubric score for almost all shuffled essays in conventions; for the others, BERT assigned scores of higher than the minimum possible to most responses. This same result occurred also for the semantic traits. In our view, these results suggest that the priority of

TABLE 2.4   Snippet of First 8 Positional Embedding Values for Each of 10 Words (Embedding size = 64)

Word position	Positional embedding values							
	0	1	2	3	4	5	6	7
0	0.00	1.00	0.00	1.00	0.00	1.00	0.00	1.00
1	0.84	0.54	0.68	0.73	0.53	0.85	0.41	0.91
2	0.91	−0.42	1.00	0.07	0.90	0.43	0.75	0.66
3	0.14	−0.99	0.78	−0.63	0.99	−0.12	0.95	0.30
4	−0.76	−0.65	0.14	−0.99	0.78	−0.63	0.99	−0.12
5	−0.96	0.28	−0.57	−0.82	0.32	−0.95	0.86	−0.51
6	−0.28	0.96	−0.98	−0.21	−0.23	−0.97	0.57	−0.82
7	0.66	0.75	−0.86	0.51	−0.71	−0.70	0.19	−0.98
8	0.99	−0.15	−0.28	0.96	−0.98	−0.21	−0.23	−0.97
9	0.41	−0.91	0.45	0.89	−0.94	0.34	−0.61	−0.79

contextual versus positional embeddings can present themselves differently in fine-tuned scoring tasks. These results also suggest that the use of condition code or non-attempt algorithms remains a critical step in automated scoring, even with the use of transformers.

TRANSFORMER APPLICATIONS

As noted in the introduction, CAI has used transformers in automated scoring of text and speech, in the detection of crisis alerts, and for providing feedback in writing. In this section, we describe the approach and results of this modeling.

Automated Scoring

At CAI, we have deployed and used models for essay scoring, short writing constructed response items, reading comprehension items, and mathematics items. We have also modeled other item types including speech responses in English Language Learner assessments, items which have students write sentences that reflect edits of one or more provided sentences, as well as science and social studies short constructed response items. We have also modeled items written in Spanish.

Across these item types, we have had success in matching human performance in essays and the associated English Language Arts constructed response items, and in speech scoring. We have had uneven success with science and social studies, and no success with Spanish language items. Our hypothesis around science scoring performance is that the language used in science does not align well with those data used to train publicly available pretrained models and that science requires a level of correctness that is not always well-suited to the fine-tuning process described earlier. Our hypothesis around social studies scoring performance is that these items elicit such a wide variety of student responses that the models struggle to map patterns in languages to the rubric score. With regard to Spanish language items, we suspect that the lack of relevant Spanish pretrained models that map onto the variations in language use by students is the core reason. Finally, we have also had no success with generic scoring (i.e., one model applied to multiple items) for rubrics that focus on what examinees write, versus how they write.

In this section, we provide small set of results to illustrate the performance of transformers in modeling. The first results are from a Fall 2022 reading comprehension competition sponsored by the National Assessment of Educational Progress (NAEP). The competition included a total of 20 items, nine in Grade 4 and eleven in Grade 8. There were twelve unique items; the same eight items were used in each of Grade 4 and 8. The datasets for training were quite large, ranging from 19,000 to 27,000 responses per item. Across the set of items, the top performers all used transformer architectures to model the responses. At CAI, we used memory-efficient models (ELECTRA, ConvBERT) that are deployed in production to help support the notion that transformer models can be used operationally to score responses. Models were trained for each item. Figure 2.10 outlines the results averaged across items.[5] While no set of models met the human quadratic weighted kappa benchmark of .905, the top few were quite close with the top engine QWK value of .888. As a comparison to classical LSA methods, when CAI modeled the items with an LSA-based approach, the QWK value was .71 on the test set, or about .17 lower than the transformer approach.

A second portion of the NAEP competition focused on how well automated scoring models could predict human scores when provided with no data beyond the responses used to train and qualify the human raters. At CAI, we trained a generic model using the item-specific responses and then fine-tuned the model using the 40 to 50 training and qualification responses provided. These results showed very poor performance for all submissions for the two items (Figure 2.11); the best performer showed an agreement .308 lower than the human agreement benchmark and CAI's model trailed behind that. These results suggest that, at least using current methods, generic modeling is not appropriate to be used as a replacement for human scoring. Future work on transformers will need to address how to train accurate generic models, and it is possible that this problem will be solved by the

**Submissions Meeting Accuracy
Requirements for Operational Use**

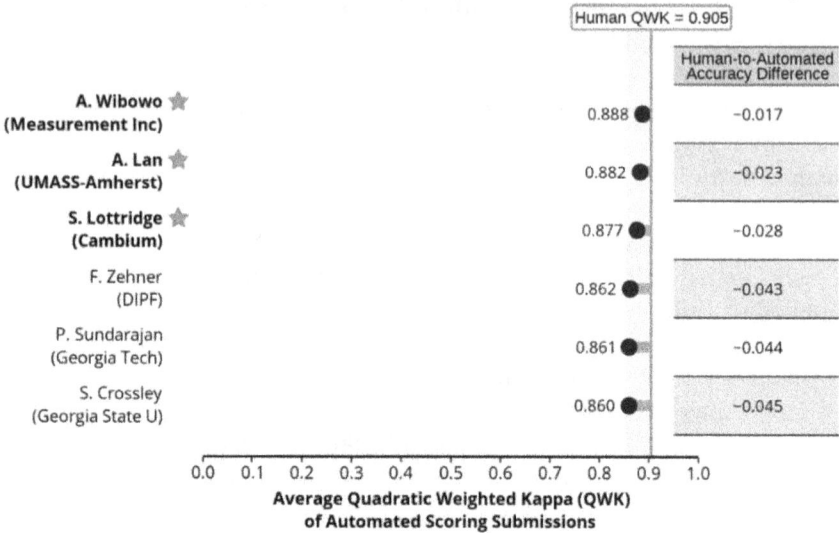

		Human QWK = 0.905	Human-to-Automated Accuracy Difference
A. Wibowo ⭐ (Measurement Inc)		0.888 ●	−0.017
A. Lan ⭐ (UMASS-Amherst)		0.882 ●	−0.023
S. Lottridge ⭐ (Cambium)		0.877 ●	−0.028
F. Zehner (DIPF)		0.862 ●	−0.043
P. Sundarajan (Georgia Tech)		0.861 ●	−0.044
S. Crossley (Georgia State U)		0.860 ●	−0.045

0.0   0.1   0.2   0.3   0.4   0.5   0.6   0.7   0.8   0.9   1.0

**Average Quadratic Weighted Kappa (QWK)
of Automated Scoring Submissions**

Figure 2.10   NAEP item-specific reading comprehension competition results. *Note:* Star symbol denotes grand prize winners. Agreement of automated scores with human scores is typically slightly lower than agreement between two human scorers. A decrease of less than 0.05 is considered acceptable to use automated models in practice. All awarded submissions have accuracy levels within this range

Generic-Level Competition Awardees

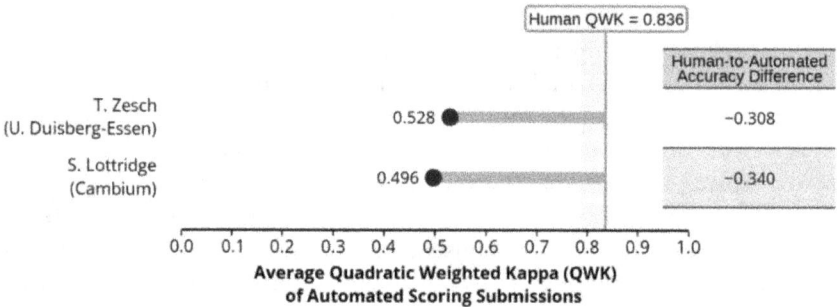

		Human QWK = 0.836	Human-to-Automated Accuracy Difference
T. Zesch (U. Duisberg-Essen)	0.528 ●		−0.308
S. Lottridge (Cambium)	0.496 ●		−0.340

0.0   0.1   0.2   0.3   0.4   0.5   0.6   0.7   0.8   0.9   1.0

**Average Quadratic Weighted Kappa (QWK)
of Automated Scoring Submissions**

Figure 2.11   NAEP generic reading comprehension competition results. *Note:* Agreement of automated scores with human scores is typically slightly lower than agreement between two human scorers. A decrease of less than 0.05 is considered acceptable to use automated models in practice. None of these models have accuracy levels within this range.

use of large language models (like ChatGPT) or by different architectural designs that can trained using smaller datasets (Gao et al., 2021).

Next, we provide results on speech scoring using transformer-based models (Lottridge et al., 2022). Fifteen items from an English Language Proficiency (ELP) assessment were modeled. Items ranged from grade 1 to grade 12, with score points ranging from 3 to 5. Three thousand responses were used to train and validate the engine, with 500 also transcribed to examine the quality of engine transcription. Responses were transcribed using each of two transformer-based engines (wav2vec2.0, Hsu et al., 2021; Unispeech, Wang et al., 2021) and then the transcribed texts were submitted to a one of two transformer-based text classification models, ELECTRA or FNet (Lee-Thorp et al., 2021). The outputs of these models were then entered into a logistic regression. The results (Table 2.5) suggest that the transformer-based architecture matched or exceeded human agreement for items grades 2 or higher but did not meet human performance for grade 1 items. The wav-2vec2.0 transcriber had an overall word error rate of 27%, while the Unispeech had a much higher word error rate of 64%. The wav2vec2.0 word error rate matched those published in other studies on children's speech (Chen et al., 2018; Metallinou & Cheng, 2014; Cheng et al., 2014).

Crisis Alert Detection

Students may disclose serious issues, such as anxiety, depression, suicide, self-harm, and abuse, in their written responses to K–12 assessments. These crisis alerts (Burkhardt et al., 2021) are identified via humans or automated engines and then routed to schools for intervention to support the student. At CAI, all written responses are processed by our Hotline engine; any response flagged as a potential alert by the engine is routed for human review

TABLE 2.5 Average Speech Scoring Results Across 15 Items

Grade Span	Word Error Rate		QWK			Exact Agreement		
	Uni-Speech	Wav2Vec 2.0	H1H2	HSAS	Diff	H1H2	HSAS	Diff
1	71%	40%	0.88	0.82	–0.06	81%	74%	–7%
2–3	71%	34%	0.87	0.89	0.02	74%	79%	5%
4–5	67%	30%	0.81	0.83	0.02	68%	74%	6%
6–8	65%	25%	0.82	0.85	0.03	65%	74%	9%
9–12	59%	22%	0.79	0.84	0.05	67%	77%	9%
All Grades	**64%**	**27%**	**0.81**	**0.84**	**0.03**	**68%**	**75%**	**7%**

and flagging. CAI processes approximately 85 million pieces of text in an academic year, and it is critical that students in crisis are identified quickly. To this end, we aim to process responses within an hour of receipt, even during times of heavy testing where millions of responses may arrive at an any given time.

At CAI, we fine-tune an ELECTRA transformer model to flag responses as potential alerts. The engine is trained on 1.2 million student responses, of which 2.1% were labeled as alerts.[6] The validation of the model uses two datasets; one set of 1,000,000 student responses that were unseen by the current engine and a set of 1,000 student responses that are known to be alerts. Because of the volume of responses, we want to minimize the responses routed for human review while also maintaining a high agreement rate on the true alerts (i.e., have a very low false negative rate). Table 2.6 illustrates the performance of the trained model when the ELECTRA threshold is set to route 0.15% of the responses. In the 1,000-alert sample, 98.4% are flagged by the engine when that that threshold is exceeded. As a reference, when using non-transformer neural networks, we needed to route 2% to obtain agreements of approximately 88%.

Feedback

Finally, we have also found that the transformer architecture can be useful in predicting more fine-grained feedback to help explain rubric-based scores. We believe that providing such feedback can help students and teachers to better understand what to do next when assessment results are reported. This feedback can take the form of Boolean trait-based scores, as highlights of elements in the student writing itself, or combinations of the two.

TABLE 2.6 Performance of ELECTRA on Correctly Classifying Alerts at Various Thresholds

ELECTRA Threshold	Normal Responses (%)	Alerts (%)
0.017850	0.05%	96.3
0.006136	0.10%	97.6
0.004451	0.125%	98.1
0.003384	**0.15%**	**98.4**
0.002353	0.20%	98.5
0.001847	0.25%	98.7
0.000438	1.00%	99.8
0.000303	1.50%	99.8

Note: Bolded threshold is operational.

The first example maps an ELA rubric to specific elements needed to obtain a correct score (Table 2.7). The potential benefit of this approach is that the elements can be combined to produce a rubric score and to indicate to the student and teacher what the student has provided (and not provided) in his or her response. A set of 4,000 responses were first scored by humans on these elements and then a transformer-based engine was trained to predict the human element labels. Table 2.8 presents the results, by element, across a set of 7 items on a held-out validation sample. These results indicate that the engine can meet or exceed human labeling of these element and reflect transformer performance across a wide variety of ELA elements we have modeled.

The second example maps an ELA writing rubric onto organizational elements in the student responses themselves. In this study, we asked human raters to identify at the sentence level seven key writing elements that are critical in crafting a well-formed argumentative essay: introduction, controlling idea, evidence, elaboration, opposing position, transitions, and conclusion. Raters labeled approximately 18,000 grades 6–8

TABLE 2.7 Exemplar Feedback Elements

Feedback Element	Feedback Element Description
cite_1	The student correctly cites Source #1.
cite_2	The student correctly cites Source #2.
det_1	The student identifies an example from Source #1 in support of the claim.
det_2	The student identifies an example from Source #2 in support of the claim.
expl_1	The student provides an explanation of how the example from source #1 supports the claim.
expl_2	The student provides an explanation of how the example from source #2 supports the claim.

TABLE 2.8 Example Feedback Agreement Results (7 items)

Feedback Element	Exact Agreement			QWK			SMD	
	H1H2	HSAS	diff	H1H2	HSAS	diff	H1H2	HSAS
cite_1	88%	90%	2%	70%	71%	1%	0.01	0.04
cite_2	89%	93%	3%	75%	82%	7%	0.00	−0.01
det_1	84%	89%	4%	63%	69%	7%	0.02	−0.02
det_2	88%	91%	3%	74%	82%	8%	0.01	0.02
expl_1	82%	89%	6%	49%	58%	9%	0.02	0.05
expl_2	87%	92%	5%	56%	65%	9%	0.00	0.07

Note: H1H2 = human–human agreement. HSAS = human–engine agreement.

TABLE 2.9 Illustrative Writing Element Annotation Human–Human and Human–Engine Agreements on a Single Item as Held-Out Set		
	Kappa	
Writing Element	Human–Human	Human–Engine
Introduction	.75	.75
Controlling Idea	.78	.80
Evidence	.66	.76
Elaboration	.64	.70
Opposing Idea	.60	.60
Transitions	.41	.55
Conclusion	.78	.85

argumentation essays (three per grade), with a 15% second read. Then, a transformer-based engine (XLNet) was trained to identify the elements in the text, with an emphasis on predicting elements in prompts the engine had not seen. While these results are preliminary, they do suggest that trained human raters can label elements with a reasonable degree of accuracy, and that an engine can do the same. The metric for evaluation was Cohen's kappa, which was computed for each writing element across the essays. For example, if rater 1 flagged two sentences as introductions in a 12-sentence essay, and rater 2 flagged three sentences as introductions in the same essay and they overlapped on two sentences, this would produce a kappa value of .75 for introduction for that essay. This process is conducted for each essay with two annotations and averaged across the essays. Table 2.9 provides example results for one item and our results indicate similar performance across other items.

Across these examples, transformers show great promise in being able to provide both labels and annotations that are aligned with human labels and annotations. In our view, this is among the most exciting developments in automated scoring as it suggests the ability to provide informative and construct-aligned feedback that teachers and students can use to understand in the learning process.

CONSIDERATIONS

While the transformer-based models have resulted in substantial improvement in scoring and feedback, they are not perfect. Transformer models have a number of issues, including lack of explainability, alignment of data used to train the pretrained model with the examinee writing, limitations on response length, and the need for technical for technical skillsets outside of those typically in the field (Lottridge et al., 2023).

Lack of Explainability

Explainability is a substantial limitation of transformer models. Because transformers are extremely complex and contain millions of parameters that have no explicit meaning, it is very difficult to identify the aspects of the model that are contributing to a score and it is very difficult to interpret them. This has a number of validity and implementation issues. First, it can be difficult to explain to stakeholders, except at a high level, how a transformer model works; in other words, the models can have poor face validity. Second, one key element in the validation of scores is the ability to show how the model features (in this case, the last prediction layer) are associated with the rubric. Third, it can be very difficult to determine the source of the problem when the model fails to accurately reproduce human scores; effort is placed on hyperparameter tuning and on processing the text prior to submitting it to the model but understanding what is happening in the model itself to explain poor performance is yet an unsolved problem. Relatedly, when issues are encountered in scoring such as a poorly scored response, it can be difficult to debug the source of the problem.

Two primary methods are used for explainability. The first method examines the relationship of text elements (e.g., words, phrases, sentences) on the predicted score by producing saliency maps that associate continuous values with the score prediction. A large (positive or negative) saliency value indicates a strong (positive or negative) relationship to the model-predicted score, and a small (positive or negative) saliency value indicates a weak (positive or negative) relationship to the model-predicted score. To produce the values, text elements are removed or replaced with non-meaningful elements and the impact of that change on the predicted score is computed. Three current approaches are LIME (Ribeiro et al., 2016), SHAP (Lundberg & Lee, 2017), and gradient methods (Danilevsky et al., 2020). A recent study examining explainability of crisis alerts illustrated that LIME and a gradient method (Integrated Gradients or IG; Sundararajan et al., 2017) showed moderate to weak ability to provide explanations aligned with those provided by humans (Lottridge, et al., 2023; Table 2.10). As an illustration of saliency predictions and how they can be mapped to annotations, Table 2.11 presents an example set of saliency values mapped to Boolean annotations when values are positive for two engine explainability models and the human annotation.

The second method considers the last layer of the transformer model, prior to the classification prediction, as implicit features (Ormerod, 2022). These features, while not directly interpretable, are representations of the

TABLE 2.10 Number of Responses, Percent of Alert Words, and Agreement Metrics for the Expert Annotator and Engine Annotation Method

Annotation Method	Percent Alert Words		Acc.	Prec.	Recall	F1	kappa	alpha
	HA	EA						
LIME_POS	63%	40%	67%	.77	.50	.56	.23	.13
IG_POS	63%	83%	67%	.65	.88	.69	.29	.18
IG_TOPN	63%	64%	74%	.69	.76	.68	.34	.29

Note: HA = Expert Human Annotator; EA = Engine Annotator; kappa = Cronbach's kappa; alpha = Krippendorff's alpha; LIME_POS = Positive saliency values computed with LIME are annotated as 1; IG_POS = Positive saliency values computed with IG are annotated as 1; IG_TOPN = Top N saliency values computed with IG are annotated as 1, where Top N set to match human labels.

Source: Lottridge et al., 2023

TABLE 2.11 Example Human and Engine Annotations on a Crisis Alert Response

Response Words	Human annotation	LIME		Integrated Gradients	
		Saliency	Annotation	Saliency	Annotation
I	1	0.060	1	0.432	1
hate	1	−0.014	0	0.040	1
my	1	0.102	1	1.264	1
life	1	0.094	1	−0.011	0
just	1	0.073	1	1.538	1
killl	1	0.105	1	4.451	1
me	1	0.081	1	1.055	1
im	0	−0.066	0	0.360	1
here	0	−0.016	0	0.398	1

Source: Adapted from Lottridge et al., 2023

responses prior to prediction, much like explicit features that are used in classical models. The contents of these features are real-valued scalars of some defined dimension (e.g., 1024) and arise out of common activation functions of the neural network model. Once a model is fine-tuned for a scoring task, the model parameters are set, and the values of the implicit features arise from the interaction of the response with the model parameters using forward propagation. The collection of the feature values for a set of responses can then be used to predict other measures, either related to the rubric (convergent validity) or not related to the rubric (divergent validity).

Length

Most transformer models limit the maximum number of tokens (e.g., 512, 256) in a response (Wolf et al., 2019). This limitation is imposed in part because of the nature of the pretrained modeling (i.e., to predict masked words) that focuses on text at the sentence or sentence-pair level. From a computational standpoint, allowing longer input requires larger models. In the case of transformer models, the amount of computing power required to implement the attention mechanism grows quadratically with the length (Vaswani et al., 2017). For items eliciting longer responses from examinees (e.g., essays or other performance tasks), responses exceeding the length limitation will be truncated in current models. Note that essays at upper grades in K–12 assessment and in many other contexts often exceed 512 tokens and so this limitation can substantially impact how these responses are processed. Workarounds to the limitation include chunking responses into smaller lengths, obtaining predictions, and then aggregating the results across those chunks for an overall score. This approach, however, is not optimal as it means the totality of the response is not considered during scoring. Still, our analysis suggests that, at least in the case of K–12 essays, the performance of the engine on long responses matches that of humans and of more classical engines. We caution that similar analyses should be conducted for the other contexts.

Alignment of Data Used to Train the Language Model With Examinee Writing

Open source pretrained models are typically trained on publicly available text resources such as Wikipedia or Books Corpus, which tend to use very formal and general language. The language in the corpora can differ from examinee writing, in terms of topic, language patterns, and grammatical quality. As a result, examinee words may not be represented in the vocabulary (i.e., are 'out of vocabulary') and/or the encoded language model may not be able to accurately represent certain topics or styles of writing. Additionally, pretrained models may have only uncased versions, meaning that words are converted to a single case (i.e., upper or lower), which may not be appropriate for some items.

The use of subwords and fine-tuning can help offset these limitations, but it is yet unclear how the choice of pretrained model can impact the quality of score prediction. As noted in Table 2.2, there are many pretrained models that are trained on varying data sources; there are far fewer models trained in other languages. Thus, when building models for, say,

Spanish, there are fewer models to choose from and these models may not map to the language usage of the examinees. This is also true of other models, such as speech, whereby pretrained models may be trained on adult speech, but then need to be applied to children's speech (Lottridge et al., 2022). Additionally, the language of science may not be well-represented in pretrained models because science language may form only a small portion of data used to train the model.

Technical Skills/Software

Another concern with transformers is the technical skills and software/hardware required for their use. The training and deployment of automated scoring models using transformers requires advanced technical expertise in software development, hardware choice (e.g., GPUs) and libraries, neural network libraries, and in neural networks themselves. The core of these challenges centers on the complexity of the models in terms of their size (i.e., number of parameters) and architecture, the need for specialized hardware and time for training and scoring (Mayfield & Black, 2020), the reliance on pretrained open-source models that can be very difficult to train, and their highly empirical focus (Church & Liberman, 2021).

The use of transformers over other neural network approaches does simplify the choices for hyperparameter tuning. Even so, identifying among the various available pretrained models or deciding whether to train one's own involves several decisions regarding compatible software and hardware library versions, deployable model size, and deployment mechanisms. The staff at CAI have spent the past four years improving our training and deployment mechanisms, and this has required the coordinated input of software engineers, data scientists, and psychometricians to ensure that the models meet accuracy, reliability, and fairness standards as well as business requirements around cost, latency, and throughput. As the use of these tools and support for their use grows, we expect that bar for organizational learning and support will lower and make them more accessible to a broader audience.

CONCLUSION

Clearly, transformer based automated scoring approaches offer substantial benefits in increasing the number and range of items that can be accurately scored by engines, and in providing more detailed feedback to examinees on what contributed to a rubric score. In our view, the future areas of research should focus on improving explainability methodology to better support efforts to validate scores, identify and correct any scoring issues, and determine how to improve scoring performance where it is lacking. It is our sincere hope that the measurement community will become acquainted with these tools, vet them for alignment with measurement concepts and practices, examine their potential in assessment (e.g., automated item generation, more authentic tasks, new measurement models), and publish this work in measurement journals and conferences. This collaboration of measurement, machine learning, software engineering, and computational linguistics stands to improve our understanding what examinees know and can do and how we measure it.

NOTES

1. https://huggingface.co/
2. https://jalammar.github.io/illustrated-transformer/
3. Perplexity is computed as $2^{entropy}$
4. An early predecessor of the recent GPT-3 and ChatGPT models.
5. https://github.com/NAEP-AS-Challenge/info/blob/952ee82cc52163b17bc cc1f12174ce246b8dff9b/results.md
6. A small portion of synthetic data are included in the modeling, but these form a very small percentage of the total number of responses (about 10k), although 5k of these responses are alerts.

REFERENCES

Burkhardt, A., Lottridge, S., & Woolf, S. (2021). A rubric for the detection of students in crisis. *Educational Measurement: Issues and Practice, 40*(2), 72–80. https://onlinelibrary.wiley.com/doi/10.1111/emip.12410.

Cahill, A., & Evanini, K. (2020). Natural language processing for writing and speaking. In D. Yan, A. Rupp, & P.W. Foltz (Eds.), *Handbook of automated scoring: Theory into practice* (pp. 69–92). CRC Press.

Chen, L., Zechner, K., Yoon, S-Y., Evanini, K., Wang, X., ... Gyawali, B. (2018). Automated scoring of nonnative speech using SpeechraterSM v. 5.0 Engine. *ETS Research Report Series, 2018*(1), 1–31.

Cheng, J., D'Antilio, Y-Z., Chen, X., & Bernstein, J. (2014). Automated assessment of the speech of young English learners. In *Proceedings of the Ninth Workshop on Innovative Use of NLP for Building Educational Applications*, Baltimore, MD.

Chung, J., Gulcehre, C., Cho, K., & Bengio, Y. (2014). *Empirical evaluation of gated recurrent neural networks on sequence modeling.* arXiv. https://doi.org/10.48550/arXiv.1412.3555.

Church, K., & Liberman, M. (2021). The future of computational linguistics: On beyond alchemy. *Frontiers in Artificial Intelligence.*

Clark, K., Luong, M-T., Le, Q., & Manning, C. (2020). *ELECTRA: Pre-training text encoders as discriminators rather than generators.* arXiv. https://doi.org/10.48550/arXiv.2003.10555

Danilevsky, M., Qian, K., Aharonov, R., Katsis, Y., Kawa, B., & Prithviraj, S. (2020). A survey of the state of explainable AI for natural language processing. *Proceedings of the 1st Conference of the Asia-Pacific Chapter of the Association for Computational Linguistics and the 10th International Joint Conference on Natural Language Processing* (pp. 447–450). Suzhou, China.

Deerwester, S. Dumais, S. T., & Landauer, T. K. (1990). Indexing by latent semantic analysis. *Journal of the American Society for Information Science, 41*(6), 391–407.

Devlin, J., Chang, M-W., Lee, K., & Toutanova, K. (2018). *BERT: Pre-training of deep bidirectional transformers for language understanding.* arXiv. https://doi.org/10.48550/arXiv.1810.04805.

Foltz, P. W., Yan, D., & Rupp, A. A. (2020). The past, present, and future of automated scoring. In D. Yan, A. Rupp, & P. W. Foltz (Eds.), *Handbook of automated scoring: Theory into practice* (pp. 1–9). CRC Press.

Gage, P. (1994). *A new algorithm for data compression.* C Users Journal.

Gao, T., Fisch, A., & Chen, D. (2021). *Making pre-trained language models better few-shot learners.* arXiv. https://arxiv.org/pdf/2012.15723v2

Goodfellow, I., Bengio, Y., & Courville, A. (2016). *Deep learning.* MIT Press.

Guthrie, D., Allison, B, Liu, W., Guthrie, L, & Wilks, Y. (2006). A closer look at skip-gram modeling. In *Proceedings of the Fifth International Conference on Language Resources and Evaluation (LREC'06)*, Genoa, Italy.

He, P. Liu, X., Gao, J., & Chen, W. (2021). *DeBERTa: Decoding-enhanced BERT with disentangled attention.* arXiv. https://arxiv.org/pdf/2006.03654.pdf

Hochreiter, S., & Schmidhuber, J. (1997). Long short-term memory. *Neural computation, 9(8),* 1735–1780.

Hsu, W-N., Sriram, A., Baevski, A., Likhomanenko, T., Xu, Q., Pratap, V., Kahn, J., Lee, A., Collobert, R., Synnaeve, G., & Auli, M. (2021). *Robust wav2vec 2.0: Analyzing domain shift in self-supervised pretraining.* arXiv. https://arxiv.org/abs/2104.01027

Jiang, Z. W., Yu, W., Zhou, D., Chen, Y., Feng, J., & Yan, S. (2020). *Convbert: Improving bert with span-based dynamic convolution.* Paper presented at the 34th Confernce on Neural Information Processing Systems (NeurIPS), Vancouver, CA. arXiv. https://arxiv.org/pdf/2008.02496.pdf

Kim, Y. (2014). Convolutional neural networks for sentence classification, in: Proc. 2014 Conf. Empir. Methods Nat. Lang. Process., pp. 1746–1751.

LeCun, Y. (1989). Generalization and network design strategies. *Technical Report CRG-TR089-4,* University of Toronto.

Lee-Thorp, J., Ainslie, J., Eckstein, I., & Ontanon, S. (2021). *FNet: Mixing tokens with fourier transforms.* arXiv. https://arxiv.org/ abs/2105.03824

Lottridge, S., Godek, B., Jafari, A., & Patel, M. (2020, September). *Comparing the robustness of deep learning and classical automated scoring approaches to gaming strategies.* Paper presented at the annual meeting of the National Council on Measurement in Education, Online. https://www.cambiumassessment.com/en/technology/machine-learning/comparing-automated-scoring

Lottridge, S., Ormerod, C., & Jafari, A. (2023). Psychometric considerations in using deep learning models for automated scoring. In Yaneva, V., & von Davier, M. (Eds.), *Natural language processing applications in assessment,* NCME Educational Measurement and Assessment Book Series.

Lottridge, S., Ormerod, C., Jafari, A., & Godek, B. (2022). *Automated speech scoring methods and results.* Cambium Assessment, Inc. https://www.cambium assessment.com/knowledge-center/news-articles/2022/09/30/16/25/ automated-speech-scoring-methods-and-results

Lottridge, S., Woolf, S., Young, M., Jafari, A., & Ormerod, C. (2023). The use of annotations to explain labels: Comparing results from a human-rater approach to a deep learning approach. *Journal of Computer-Assisted Learning.* https:// doi.org/10.1111/jcal.12784

Lundberg, S., & Lee, S-I. (2017). A unified approach to interpreting model predictions. *Proceedings of the 31st Conference on Neural Information Processing Systems* (pp. 4765–4774). Long Beach, CA.

Mayfield, E., & Black, A. (2020). Should you fine-tune BERT for automated essay scoring? In *Proceedings of the Fifteenth Workshop on Innovative Use of NLP for Building Educational Applications* (pp. 151–162), Seattle, WA.

Metallinou, A., & Cheng, J. (2014). Using deep neural networks to improve proficiency assessment for children English language learners. In *Proceedings from Interspeech,* Singapore.

Mikolov, T., Chen, K., Corrado, G., & Dean, J. (2013). *Efficient estimation of word representations in vector space.* arXiv preprint, arXiv:1301.3781

Ormerod, C. (2022). Mapping between hidden states and features to validate automated essay scoring using DeBERTa models. *Psychological Test and Assessment Modeling, 64*(4), 495–526.

Ormerod, C. M., & Harris, A. E. (2018). *Neural network approach to classifying alarming student responses to online assessment.* arXiv. preprint arXiv:1809.08899

Ormerod, C., Lottridge, S., Harris, A., Patel, M., van Wamelen, P., Kodeswaran, B., Woolf, S., & Young, M. (2022) Automated short answer scoring using an ensemble of neural networks and latent semantic analysis classifiers. *International Journal of Artificial Intelligence in Education.*

Ormerod, C., Malhotra, A., & Jafari, A. (2021). *Automated essay scoring using efficient transformer-based language models.* arXiv. https://doi.org/10.48550/arXiv .2102.13136.

Pennington, J. S. (2014). Glove: Global vectors for word representation. *Proceedings of the 2014 conference on empirical methods in natural language processing (EMNLP),* 1532–1543.

Ribeiro, M.T., Sigh, S., & Guestrin, C. (2016). *"Why should I trust you?" Explaining the predictions of any classifier.* arXiv. https://arxiv.org/pdf/1602.04938v1.pdf

Rodriguez, P., Jafari, A., & Ormerod, C. (2019). *Language models and automated essay scoring.* arXiv. https://doi.org/10.48550/arXiv.1909.09482

Rumelhart, David E. (1985). *Learning internal representations by error propagation.* Institute for Cognitive Science, University of California.

Schnable, T., Labutov, I., Mimno, D., & Joachims, R. (2015, September). Evaluation methods for unsupervised word embeddings. In *Proceedings on empirical methods in natural language processing,* 298–307, Lisbon, Portugal.

Sennrich, R., Haddow, B., & Birch, A. (2015). *Neural machine translation of rare words with subword units.* arXiv. https://doi.org/10.48550/arXiv.1508.07909

Sundararajan, M., Taly, A., & Yan, Q. (2017). Axiomatic attribution for deep networks. In *Proceedings of the 34th International Conference on Machine Learning*, Sydney, Australia. arXiv. https://arxiv.org/abs/1703.01365

Vaswani, A., Shazeer, N., Parmar, N., Uszkoreit, J., Jones, L., Gomez, A., Kaiser, L., & Polosukhin, I. (2017). *Attention is all you need*. arXiv. https://doi.org/10.48550/arXiv.1706.03762

Wang, A., Pruksachatkun, Y., Nangia, N., Singh, A., Michale, J., Hill, F., Levy, O., & Bownman, S. (2020). *SuperGLUE: A stickier benchmark for general-purpose language understanding systems*. arXiv. https://doi.org/10.48550/arXiv.1905.00537

Wang, A., Singh, A., Michael, J., Hill, F., Levy, O., & Bowman, S. (2018). *GLUE: A multi-task benchmark and analysis platform for natural language understanding*. arXiv. https://doi.org/10.48550/arXiv.1804.07461

Wang, C., Wu, Y., Wian, Y., Kumatini, K., Liu, S., Wei, F., Zeng, M., & Huang, X. (2021). Unispeech: Unified speech representation learning with labeled and unlabled data. In *Proceedings of the 38th International Conference on Machine Learning*.

Wolf, T., Debut, L., Sanh, V., Chaumond, J., Delangue, C., Moi, . . . Rush, A. (2019). *HuggingFace's transformers: State-of-the-art natural language processing*. arXiv. https://doi.org/10.48550/arXiv.1910.03771

Yan, D., & Bridgeman, B. (2020). Validation of automated scoring systems. In D. Yan, A. Rupp, & P. W. Foltz (Eds.), *Handbook of automated scoring: Theory into practice* (pp. 297–318). CRC Press.

Yang, Z., Dai, Z., Yang, Y., Carbonell, J., Salakhutdinov, R., & Le, Q., (2020). *XLNet: Generalized autoregressive pretraining for language understanding*. arXiv. https://arxiv.org/pdf/1906.08237.pdf

CHAPTER 3

INTEGRATING NATURAL LANGUAGE PROCESSING FOR WRITING ASSESSMENT

Writing Trait Model

Paul Deane
Educational Testing Service

Duanli Yan
Educational Testing Service

Writing varies across multiple dimensions. Some of these dimensions affect writing quality (Diederich et al., 1961) and must therefore be addressed during instruction. Teachers often present sample texts that model such traits (Gallagher, 2011) and train students to use them to evaluate and revise their writing (Culham, 2003). However, analyzing a text in terms of multiple traits can be both laborious and time-consuming (Weigle, 2002). This fact suggests that there may be significant instructional advantages to producing trait scores using automated writing evaluation (AWE) systems,

Machine Learning, Natural Language Processing, and Psychometrics, pages 57–92
Copyright © 2024 by Information Age Publishing
www.infoagepub.com
All rights of reproduction in any form reserved.

since AWE feedback can reduce the burden of scoring for teachers and enable fast feedback loops that supply students with personalized feedback.

For the most part, the features employed in AWE scoring models have straightforward (often linear) relations to writing quality. Essays are better, as a rule, when they are well developed and organized, when they use a richer vocabulary, and when they use language correctly, avoiding errors in grammar, usage, and mechanics. Existing AWE trait analysis systems use such features to define reportable traits, using supervised or unsupervised methods. Supervised methods predict human trait score judgments from AWE features (Shermis, Koch, Page, Keith, & Harrington, 2002). Unsupervised methods identify latent writing traits by analyzing the factor structure of AWE feature sets (Attali & Powers, 2008; Attali & Sinharay, 2015; Crossley & McNamara, 2014; Kim & Crossley, 2018). There is evidence that the resulting systems can effectively support student learning. For instance, feedback systems based upon automated trait analysis report significant improvements on specific traits when students revise their essays (Foltz & Rosenstein, 2019).

But not all dimensions of textual variation map directly onto differences in writing quality. Some differences among texts reflect differences among genres (Frow, 2014), since the same feature may occur frequently in one genre, but rarely in another (Biber, 1989, 1991; Biber, Conrad, Reppen, Byrd, & Helt, 2002). Some dimensions of text variation also have strong associations with readability (Brinton & Danielson, 1958; Deane, Sheehan, Sabatini, Futagi, & Kostin, 2006; Entin & Klare, 1978) or with patterns of linguistic development (Haswell, 2000; Reppen, 2007).

Of course, differences in genre characteristics and readability can affect text quality. A well-written text is more likely to respect the norms of its genre and be pitched at a reasonable reading level for its audience. But relations between text characteristics and writing quality may be indirect and involve tradeoffs among multiple standards of evaluation. For instance, revising a text to make it more cohesive (and hence easier to read) may cause it to seem wordy and repetitive, at least to readers with high levels of knowledge (McNamara, Kintsch, Butler-Songer, & Kintsch, 1996). Writers deal with such tradeoffs all the time. There may therefore be value in creating a writing trait model that is sensitive to other factors, such as those which account for variation among genres or differences in readability, rather than solely selecting features based on their utility as predictors of writing quality.

In this chapter, we introduce a general writing trait model that integrate natural language processing to model text quality, developmental patterns, and genre differences in student writing. This enables the extraction of key text characteristics or features from written texts to help to improve the quality of evaluation and assessment of student writing.

NATURAL LANGUAGE PROCESSING

The writing trait model and analysis were built upon three major prior lines of research:

- A series of AWE studies that explored measurement properties of the features deployed in the e-rater® essay scoring engine
- Research into genre variation and readability features that underlies the TextEvaluator® system for predicting the reading levels of texts.
- Research into the value of AWE features to predict external measures and provide useful feedback in a formative writing system (Burstein et al., 2018; Burstein, McCaffrey, Klebanov, & Ling, 2017).

e-rater

The e-rater automated essay scoring engine developed at ETS is designed to predict human essay scores from features designed to capture distinct aspects of writing quality: organization and development, discourse coherence, word choice, syntactic variety, idiomatic language, and avoidance of errors in grammar, usage, mechanics, and style. It generally achieves strong agreement with human scores, comparable to the level of agreement found between two different human raters (Attali & Burstein, 2006; Burstein, Tetreault, & Madnani, 2013). It can be viewed as measuring most of the constructs in the popular six-trait approach to evaluating student writing (Quinlan, Higgins, & Wolff, 2009), though it does not evaluate voice or the quality of ideas, nor constructs associated with an extended writing process (Deane, 2013). E-rater features have been shown to be predictive of a variety of external measures, including class grades, summative end-of-year reading and writing assessments, and high-stakes admissions tests (Burstein, McCaffrey, Beigman Klebanov, Ling, & Holtzman, 2019; Deane et al., 2019). Exploratory factor analysis of these features supports a three-factor structure: organization/development, vocabulary, and conventions (Attali, 2011; Attali & Sinharay, 2015). A study that examined essay-writing performance in 4th, 6th, 8th, 10th, and 12th grades also indicated that there is a regular increase in writing performance as measured by e-rater across grade levels (Attali & Powers, 2008).

TextEvaluator

The TextEvaluator text readability tool developed at ETS is designed to predict the grade level and the overall difficulty/readability of texts

(Sheehan, Kostin, Napolitano, & Flor, 2014). It is built on an array of AWE features designed to measure factors that affect readability, including academic language, sentence complexity, concreteness and imageability, word unfamiliarity, referential and lexical cohesion, interactive/conversational style, degree of narrativity, and argumentation. Some of the features included in TextEvaluator models are designed to help distinguish among texts from different genres, particularly literary vs. informational texts, in order to control for genre differences when assessing readability (Sheehan, Kostin, & Futagi, 2007). TextEvaluator models are trained on a corpus of adult, edited texts selected for use in high stakes state or national reading assessments, high stakes college admissions assessments, the Stanford Achievement Test, as part of the definition of the Common Core State Standards, or in previous published studies of text readability (Sheehan, 2016). TextEvaluator generates genre classifications of texts (as informational or literary), a grade-level readability estimate with an associated scale score, and a set of factor scores.

WAVES

The ETS WAVES engine was developed as part of an ongoing research project that explored differences among genres and the relationship between AWE features and broader outcomes such as GPA and college entrance examinations (Burstein, McCaffrey, Beigman Klebanov, & Ling, 2019; Burstein, McCaffrey, Beigman Klebanov, Ling, et al., 2019; Burstein et al., 2017). This work included a factor analysis that identified several components that varied across genres and reflected important aspects of the writing construct, including organization and development, coherence, argumentation, and editing (Burstein et al., 2018). The WAVES engine underlies the visualizations and feedback provided by Writing Mentor, an AWE system designed to scaffold the revision process for student writers (Burstein et al., 2018; Madnani et al., 2018).

Overlap Between e-rater and TextEvaluator Features

There is relatively little overlap between e-rater and TextEvaluator features. Both systems use word frequency features, but the word frequency measures are based upon different text corpora. Both systems use word length features, but TextEvaluator measures word length primarily using the number of syllables, whereas e-rater uses a transform of word length in characters. Both systems use measures of text coherence/cohesion, but they are constructed differently. The e-rater discourse coherence feature identifies lexical chains (sequences of repeated or related words) and uses them to build a predictive model intended to maximize association with scores (Burstein, Tetreault, Chodorow, Blanchard, & Andreyev, 2013). TextEvaluator also start with lexical overlap (word repetitions) but normalizes these inputs with respect to text length and genre. The resulting features are designed to produce valid comparisons of text cohesion across disparate students and texts (Sheehan, 2013). Otherwise, e-rater and TextEvaluator features appear to measure rather different constructs.

METHODOLOGY

There are several reasons to build a trait model for student writing that combines e-rater, TextEvaluator, and WAVES features. Perhaps the most important reason is construct coverage. TextEvaluator includes constructs that matter for English Language Arts instruction yet are not captured by the e-rater engine. Syntactic complexity is an important dimension of student writing development. Concreteness/ imageability is closely linked to vividness of language, for it is part of what teachers are interested in when they encourage students to develop a stronger writing voice. Oral/interactive style is important in many genres and social contexts, even if it is typically discouraged in formal, written essays. Similarly, the WAVES engine has a number of features that are specifically diagnostic of argumentative and complex academic texts that are not included in the other engines. As students learn to write in different genres, they need to vary what they write to increase or decrease the presence of narrative and argumentative elements. A second reason is stability of measurement. The features in the e-rater engine are designed for use in linear regression models, which means that collinearity must be minimized. The TextEvaluator and WAVES engines provide additional ways to measure shared constructs, which may yield more stable estimates of underlying student traits. Finally, the enriched feature set may make it possible to build better developmental models of student writing using features that have already been shown to be predictive on multiple criterion variables.

When creating writing trait model, one e-rater feature was excluded: the development feature, which measures the log length of essay elements in words (introduction, conclusion, thesis, topic sentences, developing sections of paragraphs). This exclusion was motivated, in part, by the fact that the development feature, when combined with the organization feature (the log number of essay elements), is very closely related mathematically to essay length in words. A potential confounding issue for automated writing evaluation systems is the typically strong relation between essay score and essay length in words (Deane, 2013). If a writing trait analysis is to support instruction, the factors that describe essay traits should be based upon features that capture constructs worth teaching, and not on simple measures like essay length that, if emphasized in instruction, might encourage students to adopt inappropriate writing strategies.

However, essay length in words is related to at least one construct worth measuring: fluency. Cognitive models of writing posit that different writing processes compete for working memory, resulting in tradeoffs in which low transcription fluency can impede idea generation and self-monitoring, and conversely, in which students working under conditions of high cognitive load may be less fluent in their writing (Kellogg, 2001; McCutchen, 1996). As a result, variations in the length of essays written to the same prompt might reflect the difficulty of the task and the impact of prior knowledge and working conditions, even for students who know how to produce essays that match expectations for the genre.

These considerations suggest that the residual role of productivity should be accounted for in a writing trait model. However, the construct as we have defined is in some sense a residual trait—it is productivity in text production that cannot be accounted for by writing knowledge, but which emerges either from (otherwise unmeasured) aspects of the writing construct, or from the impact of other cognitive factors such as prior knowledge, task difficulty, and cognitive load. It can therefore be done by examining the effect of document length on scores or other metrics after the effects of specific writing traits have been removed.

Participants

The big data set contains 1.37 million submissions to ETS' Criterion® classroom writing service by 203,144 K–12 students between 2004 and 2018. This data comprised all scored essay data submitted to Criterion at US/ North American primary and secondary schools during this timeframe.

Criterion™ is a digital writing product offered by Educational Testing Service that provides automated scoring and feedback capabilities (Burstein, Chodorow, & Leacock, 2004; Ramineni & Deane, 2016). It has been in operation since 2004, and is used in a variety of contexts, including primary and secondary schools in the United States, U.S. institutions of higher education, and various institutions around the world that use it to support instruction for English language learners. Two versions of this service have been offered: the initial version, available between 2004 and 2013, and a major revision, primarily affecting the user interface, that was released in 2013. Criterion uses ETS' e-rater automated essay scoring service to evaluate student essays and identify potential errors in grammar, usage, mechanics, and style (Attali & Burstein, 2006; Burstein, Tetreault, & Madnani, 2013).

No individual demographic data or school level demographic data was directly collected by ETS. In order to obtain school level demographic data, we matched schools as identified in the ETS operational and client relations databases with school-level data from the U.S. Department of Education's public and private school surveys (U.S. Department of Education–National Center for Education Statistics, 2003–2018a, 2003–2018b). In a few cases, districts had included students from multiple schools (typically a high school and an associated junior high school) without recording this fact in their Criterion school hierarchy, and it was necessary to correct the school list by referring to grade level and class name information that indicated data was drawn from multiple schools. There were also a few cases where there was insufficient data to match schools to the NCES data, or where the school was absent from the NCES data for the school years in question. However, we were able to obtain partial or complete school-level demographic data for 893 of the 934 schools in our dataset. Most of the schools for which data were missing were private schools not present in the NCES private school survey data for the years in which they used Criterion.

Between 2013 and 2018, students at 689 public schools, 243 private schools, and 2 homeschools made submissions to the Criterion system. Almost all the schools were in the contiguous United States, except for 4 schools in the Virgin Islands, 2 in Hawaii, and 1 in Alberta Canada. 249 of these schools were in in urban communities, 304 in suburban communities, 122 in small towns, and 248 in rural areas. The geographic distribution of schools was as follows:

- 25.2% of the schools were in the Southeast (10 in Arkansas, 1 in Delaware, 1 in the District of Columbia, 21 in Alabama, 81 in Florida, 31 in Georgia, 3 in Kentucky, 14 in Louisiana, 3 in Maryland, 5 in North Carolina, 1 in South Carolina, 43 in Tennessee, and 29 in Virginia).
- 24.9% of the schools were in the Midwest (1 in Indiana, 22 in Illinois, 96 in Indiana, 2 in Kansas, 44 in Michigan, 5 in Minnesota, 12 in Missouri, 1 in Nebraska, 28 in Ohio, 14 in South Dakota, and 8 in Wisconsin).
- 21.8% of the schools were in the Northeast (6 in Connecticut, 5 in Massachusetts, 4 in Maine, 3 in New Hampshire, 52 in New Jersey, 27 in New York, 104 in Pennsylvania, 1 in Rhode Island, and 2 in Vermont).
- 11.5% of the schools were in the Pacific states (86 in California, 10 in Oregon, and 11 in Washington).
- 8.8% of the schools were from the Southwest (27 in Arizona, 3 in New Mexico, 30 in Texas, and 22 in Oklahoma).
- 2.7% of the schools were from the Rocky Mountain states (2 in Colorado, 1 in Idaho, 1 in Montana, 15 in Nevada, and 10 in Wyoming).

The K–12 schools that used Criterion included 278 high schools, 210 middle schools, and 52 secondary (combined middle/high schools). There were 211 primary (combined elementary/middle) schools and 88 elementary schools, 28 schools that instructed all grades, and 67 schools with some other combination of grade levels.

The public schools in the Criterion data were drawn from a total of 401 school districts (including 373 independent school districts, 11 unified school districts, and 13 independent charter districts). 25.1% of these schools reported that less than 25% of their students were eligible for free or reduced school lunch, 34.9% reported that between 25 and 50% of their students were eligible for free or reduced school lunch, 26.7% reported that between 50% and 75% of their students were eligible for free or reduced lunch, and 13.4% reported that more than 75% of their students were eligible for free or reduced lunch. The private schools were predominantly Catholic parochial schools (189 out of 243). The remaining schools represented a broad array of (mostly Protestant) religious orientations, though there were also a small number of Jewish, Islamic, and nonsectarian schools. The NCES public and private school surveys indicated that 30.3% of the schools that used Criterion were majority-minority. 13.6% of Criterion schools reported that more than 25% of their students were Black, 14.9% reported that more than 25% were Hispanic, 3.3% reported that more than 25% were Asian, 1.4% reported that more than 25% were Native American, .66% reported that more than 25% were multiracial, and .1% reported that more than 25% were Pacific Islanders.

Including students who submitted to Criterion during multiple school years, and hence were counted more than once, there were 3,860 students classified as being in 4th grade, 8,670 classified as being in 5th grade, 27,737 classified as being in 6th grade, 35,518 classified as being in 7th grade, 39,671 classified as being in 8th grade, 29,924 classified as being in 9th grade, 29,158 classified as being in 10th grade, 21,599 classified as being in 11th grade, and 14,335 classified as being in 12th grade. For students from 2013 on, these classifications were derived from information provided by teachers and administrators when classes were created in the Criterion system. For students from earlier years, these classifications were imputed based upon the class name, the grade level associated with the assignment, and other information. The details of the imputation method used to create these individual classifications is detailed under the Procedures section later in this section.

Writing Tasks

The writing tasks examined included 436 standard prompts that were provided as part of the Criterion service, and approximately 2,989 locally-created prompts (reflecting 22,580 distinct class-level assignments) created and assigned by teachers or administrators. These comprised all scored locally created essay tasks assigned in Criterion by K–12 schools in the study period. Unfortunately, teacher prompts were only individuated by the title and prompt text provided by its creator. We were therefore unable to provide an analysis of prompt effects, except for topic library prompts where the prompt was indicated by the `criterion_model_id` variable. We intend in a future study to apply text clustering techniques to refine our classification of teacher-created prompts, using detailed prompt language and the teacher's instructions, so the assignment identifications used in this study should be understood as provisional.

When teachers or administrators create an assignment in Criterion, they control various options, including the genre (expository or persuasive) and assumed grade level of the task, the number of revisions allowed, whether work must be completed by a deadline or within a time limit, whether the task will be associated with peer groups, and the availability of various writing tools, such as spell-check and thesaurus, among others. These features are relevant to the conditions under which students submitted their work and were therefore recorded as part of the underlying dataset.

In addition, the writing tasks included a set of independently collected, human scored essays used to train and evaluate 73 e-rater scoring models used to provide automated scores for Criterion prompts (Burstein, Chodorow, & Leacock, 2004). This secondary dataset contained 65,372 distinct essays, divided approximately evenly by model into training and evaluation sets. Each essay was associated with at least 2 human ratings on a 6-point scale using standard Criterion rubrics. When these ratings differed by more than one point, a third, adjudication score was provided. The adjudicated score was calculated as follows: when the first and second rater differed by no more than one point, the average of the first and second rater was assigned as the final score. When they differed by two or more points, the adjudicated score was averaged with either the first or second rater's score, whichever differed less from the adjudicated score. The result was an adjudicated score on a 6-point scale that included half-point intervals.

Procedure

All submissions were made as regular submissions to assignments created by school staff, using whatever devices students at each school ordinarily used to complete online assignments. ETS' role was restricted to providing training and support to individual schools and school districts when they implemented Criterion in their classrooms. The following information was recorded at the time of submission:

- the text of the submission
- a holistic score based upon an automated scoring model associated with the prompt
- errors and advisories intended to identify cases where the automatically generated score might not be reliable
- for submissions after 2013, levels (high/medium/low) on three traits (focused on organization/development, vocabulary, and conventions).
- feedback about structural units identified in the essay, such as thesis and topic sentences
- a list of error types and locations, with associated feedback
- and finally, a timestamp indicating the time and date of submission.

Each individual submission, or attempt, was linked to a specific teacher, student, class, and assignment. If a student made multiple submissions for the same assignment (by default, unless specified otherwise for a specific assignment, up to ten submissions are allowed), a unique identifier was generated for each attempt.

Imputation of Individual Student Grade Levels

Grade levels were directly indicated (by class) only for a portion of the data (that collected since 2013). However, there were multiple sources of information that could be used to impute individual grade levels over the entire dataset. These included:

- The name of the class. A majority of classes were given names that directly or indirectly identified their grade level, such as "English I" in high school (9th grade), or "8th Grade Language Arts, period 1."
- The grade level associated with the task. The post-2013 data indicates that class grade levels and task grade levels matched in the vast majority of cases.
- The nature of the school. In a senior high school, for instance, all classes can be expected to fall between 9th and 12th grades.
- Student cohort status. Students who take the same classes are usually from the same grade (though there are exceptions, particularly in high school).

These regularities were used to create imputed grade levels for each student. First, we created a rule-base that used regular expressions to assign classes to grade levels based upon class names. Where this information was not available, grade level was imputed by task based upon the grade level assignment of the task. If a task's grade level assignment fell above or below the range of grade levels associated with the school, it was corrected to the nearest valid grade. If a student was assigned multiple grade levels across assignments, this was corrected by taking the modal grade level for the student, and if that did not resolve the conflict, it was corrected by taking the modal grade level for the class. Where class grade level assignments were available (in the post-2013 data), the resulting statistic agreed exactly with class grade levels 88.2% of the time. 95.8% of the time, the imputed grade was no more than one grade level off. We therefore used class grade levels where available and imputed grade levels otherwise. Any remaining disagreements within-student based on assigned class grade levels were resolved by taking the average of that student's grade level assignments and rounding up.

Postprocessing

When the K–12 Criterion data was extracted from the operational Criterion data, additional processing was performed to associate each essay with modern AWE features. These features comprised the features used to predict essay scores in e-rater version 19.1.1, the features used to predict genre status and reading difficulty in Text Evaluator, and selected WAVES features that help to distinguish argumentative from narratives and expository essays.

RESULTS

Extensive Analyses

What dimensions of variation can be measured in student essay writing, grades 4 to 12? We conducted both exploratory and confirmatory factor analysis using the e-rater, TextEvaluator and WAVES features identified above. Following an approach similar to that used in Sheehan et al. (2014), we used principal component analysis to extract the common factors, followed by a cluster rotation (Yamamoto & Jennrich, 2013), an oblique rotation designed to maximize the interpretability of the factors by aligning factor loadings with cluster structure present in the data. This exploratory analysis suggested a structure which we then tested, using a graphical model, which yielded our final factor model.

How are these dimensions related to criterion variables likely to matter for English Language Arts teachers, including overall writing quality, fit with genre norms, and growth across grades or after revision? We conducted the following analyses:

- Correlations between factor scores and grade level
- One-way ANOVAs to identify significant trait differences by genre
- Examination of combined trends in trait means, by genre and grade level

- Examination of trends in trait means after revision
- Multiple linear regressions in which we used factor scores to predict human essay scores on an independent essay set for which human ratings were available.

Exploratory Factor Analysis

Patterns of correlation among the features used in our analysis were investigated by conducting exploratory factor analysis – as with Sheehan et al. (2014), a principal component analysis followed by a Promax rotation. Most of the features had high levels of communality, although a few fell below recommended levels. In particular, the Topical Adjective feature from the TextEvaluator engine had a communality of .13, Cognitive Process/Perception Noun feature from the TextEvaluator engine had a communality of .15, the Section and Citation Headers feature from the WAVES engine had a communality of .11, and the Unnecessary Words feature from the WAVES engine had a communality of .12. The Sources feature from the WAVES engine had a communality of .059 on a prior run and was therefore dropped from the analysis. 38 of the 60 remaining features had communalities above .5, and 56 of the 60 features had communalities above .2. Examination of the scree plot and the factor loadings showed a plot that leveled off rapidly after 9 factors accounting for 52% of the variance, though 15 factors had eigenvalues greater than 1. A non-graphical solution, Optimal Coordinates (cf. Raiche, Walls, Magis, Riopel, & Blais, 2013), indicated that an optimal solution would extract 9 (see Figure 3.1). However, examination of the factors that would need to be collapsed to produce the 9-factor solution suggested that a 17-factor model would be clearer and more interpretable, as it would align more closely with factor structures previously identified for TextEvaluator and e-rater.

Writing Trait Model

Based on the results of our analyses, we proposed the following 17-trait model:

- **Formality** is a measure of written, academic style, characterized by longer, rarer, more Latinate vocabulary, and an avoidance of markers of oral language like first person pronouns, verbs of speaking, and contractions.
  - **Organization** is a measure of how well the essay has been elaborated in well-structured ways, using thesis and topic sentences, transition words, and chains of related ideas, varying the sentence structures to make the relationships between ideas clear.
  - **Vocabulary Length** and **Vocabulary Frequency** represent two other important aspects of formality (word length and word

Non-Graphical Solutions to Scree Test

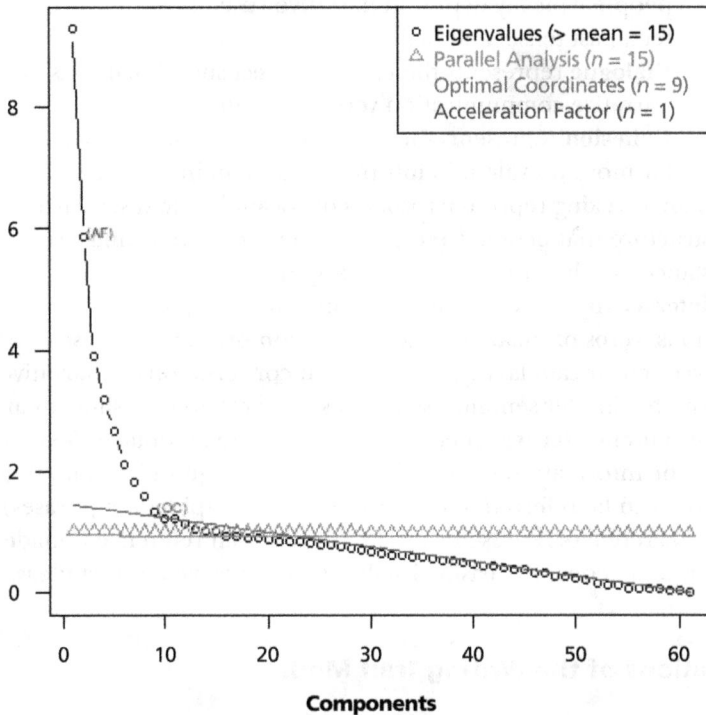

Figure 3.1 Scree plot for the joint e-rater, TextEvaluator, and WAVES feature set.

frequency), which give a sense of whether writers have deployed relatively difficulty, demanding vocabulary.

- **Sentence structure** represents all aspects of sentence construction, including sentence length, sentence complexity, and grammar/usage.
  - **Sentence Length** and **Sentence Complexity** represent aspects of sentence construction – whether the sentences tend to continue at length, and whether they keep sentence structure relatively simple, or make use of relatively complex, relatively difficult constructions.
  - **Grammar and Usage** represents another aspect of sentence construction—adherence to the grammatical norms for standard written English
- **Conventionality** and **Mechanics** represent accurate production of normal English words and phrases.
- **Narrativity** represents the group of traits and features that differentiate narratives (on one end) from argument essays (on the other).

- **Contextualization** represents aspects of sentence structure that people typically deploy in narrative (use of past tense, past perfect, past tense, and fiction verbs).
- **Dialogue** represents the use of indirect speech patterns, with narrative communication verbs and quotes
- **Cohesion** represents the repetition of key ideas across sentences, far more prevalent in informational than in narrative texts.
- **Stance Taking** represents aspects of vocabulary and sentence structure that people typically use when they are taking a subjective stance, as when they develop an argument.
- **Interactivity** represents typically oral language, marked by contractions, verbs of speaking, and first-person pronouns, by use of highly frequent vocabulary typically used in conversations or narratives, and by simpler sentence structures characterized by short themes, or sentence starts (reflecting the fact that in an oral context, thematic information early in the sentence is highly given and therefore can be referred to with pronouns or simple noun phrases).
- **Concreteness** represents the extent to which reference is made to physical, concrete, easily visualized concepts, vs. abstract ideas.

Evaluations of the Writing Trait Model

The correlations between the traits and human essay scores for human written essays for Criterion show that many are significant such as Formality (0.44), Organization (0.66), Conventionality (0.39), Mechanics (0.36), and Grammar and usage (0.35). Table 3.1 lists the correlations.

We divided the Criterion corpus randomly into a training and testing set and trained the model on the training set. We conducted a stepwise regression to predict human scores from trait scores, using half the data as a training set, and half as a test set. This model combined data across prompts. The 17-trait model demonstrated an acceptable fit (CFI = 0.934, RMSEA = .0547) in the training set. When we applied the resulting factor weights to the test set, the model fit equally well (CFI = .934, RMSEA = .0550). Appendix A lists the factor loadings for the 17-trait model.

We also created models by prompt, using the same model building and evaluation sets as Criterion's operational e-rater models. These results indicate that the trait model and the e-rater models were roughly equivalent in performance. Sometimes the trait model performed better, sometimes the e-rater model performed better, although more often than not, the e-rater model was marginally more accurate. Table 3.2 lists the performance of e-rater and trait model on Criterion prompts.

TABLE 3.1 Correlations Between Traits and Human Essay Scores for Human-Scored Essays Written to Criterion Prompts	
Trait	**Correlation With Adjudicated Human Scores**
Formality	.44
Vocabulary Length	.32
Vocabulary Frequency	−.25
Organization	.66
Sentence Structure	.21
Sentence Length	.03
Sentence Complexity	.25
Grammar and Usage	.35
Conventionality	.39
Mechanics	.36
Narrativity	.16
Contextualization	.12
Dialog	.13
Cohesion	−.02
Stance taking	−.11
Interactivity	−.20
Concreteness	.07
(Lexical Tightness)	.25

Correlations with Grade Level

Several traits (Organization, Formality, Stance Taking, Sentence Length, Sentence Complexity, Vocabulary Length, Vocabulary Difficulty, and Conventionality) show small to moderate positive correlations with grade level, while others (Interactivity and Concreteness) are negatively correlated with grade level. Table 3.3 shows the correlations between trait scores and student grade levels. Given the size of the dataset, all correlations are significant.

Patterns of Mean Trait Difference by Grade Level and Genre

By examine the way mean trait scores vary by grade level and genre, we can see large differences in mean traits across both dimensions. For instance, we see a general increase in mean Organization scores by grade, with some differentiation by genre in middle school and high school, where Narrative essays tend to have higher Organization scores than Descriptive, Persuasive, and Expository essays across all grades. Persuasive and Exposition essays have higher Organization scores than Descriptive essays. (See

TABLE 3.2 Performance of e-rater and Trait Models on Human-Scored Essays Written to Criterion Prompts

Prompt ID	N Train	N Test	Standard E-Rater Features		E-Rater Plus Supplemental Features		Trait Model	
			Adj. R²	QWK	Adj. R²	QWK	Adj. R²	QWK
ECRT1188	499	496	.78	.777	.80	.791	.80	.794
ECPT0000	2225	2224	.77	.795	.78	.795	.79	.800
ECRT1194	482	474	.80	.799	.81	.801	.81	.793
ECRT1154	233	233	.82	.848	.84	.848	.85	.836
ECRT1213	228	231	.83	.869	.84	.867	.85	.877
ECRT1101	234	232	.80	.858	.82	.880	.85	.879
ECXT0000	3212	3204	.77	.803	.78	.807	.79	.809
ECRT1175	234	235	.79	.844	.80	.851	.82	.867
ECRT0225	233	231	.85	.890	.86	.889	.86	.901
ECRT1172	487	487	.75	.787	.75	.791	.77	.803
ECRT0342	233	235	.80	.848	.81	.868	.81	.866
ECRT1219	484	476	.81	.845	.82	.834	.82	.831
ECRT1185	230	229	.83	.848	.84	.870	.87	.879
ECRT2215	233	231	.88	.843	.90	.857	.89	.859
ECRT1168	231	230	.80	.836	.83	.853	.83	.844
ECRT1246	229	228	.83	.872	.84	.865	.85	.889
ECRT1161	234	234	.79	.866	.81	.864	.83	.878
ECRT1223	231	230	.86	.856	.88	.866	.89	.872
ECRT0230	232	230	.84	.870	.86	.868	.86	.899
ECRT1190	233	233	.79	.838	.80	.848	.81	.876
ECRT1162	235	235	.81	.834	.82	.856	.83	.831
ECRT1114	232	232	.87	.872	.89	.882	.89	.887
ECRT0349	234	235	.80	.799	.81	.819	.82	.833
ECRT1234	228	226	.85	.837	.87	.856	.88	.858
ECRT1170	234	233	.84	.843	.86	.850	.86	.844
ECRT0279	231	232	.87	.848	.87	.879	.88	.866
ECRT1100	231	230	.83	.847	.84	.872	.86	.865
ECRT1215	221	228	.84	.864	.85	.866	.84	.884
ECRP0014	282	281	.58	.705	.58	.688	.56	.688
ECRP0044	500	498	.70	.708	.70	.704	.70	.724
ECRR0781	232	231	.42	.569	.43	.628	.48	.620
ECRR0612	394	220	.79	.807	.80	.810	.90	.816
ECRR0349	227	228	.69	.718	.69	.725	.70	.741
ECRR0631	256	256	.83	.818	.83	.817	.83	.790
ECRR0596	184	187	.77	.815	.77	.818	.80	.819
ECRR2342	205	209	.78	.835	.79	.844	.80	.847

TABLE 3.3 Correlations Between Trait Scores and Imputed Student Grade Level

Trait	Correlation With Grade Level (all prompts)	Correlation with Grade Level (Topic Library prompts)
Formality	.397	.468
Vocabulary Length	.330	.410
Organization	.263	.254
Interactivity	−.221	−.284
Concreteness	−.241	−.336
Sentence Complexity	.194	.241
Sentence Structure	.192	.238
Vocabulary Frequency	−.155	−.158
Sentence Length	.144	.164
Grammar and Usage	.086	.154
Stance taking	.086	.131
Conventionality	.081	.097
Narrativity	−.073	−.211
Dialog	−.068	−.193
Contextualization	−.053	−.179
Mechanics	.049	.059
Cohesion	−.040	.031

Figure 3.2). The Formality (academic language) trait shows that Persuasive essays tend to have higher scores than Descriptive, Expository, and Narrative scores. Expository essays have higher scores than Descriptive essays which have higher scores than Narrative essays (see Figure 3.3).

About essay vocabulary uses, Narrative essays have shorter vocabulary length and more frequent uses. While Persuasive essays have longer vocabulary length than Expository essays than Narrative essays (Figures 3.4 and 3.5). About essay sentence uses, Persuasive and Expository essays have higher scores on Sentence Structure, Sentence Length, and Sentence Complexity than Narrative and Descriptive essays (Figures 3.6, 3.7, and 3.8). For Gramma Usage and Mechanics, all four types of essays have similar scores with Expository and Persuasive essays having a bit higher score (Figures 3.9 and 3.10). But for Mechanics, the higher score difference of Expository essays for Grade 4 to 7 over the other types of essays vanishes at higher grades (see Figure 3.10). Similarly, Grades 4 to 8 show higher scores on Conventionality, but this difference vanishes at higher grades (see Figure 3.11).

The last set of traits show distinctive genre differences. Narrative and Descriptive essays show much higher scores than Persuasive and Expository

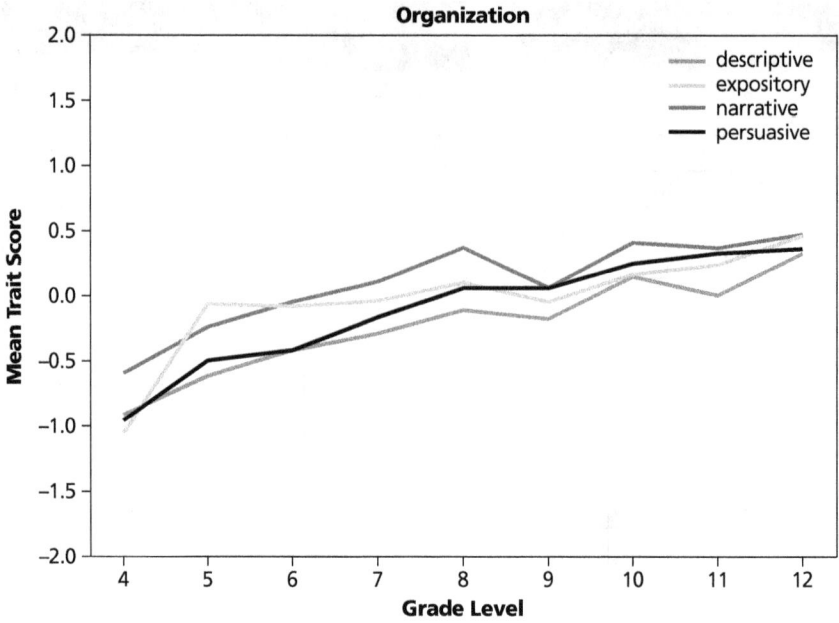

Figure 3.2   Mean organization score by grade level and genre.

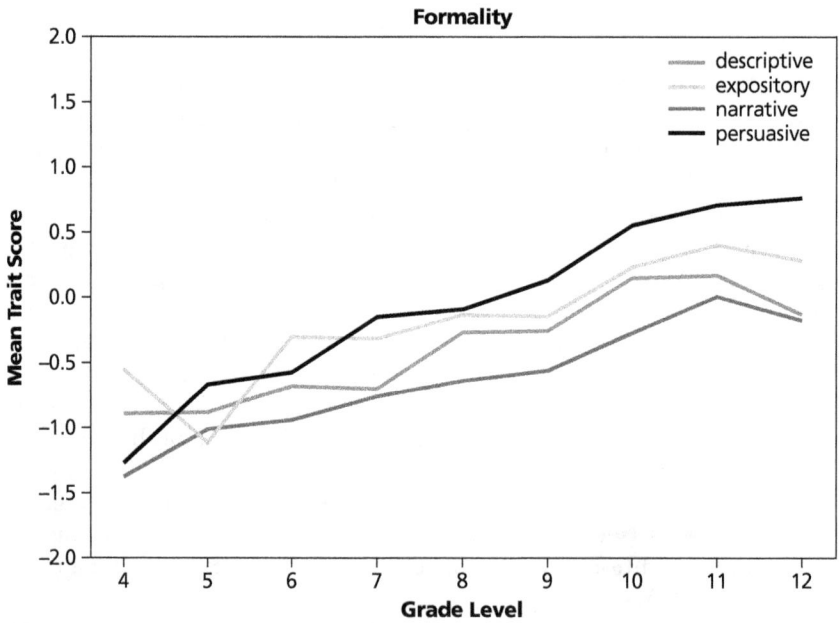

Figure 3.3   Mean formality score by grade level and genre.

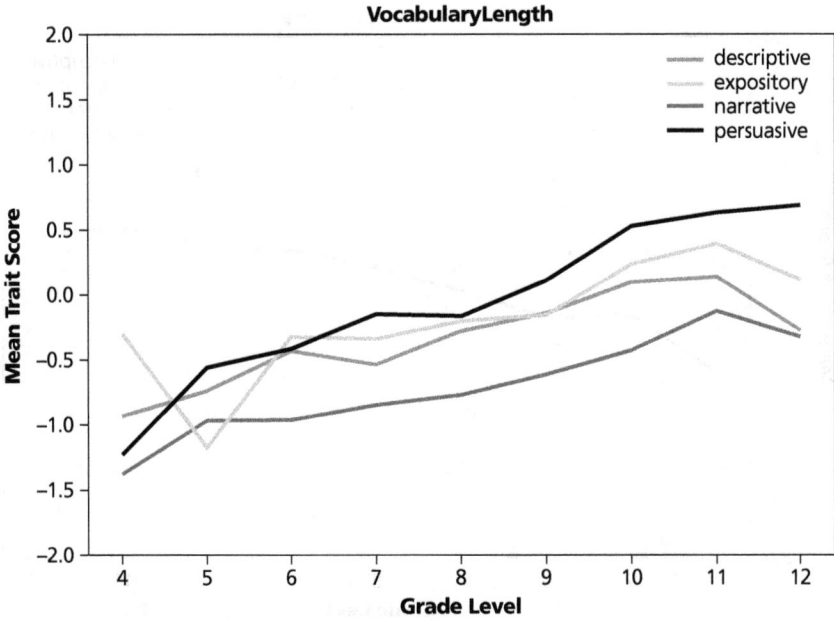

Figure 3.4 Mean vocabulary length score by grade level and genre.

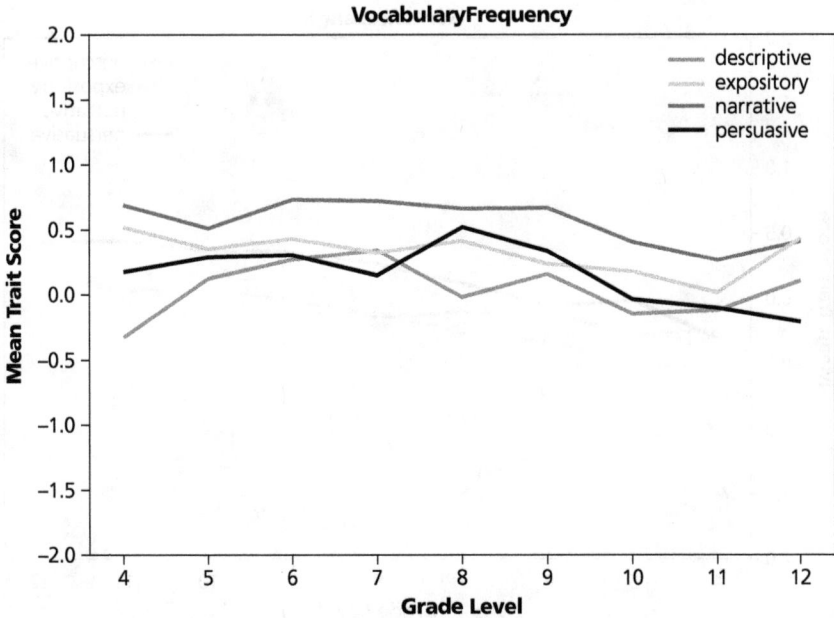

Figure 3.5 Mean vocabulary frequency score by grade level and genre.

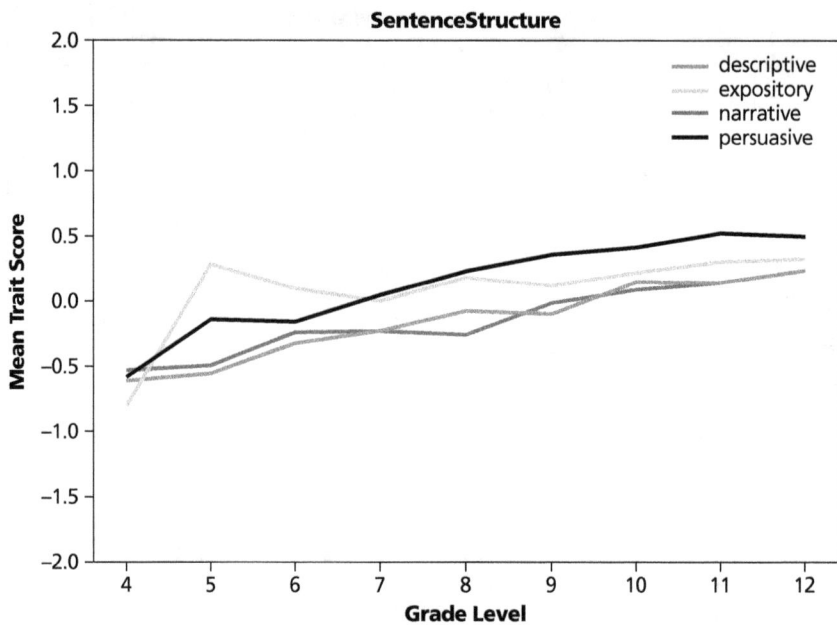

Figure 3.6   Mean sentence structure score by grade level and genre.

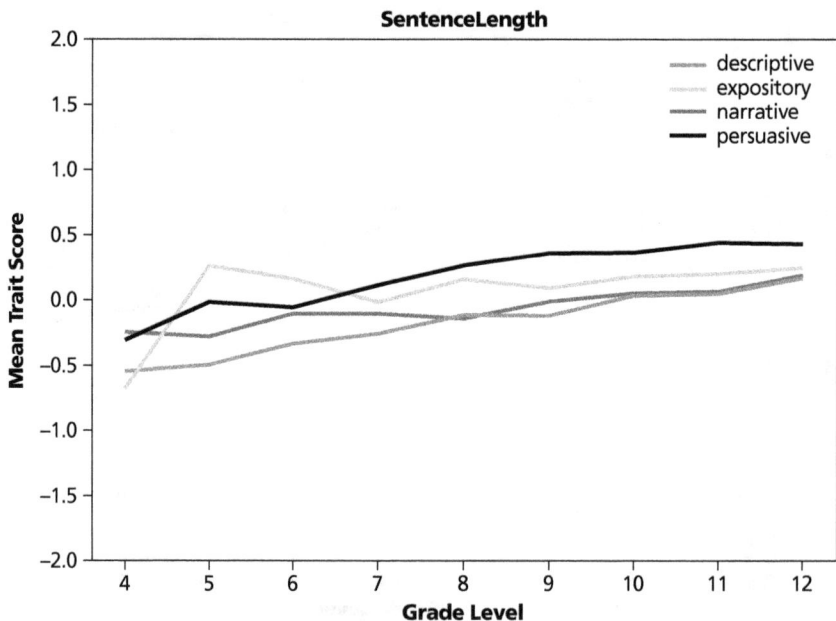

Figure 3.7   Mean sentence length score by grade level and genre.

SentenceComplexity

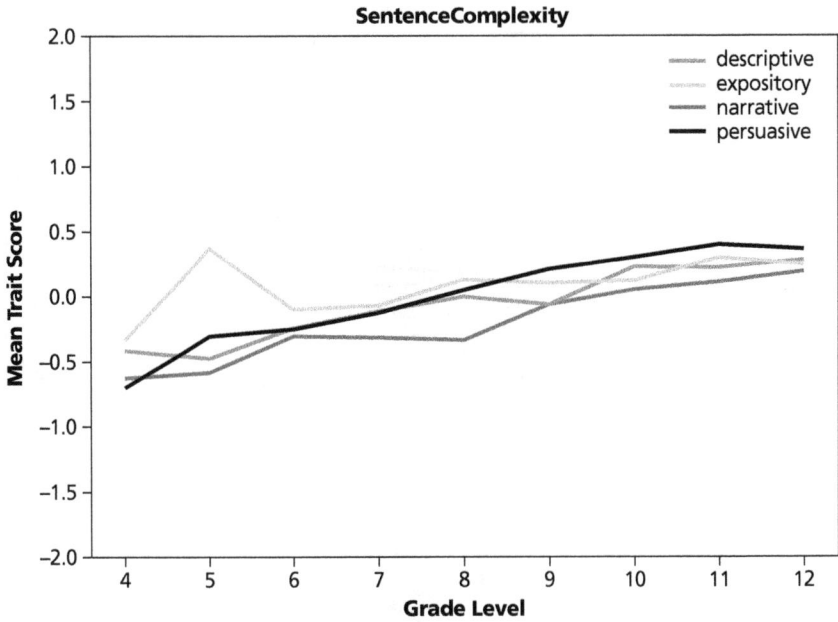

Figure 3.8 Mean sentence complexity score by grade level and genre.

GrammarUsage

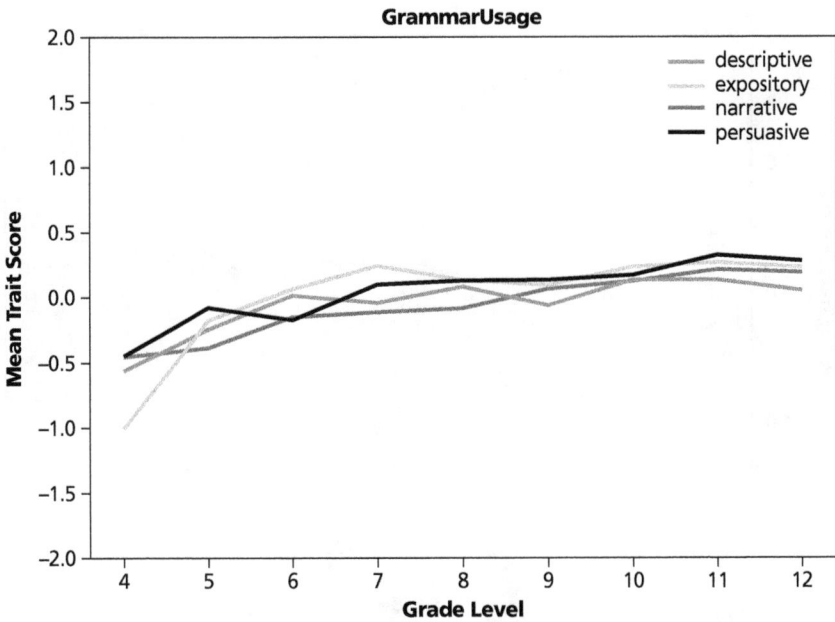

Figure 3.9 Mean gramma and usage score by grade level and genre.

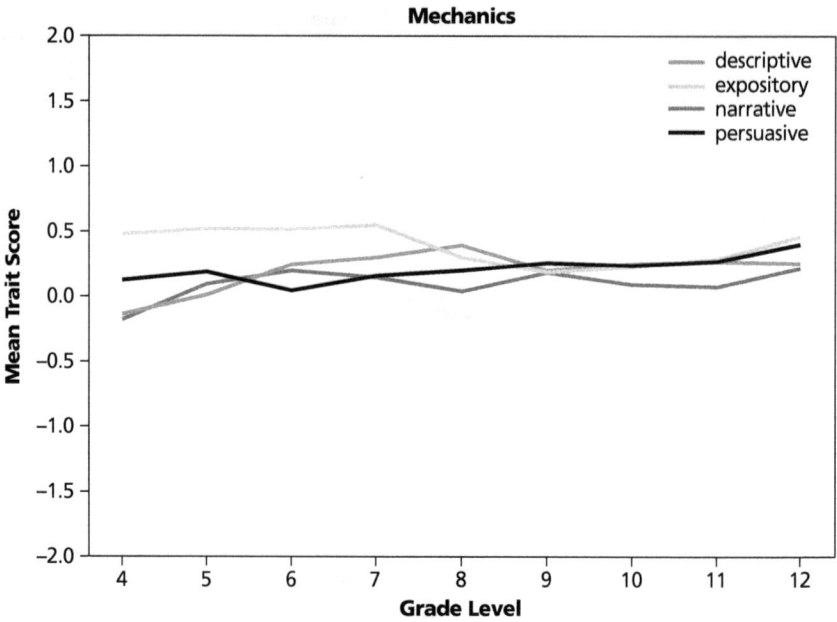

Figure 3.10 Mean mechanics score by grade level and genre.

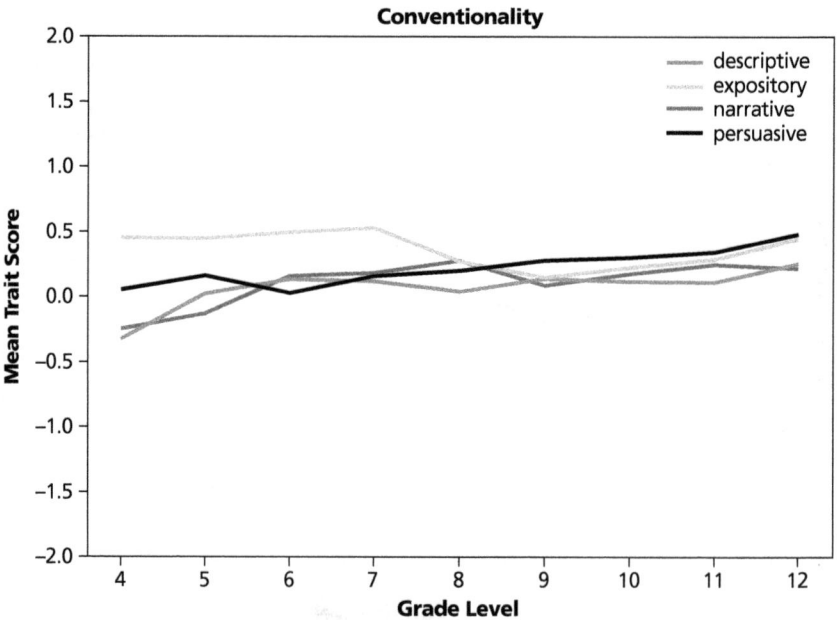

Figure 3.11 Mean conventionality score by grade level and genre.

essays on Concreteness (Figure 3.12), while Persuasive and expository essays have much higher scores than Narrative and Descriptive essays on Cohesion (Figure 3.13). On Stance Taking, the score differences are big among the four types of essays with Persuasive essays ranked as the highest, Expository the second, Descriptive the third, and Narrative the last.

Narratives essays are characteristically simpler in structure and sentences than Expository or Persuasive essays (see Figures 3.4, 3.6, and 3.8), shorter words (see Figure 3.7), and more frequent vocabulary (see Figure 3.5), but show very strong genre differences. In particular, Narrative essays show much higher mean scores than the other genres on Dialogue, Interactivity, Narrativity, and Contextualization compared to Persuasive, Descriptive, and Expository essays (Figures 3.15, 3.16, 3.17, and 3.18).

DISCUSSIONS

It is encouraging that we were able to obtain a relatively compact, interpretable factor structure when we applied the e-rater, TextEvaluator, and WAVES features to the Criterion essay data. The factors that emerged are consistent with factor analyses reported in the literature for subsets of these features. Thus, the three e-rater factors reported by (Attali, 2011; Attali

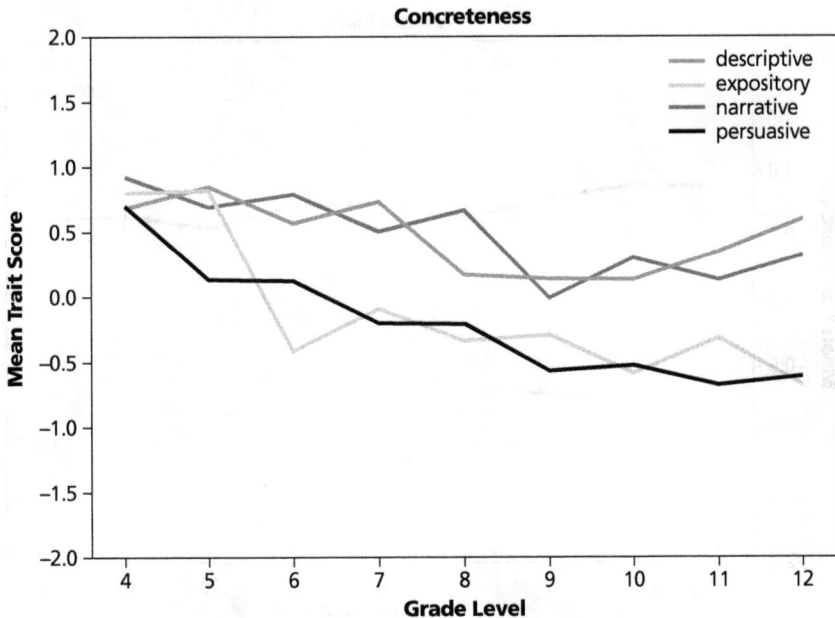

Figure 3.12   Mean concreteness score by grade level and genre.

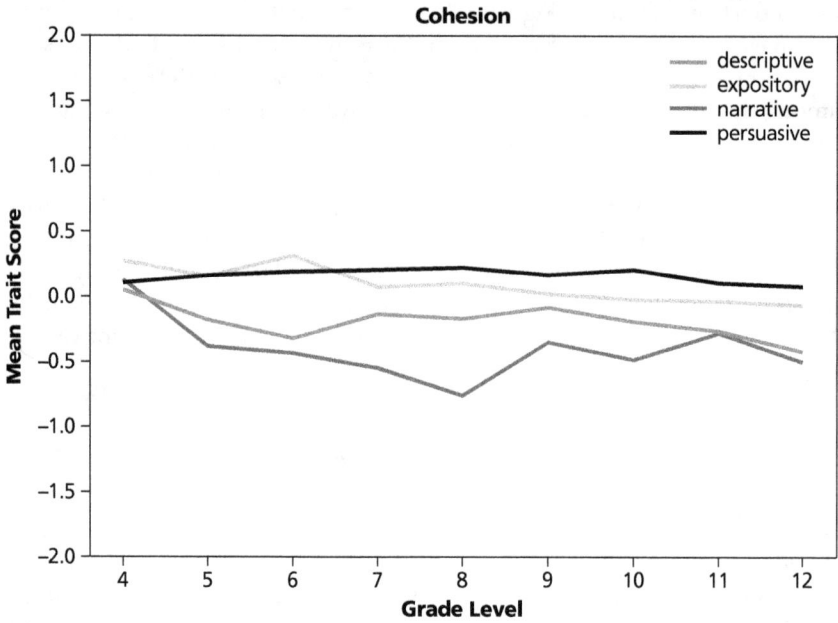

Figure 3.13 Mean text cohesion score by grade level and genre.

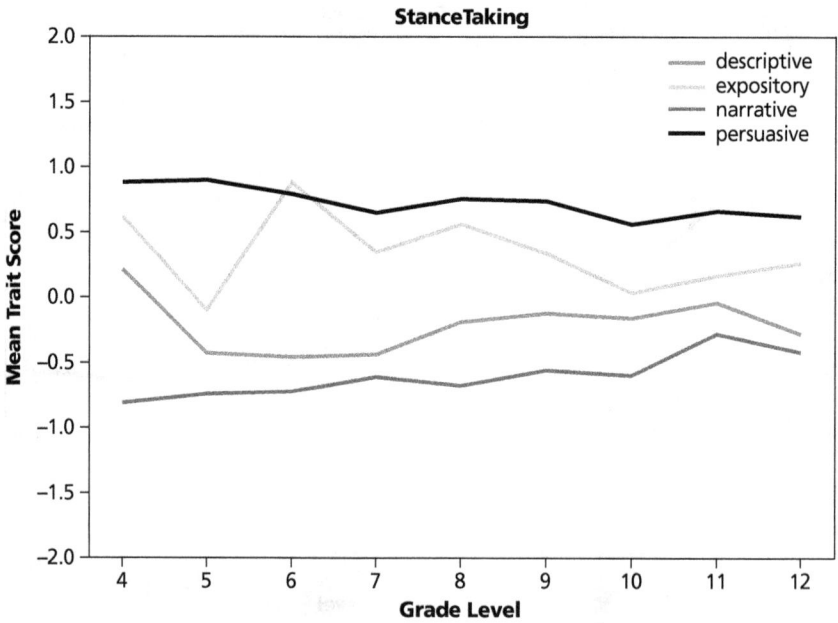

Figure 3.14 Mean stance taking score by grade level and genre.

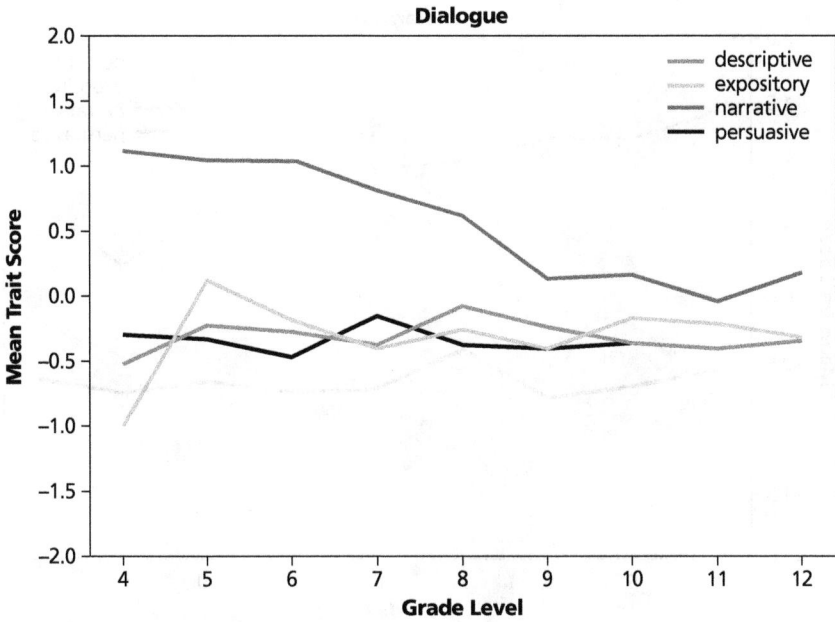

Figure 3.15   Mean dialogue by grade level and genre.

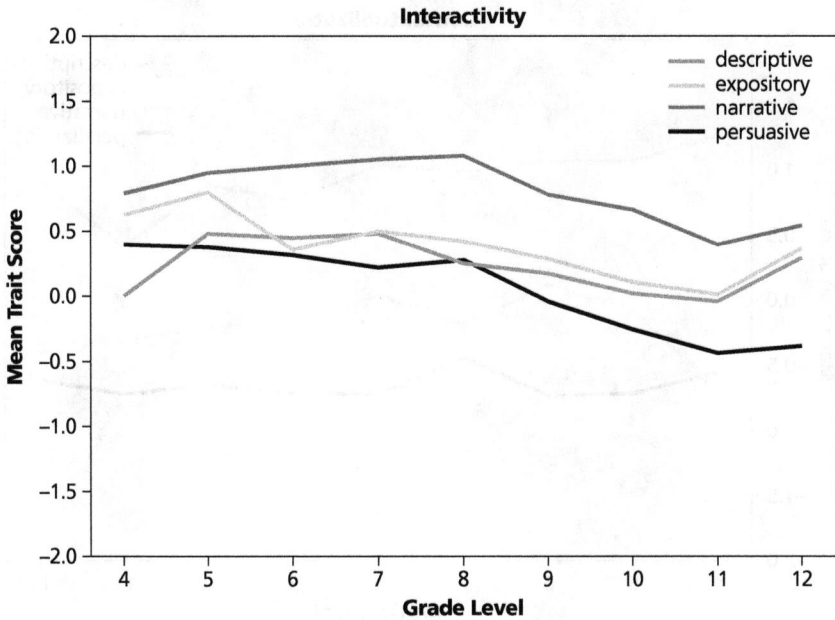

Figure 3.16   Mean interactivity score by grade level and genre.

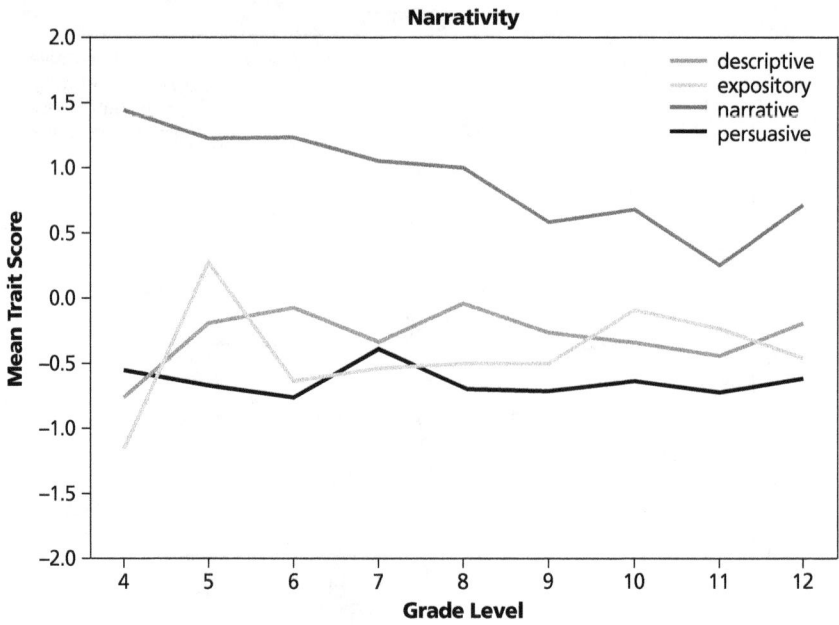

Figure 3.17   Mean narrative score by grade level and genre.

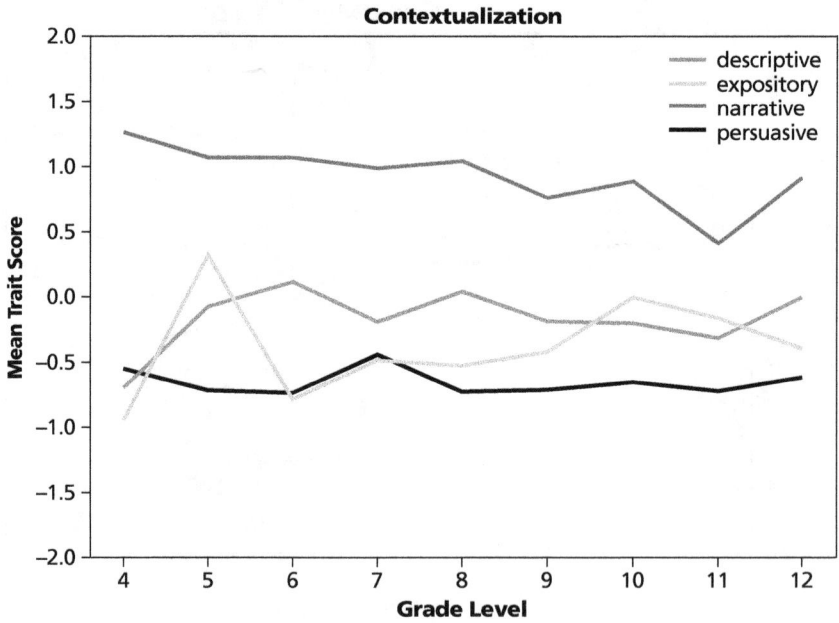

Figure 3.18   Mean contextualization score by grade level and genre.

& Powers, 2008; Attali & Sinharay, 2015) map directly onto the Organization, Formality, and Conventions factors in our analysis. Similarly, most of the TextEvaluator factors map almost directly onto factors in our analysis, though with some mergers and rearrangements. The WAVES features contribute one additional factor (stance-taking), and otherwise, map onto one of the other factors along with multiple e-rater or TextEvaluator features. The results of the factor analysis thus appear to provide a reasonable, construct-relevant way to interpret major dimensions of variation we have been able to identify in the Criterion essay data.

It is important to note, however, that the trait model does not fully account for variations in essay length. Combined, the seventeen traits account for about two-thirds of the variance essay length feature. However, this excludes the e-rater Development feature, which could not be included in the trait model since its inclusion made the factor matrix non-positive-definite. It may therefore be necessary to treat essay length (or more properly, those aspects of essay length that are not accounted for by the 17-trait model) as an extra trait, one that must be considered for certain purposes, including the prediction of essay scores.

Relations With Score and Genre

Since nearly all e-rater features were included in the factor analysis, it is not surprising that the trait model we build essentially replicates e-rater score predictions, as long as we include a feature that captures the residual effects of essay length. That is, it achieves roughly equivalent levels of accuracy. However, it is important to note that the strength of the relationship with essay quality varies across traits. Some traits (e.g., organization, text cohesion, and conventionality) have strong and consistent associations with text quality, whereas others (such as Interactivity) do not. There appears to be an inverse relationship between prediction of writing quality and prediction of genre. Many of the traits that are particularly useful for differentiating genre (e.g., Interactivity, Contextualization, Concreteness, and Stance-Taking) have relatively weak relations with essay quality.

But in a sense, that is the whole point. It may be useful to conceptualize writing performance along two meta-dimensions: adherence to genre norms, and written quality. Some students may write poor essays, while adhering to genre norms. Others may violate genre norms, and yet produce otherwise high-quality writing. The results we have reported clearly support a model in which we can compare essays both to quality norms (e.g., expected trait patterns for high-quality essays) and to genre norms (e.g., expected trait patterns for specific types of writing).

Overall, our results indicate that we can detect changes in student writing at a trait level. To the extent that this is possible, there are obvious advantages to using a trait model. Trait profiles may provide a standardized way to describe student writing, both at single time points, across revisions, or over large time periods. In principal, trait profiles might be used to support a variety of forms of feedback and reporting.

Strengths and Limitations

The seventeen-trait model proposed in this chapter has been validated using a very large sample of K–12 student writing. This is an obvious strength, though it should be born in mind that the students who attended schools that used Criterion between 2004 and 2018 may differ in various ways from the general K12 population. However, the dataset has other limitations, most notably, the following:

- We do not have human scores for operational Criterion submissions. Criterion has never collected teacher grades or scores, which means that we have to rely on ancillary datasets to evaluate the relationship between the trait scores returned by the K–12 model and overall writing quality.
- We only have school-level demographic data. It is thus impossible to explore the impact of demographic variables at an individual level.
- Information about genre is limited in important ways. We have reliable genre information only for the 40% of student submissions that used prompts from the Criterion topic library. The remaining 60% of submissions were written in response to teacher-created prompts. While teachers were asked to give their assignments a genre label, they only had two choices ('expository' or 'persuasive'), which may be misleading, as initial exploration suggests that they created a rich array of assignment types, many of which cannot accurately be described as requiring straightforward exposition or argumentation.

It is therefore important to interpret our results as preliminary in nature, to be confirmed by a series of follow-up studies that will probe different aspects of the novel, including the extent to which we can set meaningful genre norms by trait, and the extent to which a writing trait model can be used to track student responses to instruction and feedback.

CONCLUSION

Even with these caveats, our results are robust enough to suggest that we can use a writing trait model to enrich our analysis of student writing and to provide richer, and potentially more precise and effective, feedback. A writing trait model has the potential to provide meaningful ways to describe patterns of student writing (on a single assignment, or across assignments) and to describe how student writing changes as a result of instruction.

APPENDIX A
Factor Loadings for the 17-Factor Model

Factor	Features	Loadings
Formality	Average word syllables	1.00
	Long words	.89
	Nominalizations (type collapsed)	.94
	Coxhead academic words	.84
	Abstract nouns (type collapsed)	.64
	Cognitive process perception nouns	.41
	Syntactic variety	.77
	Mean TASA SFI	−.31
	Mean ETS word frequency	−.81
	(In)frequency	.37
	Length of lexical chains	.30
	Number of lexical chains	.43
	Essay elements	.25
Formality: Organization	Length of lexical chains	1.00
	Number of lexical chains	.92
	Number of Essay elements	.60
	Syntactic variety	.48
Formality: Vocabulary length	Average Word Syllables	1.00
	Long words	.49
Formality: Vocabulary frequency	Mean TASA SFI	1.00
	Mean ETS word frequency	.93
	(In)frequency	−.43
Interactivity	First person pronouns	1.00
	Conversation verbs	.88
	Contractions	.46
	(In)frequency	−.86
	Average word count before main verb	−.46
	Fiction verbs	.35
Concreteness	Proportion highly concrete	1.00
	Proportion highly imageable	.67

Factor	Features	Loadings
Narrativity	Past tense verbs	1.00
	Third person pronouns	.79
	Narrative communication verbs	.87
	Past perfect verbs	.54
	Fiction verbs	.41
	Words inside quotes	.72
	Literary cohesion	.25
Narrativity: Contextualization	Past tense verbs	1.00
	Third person pronouns	.79
	Past perfect verbs	.52
	Fiction verbs	.41
Narrativity: Dialog	Words inside quotes	1.00
	Narrative communication verbs	.79
Cohesion	Informational cohesion	1.00
	Literary cohesion	.95
Stance taking	Claims	1.00
	Argument verbs	.39
Sentence structure	Mean sentence length	1.00
	Mean clause length	.86
	Mean number of dependent clauses	.67
	Average Yngve's depth	.58
	Average word count before main verb	.32
	Grammar	.62
Sentence structure: Sentence complexity	Average Yngve's depth	1.00
	Mean sentence length	.40
	Average word count before main verb	.36
Sentence structure: Sentence length	Mean number of dependent clauses	1.00
	Mean clause length	.90
	Mean sentence length	.57
Conventionality	Grammaticality	1.00
	Mechanics	.74
	Idiomaticity of language	.31
Conventionality: Mechanics	Grammaticality	1.00
	Mechanics	.22
Conventionality: Grammar and usage	Grammar	1.00
	Usage	.84

APPENDIX B
Features Used in the Writing Trait Model

Hypothesized dimension	Features	Feature description
Formality: general (academic language)	Nominalizations	Proportion of nominalizations formed with suffixes like *-ion* and *-al.* (types collapsed: variant forms of a word treated together)
	Coxhead academic words	Proportion of words in the document that are in the Coxhead academic word list
	Abstract nouns	Proportion of word types in the document on a list of common abstract nouns
	Cognitive process perception nouns	Words for internal mental states (*thought, feeling*)
	Syntactic variety	Based on an algorithm that weights the grammatical elements present in a text by their relative distribution in a well-structured essay. (Also loads on organization)
Formality: vocabulary length	Average word syllables	Total syllables in a document, divided by the number of words
	Long words	Percentage of the words in a document that are longer than 8 characters.
Formality: vocabulary difficulty	(In)frequency	Negative one times the median word frequency in the Google Books corpus
	Mean TASA SFI	Mean standardized frequency index (SFI) in the TASA corpus
	Mean ETS word frequency	Mean log word frequency in an ETS-compiled corpus
Formality: organization	Essay elements (e-rater organization feature)	Based on an algorithm that divides the essay into major text units (introduction, thesis sentence, topic sentences, developing material, conclusion)
	Number of lexical chains	Based on an algorithm that identifies lexical chains (sequences of repeated or related words) bounded by a transition word
	Length of lexical chains	Based on an algorithm that identifies lexical chains (sequences of repeated or related words) bounded by a transition word
	Syntactic variety	Based on an algorithm that weights the grammatical elements present in a text by their relative distribution in a well-structured essay. (Also loads on academic language)

Hypothesized dimension	Features	Feature description
Sentence structure: sentence length	Avg. clause length	Number of words per clause
	Avg. sentence length	Number of words per sentence
	Avg. number dependent clauses	Number of subordinate clauses per sentence
Sentence structure: sentence complexity	Yngve's depth	Average depth of syntactic embedding
	Theme complexity	Average number of words before the main verb
	Avg. sentence length	(cross-loads on Sentence Length)
Sentence structure: grammar and usage	Grammar	Avoidance of grammar errors (negative square root of proportion of grammar errors)
	Usage	Avoidance of usage errors (negative square root of proportion of usage errors)
Conventionality (language and mechanics)	Mechanics	Avoidance of spelling and punctuation errors (negative square root of proportion of spelling and punctuation errors)
	Grammaticality	Natural phrasing (measured by the probability of word sequences—not grammaticality in the prescriptive grammar sense)
	Idiomaticity	Correct usage of collocations and prepositions
Narrativity: contextualization	Past tense verbs	Typical markers of narrative
	Past perfect verbs	Sentences built around grammatical structures typically used in arguments, such as complement clauses and infinitives
	Third person pronouns	Typical markers of narrative
	Fiction verbs	Verbs that typically appear in narratives or conversations, like *sit*, *walk*, or *look* (cross-loads on Interactivity)
Narrativity: dialog	Narrative communication verbs	Verbs typically used to express indirect speech (like *say*, *ask*, or *tell*) (also loads on the Interactivity trait)
	Words inside quotes	Proportion of words in text enclosed in quotation marks
Narrativity: cohesion	Informational cohesion	Normalized vocabulary overlap between adjacent sentences in the text, based on informational text patterns
	Literary cohesion	Normalized vocabulary overlap between adjacent sentences in the text, based on literary text patterns

Hypothesized dimension	Features	Feature description
Stance taking	Stance markers	Words like *however, seems likely, alleged*
	Argument verbs	Words like *believe, argue, claim, rebut*
Interactivity	Conversation verbs	Verbs used to mark direct speech (e.g., *ask, say*)
	First person pronouns	*I, me, my, mine, we, us, ours* . . .
	Contractions	Shortened combinations like I'm, we're, you'll
	Fiction verbs	Verbs that typically appear in narratives or conversations (cross-loads on Contextualization)
	(In)frequency	Negative one times the median word frequency in the Google Books corpus (cross-loads on Vocabulary frequency)
	Theme complexity	Average number of words before the main verb (Cross-loads on Sentence complexity)
Concreteness	Concreteness	Proportion of words in the document rated as highly concrete
	Imageability	Proportion of words in the document rated as easy to visualize

REFERENCES

Attali, Y. (2011). Automated subscores for TOEFL iBT® independent essays. *ETS Research Report Series, 2011*(2), i–16.

Attali, Y., & Burstein, J. (2006). Automated essay scoring with e-rater® V. 2. *The Journal of Technology, Learning and Assessment, 4*(3).

Attali, Y., & Powers, D. (2008). A developmental writing scale. *ETS Research Report Series, 2008*(1), i–59.

Attali, Y., & Sinharay, S. (2015). Automated Trait Scores for TOEFL® Writing Tasks. *ETS Research Report Series, 2015*(1), 1–14.

Beigman Klebanov, B., Priniski, S., Burstein, J., Gyawali, B., Harackiewicz, J., & Thoman, D. (2018). Utility-Value Score: A Case Study in System Generalization for Writing Analytics. *Journal of Writing Analytics, 2,* 314–328.

Biber, D. (1989). A typology of English texts. *Linguistics, 27*(1), 3–44.

Biber, D. (1991). *Variation across speech and writing.* Cambridge University Press.

Biber, D., Conrad, S., Reppen, R., Byrd, P., & Helt, M. (2002). Speaking and writing in the university: A multidimensional comparison. *tesol Quarterly, 36*(1), 9–48.

Brinton, J. E., & Danielson, W. A. (1958). A factor analysis of language elements affecting readability. *Journalism Quarterly, 35*(4), 420–426.

Burstein, J., Chodorow, M., & Leacock, C. (2004). Automated essay evaluation: The Criterion online writing service. *Ai Magazine, 25*(3), 27.

Burstein, J., Elliot, N., Beigman Klebanov, B., Madnani, N., Napolitano, D., Schwartz, M., . . . Molloy, H. (2018). Writing Mentor: Writing Progress Using Self-Regulated Writing Support. *Journal of Writing Analytics, 2,* 258–313.

Burstein, J., McCaffrey, D., Beigman Klebanov, B., & Ling, G. (2019). *Linking Writing Analytics and Broader Cognitive and Interpersonal Outcomes.* Paper presented at the National Conference on Measurement in Education, Toronto, ON.

Burstein, J., McCaffrey, D., Beigman Klebanov, B., Ling, G., & Holtzman, S. (2019). Exploring writing analytics and postsecondary success indicators. In L. P. Committee (Ed.), *Companion Proceedings 9th International Conference on Learning Analytics & Knowledge (LAK19)* (pp. 213–214). Tempe, Arizona: LAK.

Burstein, J., McCaffrey, D., Klebanov, B. B., & Ling, G. (2017). *Exploring Relationships Between Writing & Broader Outcomes With Automated Writing Evaluation.* Paper presented at the Proceedings of the 12th Workshop on Innovative Use of NLP for Building Educational Applications.

Burstein, J., Tetreault, J., Chodorow, M., Blanchard, D., & Andreyev, S. (2013). 16 automated evaluation of discourse coherence quality in essay writing. *Handbook of Automated Essay Evaluation: Current Applications and New Directions,* 267.

Burstein, J., Tetreault, J., & Madnani, N. (2013). The e-rater automated essay scoring system. *Handbook of Automated Essay Evaluation: Current Applications and New Directions,* 55–67.

Cahill, A., Chodorow, M., & Flor, M. (2018). Developing an e-rater advisory to detect Babel-generated essays. *Journal of Writing Analytics, 2,* 203–224.

Coltheart, M. (1981). The MRC psycholinguistic database. *Quarterly Journal of Experimental Psychology Section A, 33,* 497–505. https://doi.org/10.1080/14640 748108400805

Coxhead, A. (2000). A new academic word list. *tesol Quarterly, 34,* 213–238.

Crossley, S. A., & McNamara, D. S. (2014). Does writing development equal writing quality? A computational investigation of syntactic complexity in L2 learners. *Journal of Second Language Writing, 26,* 66–79.

Culham, R. (2003). *6+ 1 traits of writing: The complete guide grades 3 and up.* Scholastic Inc.

Deane, P. (2013). On the relation between automated essay scoring and modern views of the writing construct. *Assessing Writing, 18*(1), 7–24.

Deane, P., Sheehan, K. M., Sabatini, J., Futagi, Y., & Kostin, I. (2006). Differences in text structure and its implications for assessment of struggling readers. *Scientific Studies of Reading, 10*(3), 257–275.

Deane, P., & Song, Y. (2015). *The key practice, discuss and debate ideas: Conceptual framework, literature review, and provisional learning progressions for argumentation* (ETS RR-15-33). Retrieved from http://onlinelibrary.wiley.com/doi/ 10.1002/ets2.12079/pdf

Deane, P., Song, Y., van Rijn, P., O'Reilly, T., Fowles, M., Bennett, R., . . . Zhang, M. (2019). The case for scenario-based assessment of written argumentation. *Reading and Writing, 32*(6), 1575–1606.

Deane, P., Wilson, J., Zhang, M., Li, C., van Rijn, P. W., Guo, H., . . . Richter, T. (in press). The sensitivity of a scenario-based assessment of written argumentation to school differences in curriculum and instruction. *International Journal of Artificial Intelligence in Education.*

Diederich, P. B., French, J. W., & Carlton, S. T. (1961). Factors in judgments of writing ability. *ETS Research Bulletin Series, 1961*(2), i–93.

Elliot, N. (2005). *On a scale: A social history of writing assessment in America.* Peter Lang.

Entin, E. B., & Klare, G. R. (1978). Factor analyses of three correlation matrices of readability variables. *Journal of Reading Behavior, 10*(3), 279–290.

Flor, M., Klebanov, B. B., & Sheehan, K. M. (2013). *Lexical tightness and text complexity.* Paper presented at the Proceedings of the Workshop on Natural Language Processing for Improving Textual Accessibility.

Foltz, P., & Rosenstein, M. (2019). Data-mining large-scale formative writing. In C. Lang, G. Siemens, A. Wise, & D. Gasevic (Eds.), *Handbook of learning analytics* (pp. 199–210). www.solarresearch.com: Society for Learning Analytics Research.

Frow, J. (2014). *Genre.* Routledge.

Gallagher, K. (2011). *Write like this: Teaching real-world writing through modeling & mentor texts.* Stenhouse Publishers.

Haswell, R. H. (2000). Documenting improvement in college writing: A longitudinal approach. *Written Communication, 17*(3), 307–352.

Kellogg, R. T. (2001). Competition for working memory among writing processes. *American Journal of Psychology, 114*(2), 175–191. https://doi.org/10.2307/1423513

Kim, M., & Crossley, S. A. (2018). Modeling second language writing quality: A structural equation investigation of lexical, syntactic, and cohesive features in source-based and independent writing. *Assessing Writing, 37*, 39–56.

Madnani, N., Burstein, J., Elliot, N., Klebanov, B. B., Napolitano, D., Andreyev, S., & Schwartz, M. (2018). *Writing mentor: Self-regulated writing feedback for struggling writers.* Paper presented at the Proceedings of the 27th International Conference on Computational Linguistics: System Demonstrations.

McCutchen, D. (1996). A capacity theory of writing: Working memory in composition. *Educational Pschology Review, 8*(3), 299–325. https://doi.org/10.1007/BF01464076

McNamara, D. S., Graesser, A. C., & Louwerse, M. M. (2012). Sources of text difficulty: Across genres and grades. *Measuring up: Advances in how we assess reading ability*, 89–116.

McNamara, D. S., Kintsch, E., Butler-Songer, N., & Kintsch, W. (1996). Are good texts always better? Interactions of text coherence, background knowledge, and levels of understanding in learning from text. *Cognition and Instruction, 14*, 1–43.

National Centerfor Education Statistics. (2012). *The nation's report card: Writing 2011.*

Quinlan, T., Higgins, D., & Wolff, S. (2009). Evaluating the construct-coverage of the e-rater® scoring engine. *ETS Research Report Series, 2009*(1), i–35.

Raiche, G., Walls, T. A., Magis, D., Riopel, M., & Blais, J.-G. (2013). Non-graphical solutions for Cattell's scree test. *Methodology, 9*(1), 23–29.

Ramineni, C., & Deane, P. (2016). The Criterion® online writing evaluation service. *Adaptive Educational Technologies for Literacy Instruction*, 163.

Reppen, R. (2007). First language & second language writing development of elementary students. *Corpusbased Perspectives in Linguistics, 147–167*.

Sakia, R. M. (1992). The Box-Cox transformation technique: a review. *Journal of the Royal Statistical Society: Series D (The Statistician), 41*(2), 169–178.

Sheehan, K. M. (2013). Measuring cohesion: An approach that accounts for differences in the degree of integration challenge presented by different types of sentences. *Educational Measurement: Issues and Practice, 32*(4), 28–37. https://doi.org/10.1111/emip.12017

Sheehan, K. M. (2016). A review of evidence presented in support of three key claims in the validity argument for the TextEvaluator® text analysis tool. *ETS Research Report Series, 2016*(1), 1–15.

Sheehan, K. M., Kostin, I., & Futagi, Y. (2007). *Reading level assessment for literary and expository texts.* Paper presented at the Proceedings of the Annual Meeting of the Cognitive Science Society.

Sheehan, K. M., Kostin, I., Napolitano, D., & Flor, M. (2014). The TextEvaluator tool: Helping teachers and test developers select texts for use in instruction and assessment. *The Elementary School Journal, 115*(2), 184–209.

Shermis, M. D., Koch, C. M., Page, E. B., Keith, T. Z., & Harrington, S. (2002). Trait ratings for automated essay grading. *Educational and Psychological Measurement, 62*(1), 5–18.

Song, Y., Deane, P., & Fowles, M. (2017). Examining students' ability to critique arguments and exploring the implications for assessment and instruction. *ETS Research Report Series, 2017*(1), 1–12.

U.S. Department of Education–National Center for Education Statistics. (2003–2018a). *Private school universe survey* (PSS).

U.S. Department of Education–National Center for Education Statistics. (2003–2018b). *Public elementary/secondary school universe survey.*

Vajjala, S., & Meurers, D. (2012). On improving the accuracy of readability classifications using insights from second language acquisition. In J. Tetreault, J. Burstein, & C. Leacock (Eds.), *Proceedings of the Seventh Workshop on the Innovative Use of NLP for Building Educational Applications.* The Association for Computational Linguistics.

Weigle, S. C. (2002). *Assessing writing.* Ernst Klett Sprachen.

Yamamoto, M., & Jennrich, R. (2013). A cluster-based factor rotation. *The British Journal of Mathematical and Statistical Psychology, 66.* https://doi.org/10.1111/bmsp.12007

Yngve, V. (1972). *The depth hypothesis.*

Zeno, S. M., Ivens, S. H., Millard, R. T., & Duvvuri, R. (1995). *The educator's word frequency guide.* Touchstone Applied Science Associates.

CHAPTER 4

EMPIRICAL ENSEMBLE EQUATING UNDER THE NEAT DESIGN INSPIRED BY MACHINE LEARNING IDEOLOGY

Zhehan Jiang
Peking University

Lingling Xu
Peking University

Yuting Han
Beijing Language and Culture University

Dexin Shi
University of South Carolina

Jihong Zhang
University of Arkansas

Haiying Liang
University College London

Jinying Ouyang
Peking University

Machine Learning, Natural Language Processing, and Psychometrics, pages 93–112
Copyright © 2024 by Information Age Publishing
www.infoagepub.com

ABSTRACT

This study proposes an empirical ensemble equating (3E) approach that collectively selects, adopts, weighs, and combines outputs from different sources to take and combine advantage of equating techniques in various score intervals. The ensemble idea was demonstrated and tailored to the Non-Equivalent groups with Anchor Test (NEAT) equating. A simulation study based on several published settings was conducted. Three outcome measures- average bias, its absolute value, and root mean square difference- were used to evaluate the selected methods' performance. The 3E approach outperformed other counterparts in most given conditions, while the cautions, such as tuning weights and assuming possible scenarios for using the proposed approach were also addressed.

In high-stakes assessments (e.g., licensure and certification exams), new forms are typically created for continuing test administration. Using a new form at each administration enhances content security and item-exposure control and supports computerized mechanisms and item bank construction. From a measurement perspective, different assessment forms should be built on an identical set of content and statistical specifications for consistency purposes. Further, statistical models are adopted to support the exchangeability of scores across the forms; this process is generally called equating, allowing computations of scores projected from one form to the other.

Among many equating designs, the Non-Equivalent groups with Anchor Test (NEAT) is a highly, if not the most, popular one widely adopted in research and practice. In an application of the NEAT design, a new test x form is equated to an old test y form, a sample takes x from Group X, and a sample takes y from Group Y. In addition, an anchor test is taken by both groups and allows one to study the difference in ability between Group X and Group Y. Group X's true response data on y form and Group Y's true response data on x form are not observable, as they do not actually happen in the administration; this makes the quality evaluation of equating difficult, as no true values are available for the comparative purpose. Therefore, most studies investigating the performance of equating methods are simulation-based (e.g., Andersson & Wiberg, 2017; Moses & Holland, 2010; Sinharay & Holland, 2010). That is, researchers provide empirical conditions to find if specific methods yield better results than other counterparts; the findings are then used to assist method selections.

Statistical techniques for equating are about transformations of both modeling parameters and item responses, including the ones based on equipercentile equating, linear equating methods, item response theory (IRT) observed-score and true score equating, local equating (van der Linden, 2011), Levine nonlinear method, Kernel equating (KE), and others (see Kolen & Brennan, 2004 for details). Specifically, a post-stratification

(PSE), Levine observed-score linear, and chained equating (CE) methods are typically used in KE when the NEAT design is present (Davier et al., 2004). However, these techniques are not consistently performing better than others. In fact, the performance depends on the settings of actual tasks and different score ranges. For instance, Livingston and Kim (2009) found that differences between equating methods in accuracy were small for raw scores near the median of the distribution but large for scores far from the median, and the circle-arc method had higher accuracy in the upper and lower tails of the score distribution compared to mean equating in small samples. Kim and Livingston (2010) show that, in small sample scenarios, CE produced the most reliable results for low scores, while circle-arc ones were better choices in the upper half of the score distribution.

ENSEMBLE LEARNING

As a powerful technique, ensemble learning (EL) functions like its name suggests: utilizing multiple models to improve the reliability and accuracy of specific machine-learning predictions. The idea of the ensemble is collectively selecting, adopting, weighing, and combining outputs from different sources. Without loss of generality, in a classification task, techniques such as logistic regression, support vector machine, random forests, and neural network are all set into EL to improve the stability of the overall performance. Tremendous studies across fields show that EL is frequently more reliable than individual models. For instance, Borovkova and Tsiamas (2019) classify different companies in the stock market via EL; Lessmann and colleagues (2021) propose an EL framework to support marketing decision-making; Priore and colleagues (2018) construct scheduling of flexible manufacturing systems using ensemble methods. Unsurprisingly, EL often ranks at the top in machine-learning competitions such as Kaggle (Kumar & Mayank, 2020; Stamp et al., 2021).

EL can be framed in multiple ways. The simplest one is averaging the outputs of different models, while complex ones devising weights and adaptive algorithms to empower the engineer. The concept of EL has been extended to a broader sense, meaning it is not limited to models, but also data and hypotheses. In this chapter, we limit EL in the context of a modeling ensemble, where each model is termed a "learner." There are two EL sub-types: sequential EL and parallel EL. The former considers the dependence between learners, each of which is exploited sequentially to obtain more accurate predictions. To illustrate with a classification example again, mislabeled cases have their weights adjusted while the weights for properly labeled sets stay unchanged. Each time a new learner is generated, the weights are updated to improve the classification performance. On the

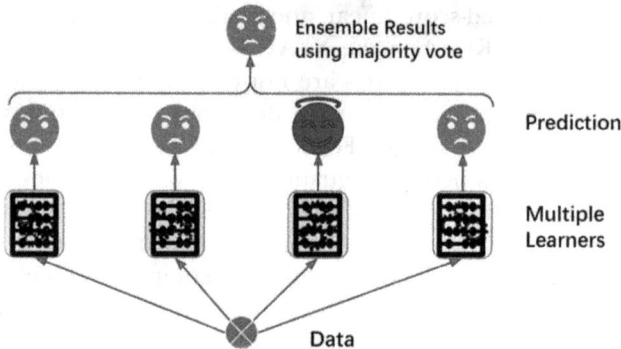

Figure 4.1 A simple ensemble learning using majority vote.

other hand, parallel EL drives learners in parallel. When rendering parallel EL, the idea is to exploit the learners' independence, as the overall error rates can be reduced by drawing on "good" learners' strengths and offsetting "bad" learners' weaknesses. Figure 4.1 shows a simple EL: four learners (i.e., classification techniques such as logistic regression, support vector machine, and so on) are used to predict a binary variable with a value of red or blue, while the third one yields a different label (blue) to others (red). If one uses majority vote as the ensemble schema, the aggregated result is colored red, as three learners endorse red and only one endorses blue.

It's self-evident that different weighting schemes can lead to unidentical conclusions, even if the learners are identical in two EL models. "Simple weighted average (SWA)" is that the weights are proportional to the precisions of each learner. "Weight proportional to the square of the precision (SqrWA)" squares the precisions to obtain weights. In contrast, "weight proportional to the precision's powers of N (PrWA)" further extends square to an arbitrary integer N. Other schemes, such as considering data collection time (i.e., "age" of the data) and polynomial functions on data variance, are also available but not applicable to the present study (see Wagner, 1975, p. 289). Let's consider a situation where the precisions are wrapped into values larger than 1 (the inversed effect exhibits when the precisions are presented as ratios or percentages); the three weighting schemes (SWA, SqrWA, and PrWA) incrementally entrust the learners that perform the best at a specific estimate more; for example, the same precision will be given more considerable weight in SqrWA than in SWA. An extreme choice is brutally picking the best one and neglecting others; that said, all non-optimal learners receive zeros and 100% for the optimal one when calculating weights.

EL has been applied to different areas and inquiries in educational and psychological studies. Ragab and colleagues (2021) use EL algorithms to predict student failure and enable customized educational paths; Abidi and colleagues (2020) adopt ensemble classifiers to quantify academic procrastination through big data assimilation; Premalatha and Sujatha (2021) predict the employment status of graduates in higher educational institutions via EL; Pearson and colleagues (2019) estimate treatment outcomes following an internet intervention for depression through a machine learning ensemble. These successful applications primarily lie in prediction and classification; engrafting EL to equating tasks remains unknown such that the topic per se is practically beneficial and methodologically meaningful to the field.

METHOD

The method section outlines the steps involved in constructing the proposed ensemble approach and highlights the rationales and consequences of this method through a walkthrough case study. This case study uses the scenario depicted in Figure 4.2 for illustration purposes. The first part of Figure 4.2 displays the true scores ranging from 20 to 23, along with the estimated scores generated by three equating models (referred to as learners in this study) represented by M1, M2, and M3. The second and third parts of Figure 4.2 present the biases (i.e., the equating result minus the true score) and their absolute values, along with their averaged values highlighted in the last row. It can be observed that the lowest values of the averaged bias and absolute bias are 0.15 and 0.25, respectively (see the last row in the second and third part of Figure 4.2). Thus, a better approach would ideally produce values lower than these two numbers.

The proposed approach employs a "simple weighted average" schema and requires absolute bias values to generate comparable measures, enabling the calculation of relative contributions to ensemble weights. Theoretically, models with smaller absolute biases should be trusted more and given greater weight in the final ensemble. Thus, contributions to the weights should be inversely related to absolute biases. In the fourth part of Figure 4.2, the inversions of the absolute biases (e.g., 1.0/0.5, 1.0/0.3, and 1.0/0.4 in the first row) are calculated and summed across each row. These inversions, as shown in the fourth part of Figure 4.2, are divided by their sums for each row (e.g., 2.0/7.8, 3.3/7.8, and 2.5/7.8 in the first row) to create ensemble weights, which are listed in the fifth part of Figure 4.2. Consequently, the sum of the weights in each row equals 1, as shown in the last column.

Finally, the weights are applied to the corresponding estimated scores presented in the first part of Figure 4.2. The ensemble equating is completed by summing the weighted scores, resulting in the last column in the sixth part of Figure 4.2. It is straightforward to calculate that the average bias and absolute bias values of the ensemble score, as seen in Figure 4.2 (across the case's 20–23 range), are 0.05 and 0.15. As expected, these aggregated accuracy

TRUE	M1	M2	M3
20.0	20.5	20.3	19.6
21.0	21.2	21.4	20.8
22.0	22.4	22.1	22.2
23.0	22.9	22.8	22.7

$BIAS = estimated\ score - true\ score$

	BIAS1	BIAS2	BIAS3
	0.5	0.3	-0.4
	0.2	0.4	-0.2
	0.4	0.1	0.2
	-0.1	-0.2	-0.3
Average	0.25	0.15	-0.175

$AbsBIAS = abs(BIAS)$

	AbsBIAS1	AbsBIAS2	AbsBIAS3
	0.5	0.3	0.4
	0.2	0.4	0.2
	0.4	0.1	0.2
	0.1	0.2	0.3
Average	0.3	0.25	0.275

$$revAbsBIAS = \frac{1}{AbsBIAS}$$

revAbsBIAS1	revAbsBIAS2	revAbsBIAS3	Sum
2.0	3.3	2.5	7.8
5.0	2.5	5.0	12.5
2.5	10.0	5.0	17.5
10.0	5.0	3.3	18.3

$$Weight = \frac{revAbsBIAS}{rowsum(revAbsBIAS)}$$

M1Weight	M2Weight	M3Weight	Sum
0.26	0.43	0.32	1.0
0.40	0.20	0.40	1.0
0.14	0.57	0.29	1.0
0.55	0.27	0.18	1.0

$Weighted\ score = estimated\ score \times Weight$
$Ensemble = rowsum(Weighted\ score)$

WeightedM1	WeightedM2	WeightedM3	Ensemble
5.23	8.64	6.26	20.1
8.48	4.28	8.32	21.1
3.20	12.63	6.34	22.2
12.49	6.22	4.13	22.8

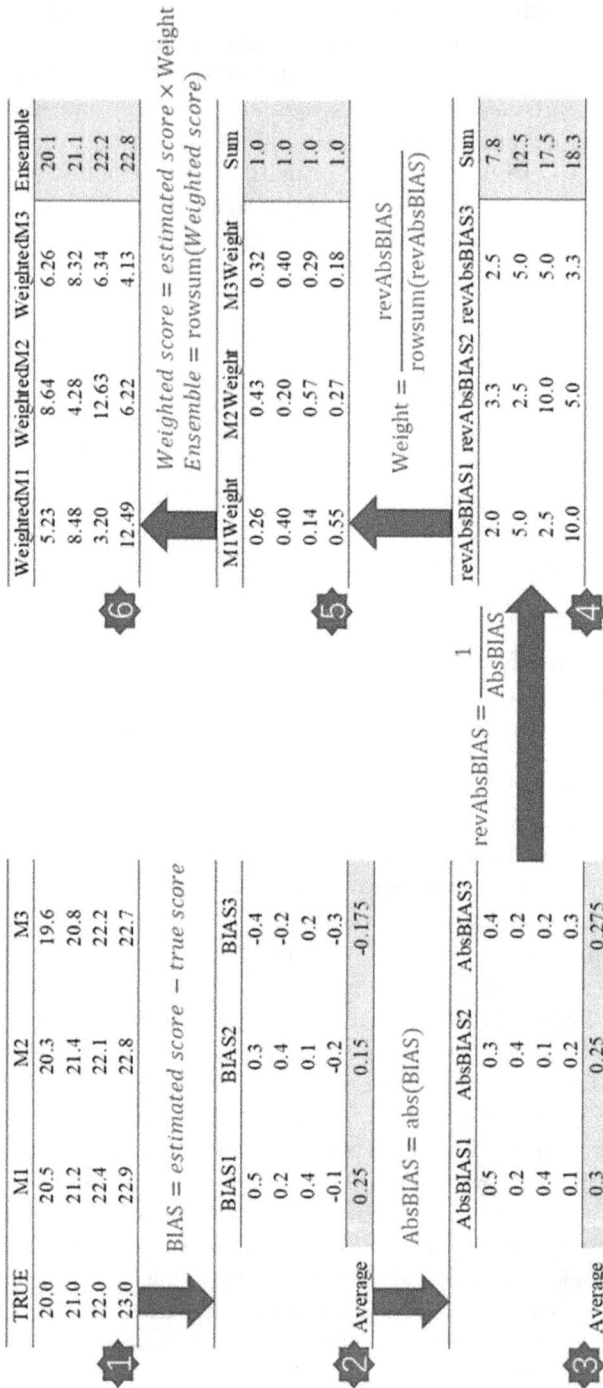

Figure 4.2   The steps of a walkthrough case using simple weighted average schema.

measures are both lower than those of any individual model, as shown in the last row of the second and third parts of Figure 4.2. This indicates that the ensemble approach effectively improves the equating accuracy compared to relying on a single model, thus validating the proposed method.

The walkthrough case in Figure 4.2 shows one scenario only, of which the result is not comprehensive enough to generalize. Figure 4.3 contains two more scenarios: the first one further amplifies the advantage, as all the aggregated absolute bias values for the three learners (0.325, 0.725, and 0.75) are larger than that of the ensemble score (0.26); while the second one, although not producing the optimal results (0.56) when compared with other individual learners (0.5, 0.75, and 0.75), remains robust as it outperforms many counterparts.

As introduced above, different weighting schemes likely result in inconsistent estimates. If one uses the "weight proportional to the square of the value/precision (SqrWA)" scheme, the white cells in the fourth part of Figure 4.2 should be squared before summing, and the rest of the calculations, follow the same flow. The PrWA_N scheme calculates the Nth power for the reversed absolute bias values in the fourth part of Figure 4.2 to increase the impact of top-performing learners in the ensemble procedure.

In practice, however, true scores are unknown in an equating setting. Therefore, constructing an ensemble equating model demands a mechanism to account for the plausible variability in observed responses. That said, this mechanism should deliver weights for each learner. Based on the ideology of the walkthrough case, we propose an empirical ensemble equating (3E) approach to handling the NEAT design's inquiry.

Like power analysis in complex scenarios where mathematical deriving fails to provide viable solutions, the 3E approach is simulation-based and rooted in empirical estimates from item response theory (IRT). Let $\{x, y, anchor\}$ be observed responses from a NEAT design and, correspondingly, $\{\beta, \theta\}$ be estimates of item parameters and latent traits via a IRT model (e.g., three-parameter logistic model) where the observed responses are fed. We adopt the famous "KBneat" dataset to demonstrate the 3E approach. This dataset contains responses for two forms (one for each group) of a 36-item NEAT-based examination, while 12 anchor items were taken by both groups (Kolen & Brennan, 2004).

In this study, eight learners were used for both comparative purposes and 3E construction, including linear equating methods (the Tucker linear equating and the chained linear equating), equipercentile equating methods (the equipercentile equating using frequency estimation method with log-linear smoothing and the equipercentile equating using a chained method with log-linear smoothing), mean equating methods (the Tucker mean equating and the chained mean equating), and the circle-arc ones (the Tucker circle-arc equating and the chained circle-arc equating). These

1

TRUE	M1	M2	M3
20.0	20.5	20.3	21.0
21.0	21.2	21.4	21.8
22.0	22.4	21.8	22.2
23.0	22.8	25.0	24.0
Average AbsBIAS	0.325	0.725	0.75

WeightedM1	WeightedM2	WeightedM3	Ensemble
6.47	10.68	3.32	20.5
12.11	6.11	3.11	21.3
4.48	8.72	8.88	22.1
17.54	1.92	3.69	23.2
		Average AbsBIAS	0.26

2

TRUE	M1	M2	M3
20.0	20.5	20.3	21.0
21.0	21.2	21.4	21.8
22.0	22.4	22.3	22.2
23.0	23.9	25.0	24.0
Average AbsBIAS	0.5	0.75	0.75

WeightedM1	WeightedM2	WeightedM3	Ensemble
6.47	10.68	3.32	20.5
12.11	6.11	3.11	21.3
5.17	6.86	10.25	22.3
10.17	4.79	9.19	24.1
		Average AbsBIAS	0.56

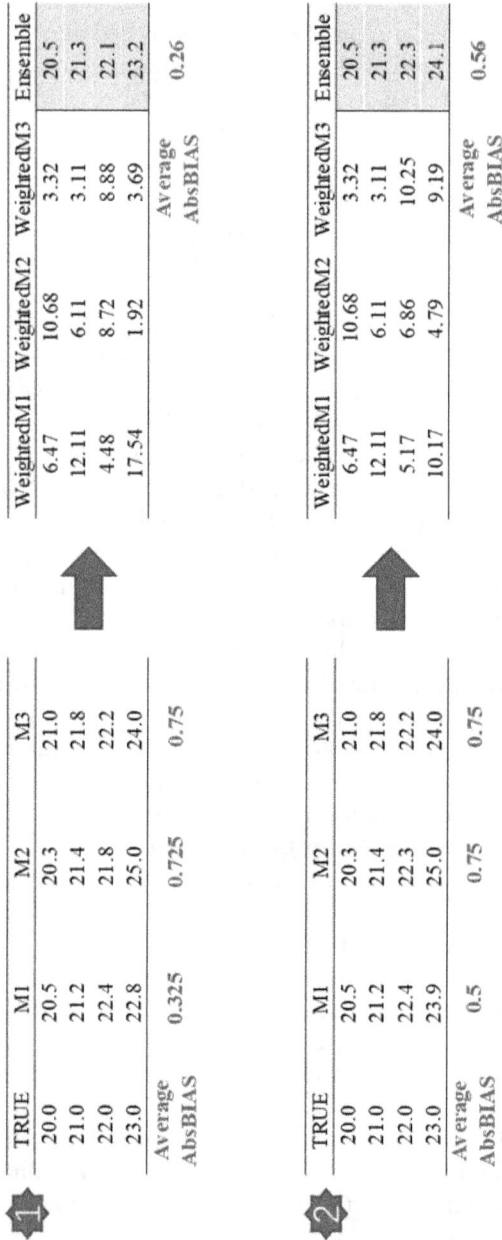

Figure 4.3 Two possible scenarios in the use of ensemble learning.

learners have been substantially studied and proved useful in many environments. Employing a diverse set of learners allows the ensemble approach to benefit from collective wisdom, as it can potentially reduce the impact of any shortcomings associated with a single method. By combining the outputs of these learners, the ensemble method can achieve better overall performance, ultimately improving the accuracy and robustness of the equating process.

Each learner was applied to "KBneat," and the equated results were standardized to serve as the ability difference between the two groups: the mean of the standardized differences was 0.3. The "KBneat" data of both groups were calibrated via two separate three-parameter logistic (3-PL) IRT models, resulting in β_X and β_Y (see Kolen & Brennan, 2014, p. 203 for item parameter estimates). θ_X is sampled from *Normal* $(0, 1)$, while the θ_Y is assumed to drift from θ_X by 0.3 and therefore the distribution was set to *Normal* $(0.3, 1.5)$. θ_X was used with β_Y in Group Y's 3-PL model to generate Group X's *true* responses in y form (called *x.y*), such that each learner's precision was calculated. 10,000 individuals per group were generated as the pool. To summarize, these simulation-based steps were functioning as a basis for learners' weights calculation.

The 3E approach is simulation-based, yet evaluating its performance demands a simulation study, too. Sample size directly affects random equating error, and different equating methods are suitable for different sample sizes. For example, when sample sizes are relatively small, the circle-arc equating and mean equating might be considered (Livingston & Kim, 2009). However, Diao and Keller (2020) suggested that sample sizes between 100 and 400 are sufficient for all classical equating methods. Sample sizes larger than 1,000 (e.g., 1,000, 1,500, 2,000) are not well investigated in previous equating research. To fully consider the impact of various sample sizes on the learners (traditional equating methods), the simulation study set the sample size per group equally to [200, 500, 1,000, 1,500, 2,000]. For example, if sample size was 500, 500 rows of the observations were randomly drawn from {*x, y, anchor, x.y*}. As an empirical approach, it's reasonable to assume that item parameters functioned stable. However, the ability difference could vary from cohort to cohort, especially when the sample size was small. Therefore, in addition to 0.3, two more θ drifts—0.1 and 0.5—were used. Finally, the SWA, SqrWA, and PrWA (powers set to 5, 50, and 100) were deployed as weighting schemes of the 3E approach, which adjusted the impact of top-performing learners in the ensemble procedure. Each condition was replicated 100 times. Three measures were used according to the literature (i.e., Wolkowitz & Wright, 2019; Zeng, 1993)—the average bias and its absolute value (BIAS and AbsBIAS) and root mean square difference (RMSD):

$$BIAS = \frac{\sum_p^{SS}(x.y_p - \widehat{x.y}_p)}{SS} \tag{4.1}$$

$$AbsBIAS = \frac{\sum_p^{SS}|x.y_p - \widehat{x.y}_p|}{SS} \tag{4.2}$$

$$RMSD = \sqrt{\frac{\sum_p^{SS}(x.y_p - \widehat{x.y}_p)^2}{SS}} \tag{4.3}$$

where SS was the sample size, and $\widehat{x.y}_p$ was the equated score of an individual examinee. The true responses of individual p from group X on test $y(x \cdot y_p)$ was generated through the (3E) approach as described previously. Based on the repeated samples, the measures were calculated by averaging over 100 repetitions. The analysis was implemented using R (Version 4.2.2 64-bit; R Core Team, 2016) and the R code was given in the supplementary material.

ANALYSIS

Since this study aims to explore the performance of the ensemble method and compare the ensemble method with traditional methods, rather than comparing among traditional methods (learners), in each repetition, we choose the learner with the highest equating accuracy as a reference. The reference method does not explicitly refer to a specific method, which may differ across conditions and repetition. Still, it is always the best learner, and the ensemble method is always compared with the best learner.

The average equating errors for the reference method and five 3E approaches utilizing various weighting schemes across different conditions are displayed in Tables 4.1 to 4.3. It is important to note that the reference method does not correspond to a specific equating method. Instead, it represents the method that produced the minimum equating error (i.e., the smallest absolute BIAS, RMSD, and BIAS values) among the eight learners in each repetition, and the values were calculated via averaging over all repetitions. It is crucial to emphasize that these bias measures are used to gauge the equating accuracy, with smaller values indicating higher precision in the equating process. As shown in Table 4.1, with the increase of the power in the weighting scheme for the 3E approaches, the smaller the absolute BIAS value, the higher the equating accuracy. This trend weakens until the power increases to 50, and the absolute BIAS value may no longer

TABLE 4.1   The Averaged Absolute BIAS for Different Equating Methods

Ability Difference	Equating Method	Sample Size				
		200	500	1,000	1,500	2,000
0.1	Reference	2.263	2.213	2.134	2.151	2.149
	PrWA_100	2.247	2.168	2.094	2.111	2.102
	PrWA_50	2.244	2.171	2.096	2.113	2.106
	PrWA_5	2.506	2.552	2.475	2.505	2.521
	SqrWA	2.648	2.738	2.665	2.691	2.711
	SWA	2.708	2.815	2.744	2.766	2.785
0.3	Reference	2.501	2.449	2.366	2.368	2.365
	PrWA_100	2.483	2.417	2.338	2.347	2.339
	PrWA_50	2.480	2.419	2.341	2.350	2.343
	PrWA_5	2.683	2.744	2.652	2.675	2.692
	SqrWA	2.811	2.907	2.811	2.831	2.850
	SWA	2.869	2.977	2.879	2.895	2.914
0.5	Reference	2.765	2.739	2.684	2.675	2.658
	PrWA_100	2.746	2.694	2.645	2.644	2.627
	PrWA_50	2.739	2.693	2.645	2.645	2.630
	PrWA_5	2.825	2.915	2.839	2.856	2.864
	SqrWA	2.920	3.035	2.951	2.966	2.976
	SWA	2.969	3.092	3.004	3.017	3.026

Note: PrWA_100, PrWA_50, and PrWA_5 reparented the 3E approaches with weight proportional to the precision's powers of 100, 50 and 5, respectively.

decrease. The difference in the absolute BIAS values among powers 1, 2, 5, and 50 is relatively large. The difference in the absolute BIAS values between powers 50 and 100 is fairly close. Their equating accuracy is higher than that of the reference method, for their absolute BIAS values are smaller than that of the reference method. That is, in the practical equating work with similar conditions, selecting the power of 50 can obtain better equating performance than the reference method.

The absolute BIAS values for all methods increased as the ability difference between the two groups increased. It is worth noting that even though 0.3 is the preset ability difference between the two groups—that is, the weights used in the 3E approaches were calculated under the same setting—the equating deviation of all approaches is still greater than that of the condition that the ability difference between the two groups is 0.1. However, the difference between the reference method and the worst-performing 3E approaches decreases with increasing ability drift. Taking the sample size of 200 as an example, when the ability difference was 0.1, 0.3, and 0.5, the absolute BIAS values between the SWA method and the reference method were 0.445, 0.368, and 0.203, respectively.

Regardless of the ability difference, the absolute BIAS values of the reference, the PrWA_100, and PrWA_50 methods decreased as the sample size increased from 200 to 1,000. However, larger samples did not always lead to better equating when the sample size was greater than 1,000. For example, when the ability difference between the two groups was 0.1 and 0.3, the absolute BIAS values of the reference, the PrWA_100 and the PrWA_50 methods decreased when the sample size increased from 200 to 1,000 but increased when the sample size increased from 1,000 to 1,500. And when the ability difference was 0.5, the absolute BIAS values of the reference, the PrWA_100, and the PrWA_50 methods showed a downward trend with increasing sample size. Larger sample sizes do not always lead to better equating results when the sample size exceeds 1,000 may be due to a phenomenon known as the "law of diminishing returns." As the sample size increases, the estimates derived from the equating methods become more stable and closer to their true values. However, after a certain point, the estimates are already stable enough, and further increasing the sample size provides minimal additional information. Besides, the equating methods may have inherent limitations that prevent them from achieving perfect accuracy, regardless of the sample size. In these cases, increasing the sample size may not lead to significant improvements in equating accuracy, as the limitations are related to the methods rather than the sample size.

In addition, the effect of sample size on the absolute BIAS values of the PrWA_5, SqrWA, and SWA methods did not show a uniform pattern. The RMSD results present a similar pattern to the absolute BIAS values and are shown in Table 4.2.

Table 4.3 shows that regardless of which equating method was used, the BIAS value increased as the ability difference between the two groups increased. The greater the difference in ability between the two groups and the smaller the sample size, the more pronounced the advantage of the 3E approaches. When the ability difference between the two groups was 0.1, only when the sample size was 200, the BIAS values of the PrWA_100 and PrWA_50 methods were smaller than that of the reference method; when the ability difference was 0.3, and the sample size was 200, 500 and 1,000, the BIAS values of the PrWA_100 and PrWA_50 methods were smaller than that of the reference method. Whereas, when the ability difference was 0.5, the BIAS values of the PrWA_100 and PrWA_50 methods were smaller than that of the reference method, regardless of the sample size.

Among the five 3E approaches, the BIAS values tended to decrease as the powers of the precision used in the weighting schemas increased. Still,

TABLE 4.2   The Averaged RMSD for Different Equating Methods

Ability Difference	Equating Method	Sample Size				
		200	500	1,000	1,500	2,000
0.1	Reference	2.810	2.787	2.722	2.728	2.719
	PrWA_100	2.801	2.735	2.675	2.687	2.670
	PrWA_50	2.799	2.738	2.678	2.691	2.675
	PrWA_5	3.111	3.189	3.107	3.132	3.137
	SqrWA	3.289	3.403	3.315	3.333	3.339
	SWA	3.362	3.485	3.396	3.410	3.416
0.3	Reference	3.083	3.065	2.983	2.982	2.966
	PrWA_100	3.078	3.031	2.959	2.963	2.943
	PrWA_50	3.076	3.033	2.961	2.966	2.947
	PrWA_5	3.316	3.406	3.298	3.317	3.321
	SqrWA	3.466	3.583	3.468	3.481	3.485
	SWA	3.532	3.655	3.538	3.548	3.550
0.5	Reference	3.369	3.385	3.322	3.312	3.280
	PrWA_100	3.377	3.346	3.293	3.288	3.255
	PrWA_50	3.371	3.346	3.293	3.289	3.257
	PrWA_5	3.476	3.587	3.492	3.506	3.499
	SqrWA	3.580	3.717	3.609	3.621	3.614
	SWA	3.632	3.775	3.664	3.673	3.665

Note: PrWA_100, PrWA_50 and PrWA_5 reparented the 3E approaches with weight proportional to the precision's powers of 100, 50 and 5, respectively.

the values may not continue to fall as the power increased to 50, especially when the ability difference between the two groups was large.

The sample size has no uniform effect on the reference method, and for the 3E approaches, their BIAS values at a sample size of 2000 were always greater than those at a sample size of 200. However, this did not mean the BIAS value consistently increased according to the sample size. For example, the BIAS values of all the compared 3E approaches under the condition of 1,000 sample size were all smaller than that for the 500-sample size condition.

In summary, in terms of equating accuracy, the higher the power of precision used in the weighting schemas for the 3E approaches, the better the performance. When the number of powers reaches 50, it is enough to outperform the eight reference learners in most cases. In addition, the greater the ability difference between the two groups and the smaller the sample size, the more noticeable the advantages of the 3E approaches (i.e., the PrWA_100 and PrWA_50 methods) over the reference method.

TABLE 4.3   The Averaged BIAS for Different Equating Methods

Ability Difference	Equating Method	Sample Size				
		200	**500**	**1,000**	**1,500**	**2,000**
0.1	Reference	0.910	0.970	0.937	0.954	0.930
	PrWA_100	0.839	1.031	1.021	1.070	1.088
	PrWA_50	0.849	1.044	1.031	1.081	1.100
	PrWA_5	1.342	1.698	1.618	1.688	1.737
	SqrWA	1.523	1.914	1.813	1.887	1.938
	SWA	1.592	1.990	1.881	1.955	2.007
0.3	Reference	1.560	1.602	1.538	1.537	1.507
	PrWA_100	1.421	1.577	1.522	1.554	1.565
	PrWA_50	1.424	1.584	1.526	1.560	1.573
	PrWA_5	1.729	2.044	1.924	1.981	2.024
	SqrWA	1.857	2.205	2.065	2.126	2.172
	SWA	1.911	2.265	2.117	2.180	2.226
0.5	Reference	2.053	2.152	2.122	2.107	2.058
	PrWA_100	1.880	2.043	2.022	2.032	2.022
	PrWA_50	1.878	2.046	2.021	2.033	2.024
	PrWA_5	1.986	2.311	2.227	2.266	2.287
	SqrWA	2.057	2.415	2.310	2.356	2.382
	SWA	2.096	2.460	2.346	2.395	2.421

Note: PrWA_100, PrWA_50, and PrWA_5 reparented the 3E approaches with weight proportional to the precision's powers of 100, 50 and 5, respectively.

EMPIRICAL STUDY

To showcase the performance of the new method in a practical setting, we present an empirical study using the final examination scores of fifth-year undergraduate students from a medical school. The surgery exam consisted of two rounds, corresponding to two tests, each containing 40 dichotomously scored items, with 12 common items between them. A total of 201 students were randomly assigned to the two tests. The descriptive information of raw scores can be found in Table 4.4.

The eight equating methods used in the simulation study, along with the PrWA_50 method, were employed to equate the scores of the first round to those of the second round. The dataset and the code used can be obtained by contacting the corresponding author. The equating results are displayed in Figure 4.4. Since no student's total score was below 10, the figure only shows the raw scores from 10 to 40. Although the true equating

TABLE 4.4		Descriptive Statistics of the Total Scores for Each Group			
		Raw scores			Average score on the anchor test
Round	N	Minimum	Mean	Maximum	
1	100	13.0	27.9	38.0	8.3
2	101	13.0	29.1	38.0	9.1

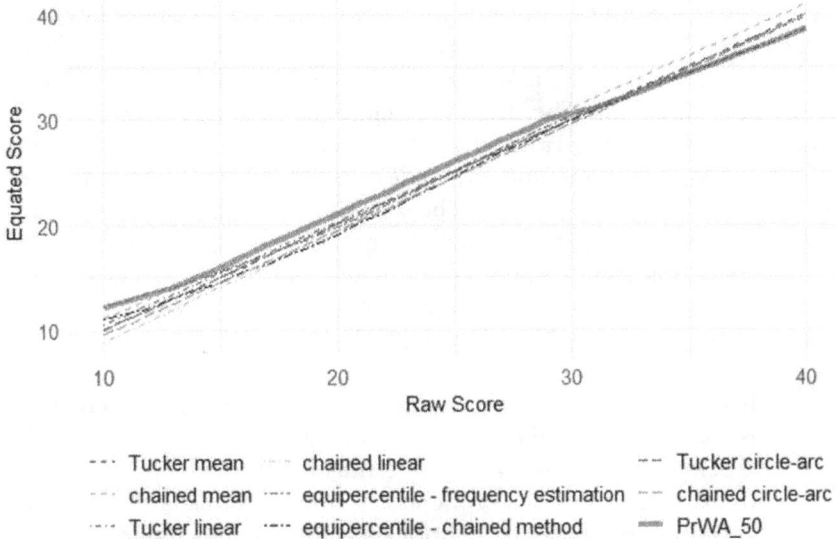

Figure 4.4 Equating results for a real-world dataset.

transformation is not known in the real dataset, it can be observed that the differences among various equating methods are not substantial. The PrWA_50 method is shown with a thicker red line, and in the score range of 10 to 30, it is closest to the results of the chained mean equating method. When the scores are above 30, it is more similar to the results of the two equipercentile equating methods. In other words, the PrWA_50 method can combine the results of various equating methods with different weights across different score ranges.

DISCUSSION AND CONCLUSION

EL is a powerful technique that utilizes multiple models to improve the reliability and accuracy of individual models. This study proposed an empirical ensemble equating (3E) approach that treats multiple equating functions as learners in EL and adopted several weighting schemes to improve the equating accuracy under the NEAT Design. The simulation study found that the 3E approach with weights proportional to the precision's powers of 50 or 100 can yield more accurate equating results than the eight ensembled equating methods in most cases. The 3E equating approach proposed in this study can better support the exchangeability of scores across different forms of an assessment, thereby guaranteeing the fairness of the assessment and providing support in constructing item banks more scientifically.

Holland and Strawderman (2009) introduced several approaches to averaging two or more equating functions, provided details on how to weigh the equating parameters, and discussed some properties of the averages of equating functions. The traditional methods of averaging equivalence functions introduced by Holland and Strawderman (2009) (e.g., the pointwise weighted average method, the angle bisector method, and the symmetric weighted average method) can be seen as following the ensemble idea but limited to linear equating functions or two nonlinear equivalence functions. The 3E approach proposed in this study can ensemble various linear or nonlinear equating methods and adopt various weighting schemes, which is more generalized and flexible, as the 3E eventually turns an equated score sheet in rather than a model.

Another perspective of understanding the utility of the proposed 3E approach is comparing it to the prior sensitivity analysis in Bayesian analysis. From the perspective of Bayesian analysis, the ideal priors should accurately reflect preexisting knowledge of the world, both in terms of the facts and the uncertainty about those facts. Priors that do not correspond to reality, however, can lead to severe bias (e.g., Baldwin & Fellingham, 2013; van Erp et al., 2018). Thus, a prior sensitivity analysis aiming to update one's prior beliefs with the data is vital to improve the performance of Bayesian modeling. Compared to typical prior sensitivity analysis, improving equating performance by proposing multiple equating designs is scarce in equating studies. There are commonalities between the proposed ensemble learning method with Bayesian prior sensitivity analysis. First, both utilize multiple methods (frequentist perspective) or priors' settings (Bayesian perspective) to improve prediction accuracy. The selection process could be arbitrary or purposeful for both frameworks depending on the research purpose. For instance, researchers may include the chained linear equating method as one learner because she/he, as an equating expert, believes the method is appropriate. Previous Bayesian literature has shown that some models perform better than the frequentist model when priors reflect researchers' beliefs appropriately (van Erp et al., 2018). Second, selecting those sources reflects different hypotheses (frequentist perspective) or beliefs (Bayesian perspective). In the simulation study, eight learners are chosen for learning. Like informative and uninformative prior, in ensemble learning, each learner reflects strong or weak hypotheses and thus performs better in specific scenarios than others. Third, some methods are needed to summarize the outputs of different outputs and obtain the best result. This study shows that EL is very flexible when adopting different average schemas. At the same time, in Bayesian analysis, the prior setting could be updated using the information of previous prior settings to get better performance.

To develop further from this initial attempt, research directions can extend to setting comparison and monotonicity constraints. The former question relates to the assumptions for empirical settings of the 3E simulation scenarios; Are large-scale assessments more appropriate than the smaller ones as the estimated parameters are more stable and trackable due to their standardized nature? The second problem is that the equated scores do not grant a straight ascending/descending order; Can smoothing functions be used to ease the monotonicity violation? Thirdly, only the absolute bias has been used to calculate weights. It might be beneficial to consider both the equating bias and standard deviation when determining the weights for the ensemble approach. Finally, it's essential to remember that the 3E approach highly relies on the learners' qualities. Even though the contaminations by bad learners can be well controlled within the 3E approach's framework, a relatively large number of bad learners can still be detrimental to the final equated estimates.

ACKNOWLEDGMENTS

Financial Disclosure:

This work was funded by the National Natural Science Foundation of China for Young Scholars (Grant No. 72104006), Peking University Health Science Center (Grant No. BMU2021YJ010), and the Peking University Health Science Center Medical Education Research Funding Project (Grant No. 2022YB41).

Competing Interests:

The authors have declared that no competing interests exist.

Data Availability Statement:

The datasets analyzed during the current study are not publicly available but are available from the corresponding author on reasonable request. Requests to access these datasets should be directed to YH, hanyuting716@gmail.com.

REFERENCE

Abidi, S. M. R., Zhang, W., Haidery, S. A., Rizvi, S. S., Riaz, R., Ding, H., & Kwon, S. J. (2020). Educational sustainability through big data assimilation to quantify academic procrastination using ensemble classifiers. *Sustainability, 12*(15), Article 6074. https://doi.org/10.3390/su12156074

Andersson, B., & Wiberg, M. (2017). Item response theory observed-score kernel equating. *Psychometrika, 82*(1), 48–66. https://doi.org/10.1007/s11336-016-9528-7 PubMed

Baldwin, S. A., & Fellingham, G. W. (2013). Bayesian methods for the analysis of small sample multilevel data with a complex variance structure. *Psychological Methods, 18*(2), 151.

Borovkova, S., & Tsiamas, I. (2019). An ensemble of LSTM neural networks for high-frequency stock market classification. *Journal of Forecasting, 38*(6), 600–619. https://doi.org/10.1002/for.2585

Davier, A. A., Holland, P. W., & Thayer, D. T. (2004). *The kernel method of test equating.* Springer.

Diao, H., & Keller, L. (2020). Investigating repeater effects on smallsample equating: Include or exclude? *Applied Measurement in Education, 33*(1), 54–66. https://doi.org/10.1080/08957347.2019.1674302

Holland, P. W., & Strawderman, W. E. (2009). How to average equating functions, if you must. In *Statistical models for test equating, scaling, and linking* (pp. 89–107). Springer.

Kim, S., & Livingston, S. A. (2010). Comparisons among small sample equating methods in a common-item design. *Journal of Educational Measurement, 47*(3), 286–298. https://doi.org/10.1111/j.1745-3984.2010.00114.x

Kolen, M. J., & Brennan, R. L. (2004). *Test equating, scaling, and linking: Methods and practices.* Springer-Verlag.

Kolen, M. J., & Brennan, R. L. (2014). *Test equating, scaling and linking: Methods and practices* (3rd ed.). Springer.

Kumar, A., & Mayank, J. (2020). *Ensemble learning for AI developers.* BA Press.

Lessmann, S., Haupt, J., Coussement, K., & De Bock, K. W. (2021). Targeting customers for profit: An ensemble learning framework to support marketing decision-making. *Information Sciences, 557*, 286–301. https://doi.org/10.1016/j.ins.2019.05.027

Livingston, S. A., & Kim, S. (2009). The circle-arc method for equating in small samples. *Journal of Educational Measurement, 46*, 330–343 https://doi.org/10.1111/j.1745-3984.2009.00084.x

Moses, T., & Holland, P. W. (2010). The effects of selection strategies for bivariate loglinear smoothing models on NEAT equating functions. *Journal of Educational Measurement, 47*(1), 76–91. https://doi.org/10.1111/j.1745-3984.2009.00100.x

Pearson, R., Pisner, D., Meyer, B., Shumake, J., & Beevers, C. G. (2019). A machine learning ensemble to predict treatment outcomes following an Internet intervention for depression. *Psychological Medicine, 49*(14), 2330–2341. PubMed https://doi.org/10.1017/S003329171800315X

Premalatha, N., & Sujatha, S. (2021, September). An effective ensemble model to predict employment status of graduates in higher educational institutions. In *2021 Fourth International Conference on Electrical, Computer and Communication Technologies (ICECCT)* (pp. 1–4). IEEE. https://doi.org/10.1109/ICECCT52121.2021.9616952

Priore, P., Ponte, B., Puente, J., & Gómez, A. (2018). Learning-based scheduling of flexible manufacturing systems using ensemble methods. *Computers & Industrial Engineering, 126,* 282–291. https://doi.org/10.1016/j.cie.2018.09.034

Ragab, M., Abdel Aal, A. M., Jifri, A. O., & Omran, N. F. (2021). Enhancement of predicting students performance model using ensemble approaches and educational data mining techniques. *Wireless Communications and Mobile Computing, 2021.* https://doi.org/10.1155/2021/6241676

R Core Team. (2016). *R: A language and environment for statistical computing.* R Foundation for Statistical Computing.

Sinharay, S., & Holland, P. W. (2010). A new approach to comparing several equating methods in the context of the NEAT design. *Journal of Educational Measurement, 47*(3), 261–285. https://doi.org/10.1111/j.1745-3984.2010.00113.x

Stamp, M., Chandak, A., Wong, G., & Ye, A. (2021). On ensemble learning. In *Malware analysis using artificial intelligence and deep learning* (pp. 223–246). Springer.

van der Linden W (2011). Local observed-score equating. In A von Davier (Ed.), *Statistical models for test equating, scaling, and linking* (pp. 201–223). Springer-Verlag.

Van Erp, S., Oberski, D. L., & Mulder, J. (2019). Shrinkage priors for Bayesian penalized regression. *Journal of Mathematical Psychology, 89,* 31–50.

Wagner, J. G. (1975). *Fundamentals of clinical pharmacokinetics.* Drug Intelligence Publications.

Wolkowitz, A. A., & Wright, K. D. (2019). Effectiveness of equating at the passing score for exams with small sample sizes. *Journal of Educational Measurement, 56*(2), 361–390. https://doi.org/10.1111/jedm.12212

Zeng, L. (1993). A numerical approach for computing standard errors of linear equating. *Applied Psychological Measurement, 17*(2), 177–186. https://doi.org/10.1177/014662169301700207

CHAPTER 5

TEST SECURITY IN REMOTE TESTING AGE

Perspectives From Process Data Analytics and AI

Jiangang Hao
Educational Testing Service

Michael Fauss
Educational Testing Service

ABSTRACT

The COVID-19 pandemic has accelerated the implementation and acceptance of remotely proctored high-stake assessments. While the flexible administration of the tests brings forth many values, it raises test security-related
concerns. Meanwhile, artificial intelligence (AI) has witnessed tremendous
advances in the last five years. Many AI tools (such as the very recent Chat-
GPT) can generate high-quality responses to test items. These new developments require test security research beyond the statistical analysis of scores
and response time. Data analytics and AI methods based on clickstream process data can get us deeper insight into the test-taking process and hold great

Machine Learning, Natural Language Processing, and Psychometrics, pages 113–131 promise for securing remotely administered high-stakes tests. This chapter uses real-world examples to show that this is indeed the case.

Test security is an integrated component of high-stakes assessments and is critical to ensure test results' validity, reliability, and fairness. Test security breaches can happen at different parts of a testing, such as testing sites, testing items, and testing processes. Therefore, a good test security solution often involves coordinated efforts around the prevention, detection, and remediation of security breaches. Among these efforts, data-based detection of security breaches plays an essential role in large-scale tests and the methods used in this area have evolved over the years as the available data changed.

Before the advent of digital technology, high-stakes tests were in paper-pencil format and administered in proctored sites. The data is limited to the final responses on the test papers. Statistical analyses were primarily used to detect test irregularities, such as similar response sequences due to answer copying. Since the late 1990s, the advance of digital technology has enabled computed-based and Internet-based tests. For example, Educational Testing Service (ETS) started offering the computer-based edition of TOEFL in 1998 and the internet-based edition in 2005 (TOEFL Report, 2005). When tests are delivered through computers, collecting more data is possible. In addition to the final response data collected in paper-pencil tests, computer-based tests also capture response process data, such as response time, change of responses, navigation activities, and other clickstream activities. A number of statistical methods have been developed for detecting test irregularity, such as examining similar responses (Sotaridona & Meijer, 2003; Wollack, 1997; Cizek & Wollack, 2017; Kingston & Xlark, 2014; Wollack & Fremer, 2013; Haberman & Lee, 2017), item pre-knowledge (Lee & Lewis, 2021), score gains and anomalies (Skorupski & Egan, 2011; Wollack & Eckerly, 2017; Lee & von Davier, 2013), response time (van der Linden & Guo, 2008; Meijer & Sotaridona, 2006; Man, Harring, et al., 2018), and answer revision patterns (Primoli et al., 2011; van der Linden & Jeon, 2012; Wollack et al., 2015; Sinharary et al., 2017; Sinharay & Johnson, 2017). Data mining methods such as cluster analysis have also been suggested(Man et al., 2019). Readers should be aware that the above is an incomplete list of the relevant literature in the public domain. There are many methods and practices being used by different testing companies or organizations, but they are not in the public domain due to the sensitivity of test-security related research.

Since 2020, the COVID-19 pandemic has accelerated the implementation and acceptance of remotely proctored high-stakes tests. For example, ETS started offering TOEFL and GRE at-home editions in March 2020(ETS News, 2020).In remotely proctored tests, test takers can take the tests from places (often at home) based on their convenience, as long as the site meets some requirements specified by the test administrator. While the flexible administration of the tests brings forth many values, it also raises concerns, such as security breaches and test interruption, which may impact the tests' validity, reliability, and fairness. Generally, we cannot control the hardware and environment in remotely proctored tests as tightly as in testing centers. This opens the doors for many possible unintended test-taking strategies to gain an advantage in the tests, creating many security concerns that do not exist for test-center administrations. However, addressing the hardware and environment issues often involves a non negligible burden for test takers. For example, bringing in a second or third camera can help to reduce the blind spots, but requires an extra cost for acquiring the cameras as well as improving the Internet infrastructure to meet the needs of the increased WiFi bandwidth to transmit the video data.

On the other hand, click stream process data contain rich information about the test-taking process. Analyzing these process data allows us to develop indicators that can be used to flag suspicious test-taking behaviors to defend test security at a much lower cost compared to hardware enhancement. To extract useful information from the big clickstream data, one should go beyond the traditional psychometric/statistical methods and leverage techniques from data science, artificial intelligence (AI), and natural language processing (NLP), as is done in, e.g., computational psychometrics (von Davier, et al., 2021). ETS researchers conducted comprehensive research projects in this area (Hao, 2022), and some examples include clickstream data-based detection of remote computer access (Hao & Li, 2021), automated essay similarity detection (Novak, et al., 2022), using keystroke as biometrics to detect imposters (Choi et al., 2019), detection of AI generated essays (Yan et al., 2022), and the detection of retyping vs. drafting using keystroke (Zhang et al., 2022).

Despite the great promises, we want to caution that the current level of AI and analytics (even in the near foreseeable future) cannot completely replace human proctors for high-stake assessments, though AI and analytics can assist human proctors in improving their efficiency and accuracy in the proctoring process. Furthermore, joint consideration of innovations in item types, assessment design, and reporting is necessary to ensure the success of remote testing. In this chapter, we first outline the general methodology for using clickstream process data to support remotely proctored tests. Then we introduce how these new techniques can be applied in practice with some real-world examples.

A GENERAL ROADMAP

Based on the data flow, there are four critical steps in using clickstream process data. Figure 5.1 shows these steps. The first step is to get all the

```
┌─────────────────────────────────────────┐
│ 1. Data acquisition and evaluation        │
└─────────────────────────────────────────┘
                    ⬇
┌─────────────────────────────────────────┐
│ 2. Data wrangling                         │
└─────────────────────────────────────────┘
                    ⬇
┌─────────────────────────────────────────┐
│ 3. Data mining and feature engineering    │
└─────────────────────────────────────────┘
                    ⬇
┌─────────────────────────────────────────┐
│ 4. Connecting features with different     │
│    claims through machine learning/AI     │
└─────────────────────────────────────────┘
```

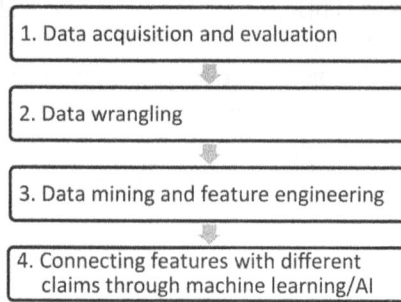

Figure 5.1   Critical steps in using process data to support remotely proctored tests.

relevant data and do a preliminary evaluation of their usefulness for different purposes. The second step is to transform the data and organize them in an appropriate format to feed into further analyses. The third step is to conduct extensive data mining work to develop features to characterize the process data. The last step is to connect the features developed in step 3 to scientific and business claims and present the results to stakeholders through interactive forms, such as dashboards. These four steps are not specific to the application for remotely proctored tests; they are the general steps of almost all data science projects. The steps are usually not a one-way process but an iterative one, meaning that the feedback from later steps often leads to adjustments (or reruns) of the earlier steps. As such, a close and agile collaboration among different parties involved is critical for moving the project forward.

For the data collection and evaluation step, it is important to differentiate two types of data, namely, the outcome and process data. The outcome data refers to the final responses used for scoring, and there are well-established psychometric procedures to analyze them, which we will not cover in this chapter. The process data, however, capture the timestamped interactions between the test takers and the system. The process data could include the system telemetry log data and multimodal data such as video or audio. Traditional psychometric/statistical methods are not enough to fully extract the values of these process data, and new methods from data science, machine learning/AI, and NLP are generally needed. These process data and new methods lead to many security-related applications, such as detecting abnormal activities, excessive similarity of constructed responses, and AI-generated responses. Figure 5.2 is a schematic that outlines some of the major applications.

The methods for handling process data in test security applications could be roughly categorized into data analytics and AI (supervised machine learning). The data analytics approach refers to discovering meaningful features or patterns in data through data mining and making decisions

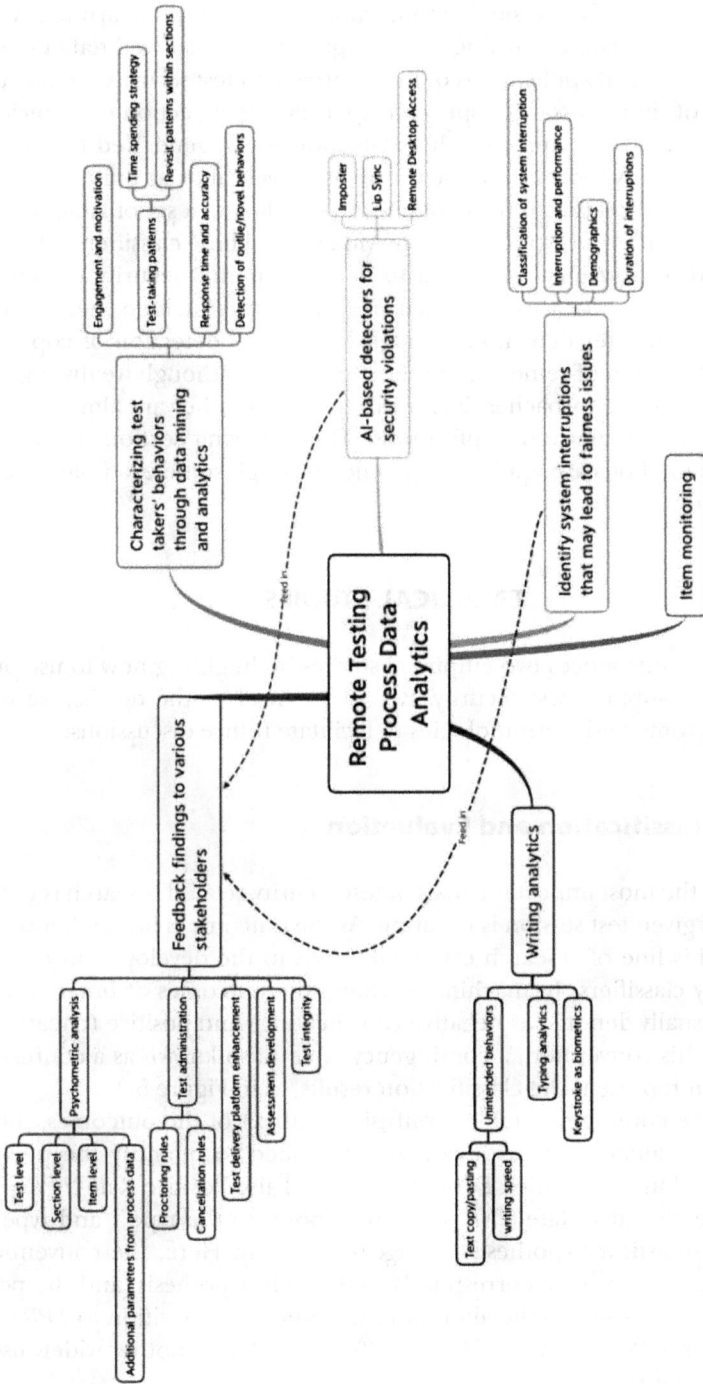

Figure 5.2 A summary of possible applications of process data in supporting remote testing.

based on these patterns, similar to unsupervised machine learning. As in unsupervised machine learning, there is generally no labeled data beforehand. Some typical applications of this approach in test security include the detection of similar essays or speech responses, the detection of suspicious test-taking behaviors, and zero-shot detection of AI- generated responses. The AI or supervised machine learning approach aims at building classifiers to map the feature representations of the data to a set of labels corresponding to different types of security violations. These classifiers will then be applied to new unlabeled data to detect potential security violations. Some applications of this approach in test security include, but are not limited to, imposter detection through biometrics, detection of copywriting, and detection of remote computer access. Even though we distinguish the two different approaches, it is worth noting that they are almost always used jointly in real-world applications. The following section introduces how these methods are applied in practice through some examples of empirical study.

EMPIRICAL STUDIES

This section introduces two empirical studies highlighting how to use process data to support test security. Before we head to the details, we first introduce some basic terminologies to facilitate future discussions.

Binary Classification and Evaluation

One of the most important goals of test security-related research is to tell whether a given test session is cheating. As the outcome is binary (cheating or not), this line of research eventually leads to the development of various binary classifiers. In machine learning, the outcomes of binary classifiers are usually denoted as negative (no cheating) and positive (cheating). Based on this convention, a contingency table (also known as a confusion matrix) can represent the classification results, as in Figure 5.3.

From the contingency table (confusion matrix) of the outcomes, some important evaluation metrics can be established to quantify the performance of a binary classifier. For example, the False Positive Rate($FPR = \frac{FP}{N}$)and False Negative Rate($FNR = \frac{FN}{P}$)correspond to the type I and type II errors in statistical hypothesis testing, respectively. Here, the convention is that the negative case corresponds to the null hypothesis, and the positive case corresponds to the alternative hypothesis. In addition to FPR and FNR, the True Positive Rate ($TPR = 1 - \frac{TP}{P} = 1 - FNR$) is another widely used evaluation metric.

		Predicted condition	
	Total population = P + N	Positive (PP)	Negative (PN)
Actual condition	Positive (P)	True positive (TP), hit	False negative (FN), type II error, miss, underestimation
	Negative (N)	False positive (FP), type I error, false alarm, overestimation	True negative (TN), correct rejection

Figure 5.3 Confusion matrix for binary classifier outcomes. Adapted from https://en.wikipedia.org/wiki/Evaluation_of_binary_classifiers

The direct output of a binary classifier is often not a binary class but a continuous decision function. The algorithm usually applies a threshold on the decision function to assign positive or negative labels. As one changes the threshold, the positive and negative labels change accordingly, and so do the *FPR* and *TPR* of the classification result. The receiver operating curve (ROC) is introduced to characterize how *FPR* and *TPR* change as the decision threshold varies. Figure 5.4 illustrates the ROCs of good and poor classifiers. Two important statistics based on the ROC are widely used to quantify the performance of a classifier. One is the area under the ROC, usually denoted as AUC, which ranges from 0.5 for a random classifier to 1

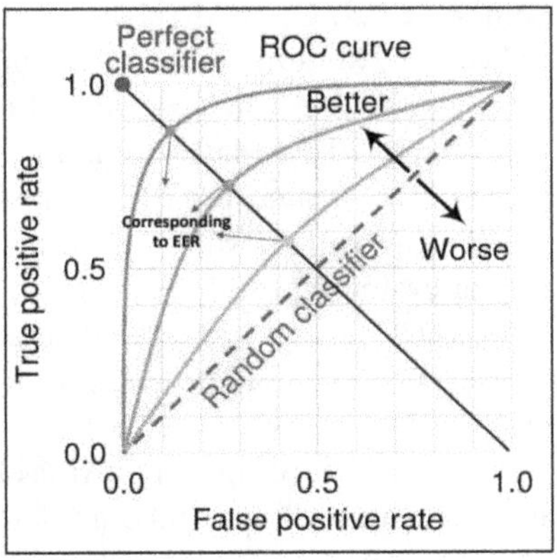

Figure 5.4 ROC curves of different classifiers adapted from https://en.wikipedia.org/wiki/Receiver_operating_characteristic

for a perfect classifier. Generally, an AUC greater than 0.9 is considered an outstanding classifier, while an AUC from 0.7 to 0.8 is considered acceptable (Bradley, 1997).

Another important statistic from the ROC is the equal error rate, EER, which denotes the point where the *FPR* equals *FNR*. In Figure 5.4, three points corresponding to the EERs of the three classifiers are marked. Note that these points are not precisely EERs as the *y*-axis is not FNR but 1-FNR (e.g., TPR). EER is widely used in biometrics to characterize the classifier's performance;the smaller, the better. For example, the EER of the fingerprint is around 0.2%, and that of the iris is around 0.01%, though the actual numbers may be affected by the specific implementations (Walker, 2002).

In the following, we introduce three empirical studies to showcase how data analytics and AI/machine learning approaches can be used in the real world to support test security.

Detection of ChatGPT-generated Essays

The revolutionary advance of AI technology is changing learning and assessment in both positive and negative ways. There have been increasing concerns about test takers using AI-generated responses in writing tests, especially in remote testing. ETS researchers have conducted a systematic study to detect essays generated by a large language model, GPT-3(Yan, et al., 2022). Two approaches were explored for the detection, one is a support vector machine classifier based on features generated by ETS' e-rater system (Attali & Burstein, 2006), and another is based on fine tuning a pre-trained LLM, RoBERTa (Liu et al., 2019). The two methods achieved a classification accuracy of 95% and 99%, respectively (Yan, et al., 2023)

At the end of November 2022, OpenAI released another revolutionary AI product, ChatGPT(https://openai.com/blog/chatgpt/), which became an instant hit since its release. ChatGPT introduced a reinforcement learning with human feedback (RLHF) layer to handle user prompts/questions better than its predecessors, such as GPT-2 and 3, and can generate high- quality texts in a different context which has already put a serious challenge to the current way of evaluating students' writing. As a result, developing detectors that can detect ChatGPT- generated responses has become a hot research topic, and several detectors have been developed by different individuals and organizations in the public domain (Crothers et al., 2022; Slashdot, 2023; Tian, 2023). Most recently, OpenAI itself also released a detector for AI-generated texts (https://openai.com/blog/new-ai-classifier-for -indicating-ai-written-text). In addition, there are many other detectors being developed but have not yet been opened to the public, such as those developed at ETS and other organizations.

Three important up front issues must be kept in mind while developing a serious detector of AI-generated essays (Hao, 2023). To clarify, we refer to a detector as "serious" if it is supposed to be used in a high-stakes application in which the detection outcome needs to be well justified and can lead to significant consequences. The first requirement is that a serious detector needs to have clear performance metrics, such as FPR and TNR, as discussed in the preceding subsection. A contrast sample must be specified to establish such metrics, e.g., against which sample the detector is trying to detect ChatGPT-generated essays. The second requirement is that the detector should be robust against reasonable human edits on top of the AI-generated texts, as this is how people use AI language models in the real world. The extent to which the detector should be robust against human edits is an open question and requires some consensus among the stakeholders in different use cases. Fundamentally, there is no way to tell for sure whether an AI or a human generated a text if enough paraphrases or revisions are applied. The third issue is the most challenging, namely, what evidence is necessary for one to confidently and justifiably claim that an essay is generated by AI in high-stakes applications. After all, it could cause more damages if someone is incorrectly accused of cheating using ChatGPT-generated responses. All these issues take work to address and generally require the consensus of stakeholders in specific use cases. In what follows, we introduce our work on developing a ChatGPT detector by keeping these three issues in mind.

We chose a specific contrast sample when developing our detector. First, we randomly sampled two thousand essays from two prompts in the writing section of a high-stakes test. Then, we generated two hundred essays from each prompt using ChatGPT. These procedures guarantee a clear context for our detector. Furthermore, while we generated these essays from ChatGPT, we explicitly prompted the system to add some typos and grammar errors, by which we aim to mimic some level of human edits. Finally, once we had all the data ready, we conducted data analytics to identify features that could be used to detect the ChatGPT-generated essays.

We start with the simplest one of all possible features that can characterize the texts. As our goal is to detect whether a text is generated by AI, there is already a well-established quantity, perplexity (Mao, 2019), which characterizes how unlikely a sequence is generated by a given language model. The higher the perplexity, the less likely the sequence is from a given language model. When we have the essays from humans and ChatGPT, the simplest classifier is to compute the perplexity of the essays based on a given language model and then find out where to set the threshold as we know which essay is from ChatGPT. In the left panel of Figure 5.5, we show the density plot of the perplexity of essays from humans and ChatGPT, respectively. As one can read from the distribution, human-generated essays show a much broader range of perplexity, while ChatGPT-generated essays show a much narrower range. If we use the thresholds of the essay perplexity to control the two error probabilities of the decision function, the resulting ROC of the classification results is shown in the right panel of Figure 5.5. The results suggest that the essay perplexity alone already works very well for detecting ChatGPT-generated essays.

The essays used in the above analysis are relatively long, from 400 to 600 words on average. Can we still see the clear separation when the texts are shorter, e.g., at the sentence level? To verify this, we use the same essays but look at the distribution of the sentence perplexity. The results are shown in Figure 5.6. It is not unexpected that the detection power decreases at the sentence level, as the fewer words there are, the more difficult it is to tell whether a text was written by a human or an AI. There is no chance of detecting this in the extreme case of only one word.

The above detector does not involve supervised machine learning/AI but applies data analytics to identify the right features to detect essays generated from ChatGPT, and it already performs very well, as measured by an almost perfect ROC. However, as we highlighted earlier, if more human edits are made to ChatGPT-generated essays, a more sophisticated detector is required. More features based on sentence-level perplexity and other language features should be combined with machine learning/AI algorithms to deliver a robust detector (Hao, Fauss, & Yan, in preparation).

Keystroke-Based Detection of Suspicious Writing Behaviors

In the preceding subsection, we introduced a simple detector of ChatGPT-generated essays. However, as we pointed out earlier, if a person makes many edits on top of AI-generated essays, we will surely lose the power of detection at a certain point, even with more robust detectors based on more language features and machine learning models. Therefore, additional information is needed to rescue the case, especially from another modality. Among them, the data captured in the keystroke logs could provide valuable information about the writing process. It could be used to help with the detection when human edits are there. In the following, we show two applications of keystroke process data in test security, using it as a biometric to identify test takers and as a detector to uncover copywriting behaviors.

ETS researchers have extensively researched using keystroke data to understand students' writing process (Deane, 2014; Zhang & Deane, 2015). Recently, this line of keystroke capability has been applied to test security-related applications. For example, the possibility of using keystroke pattern as biometrics to identify test takers has been demonstrated (Choi, et al.,

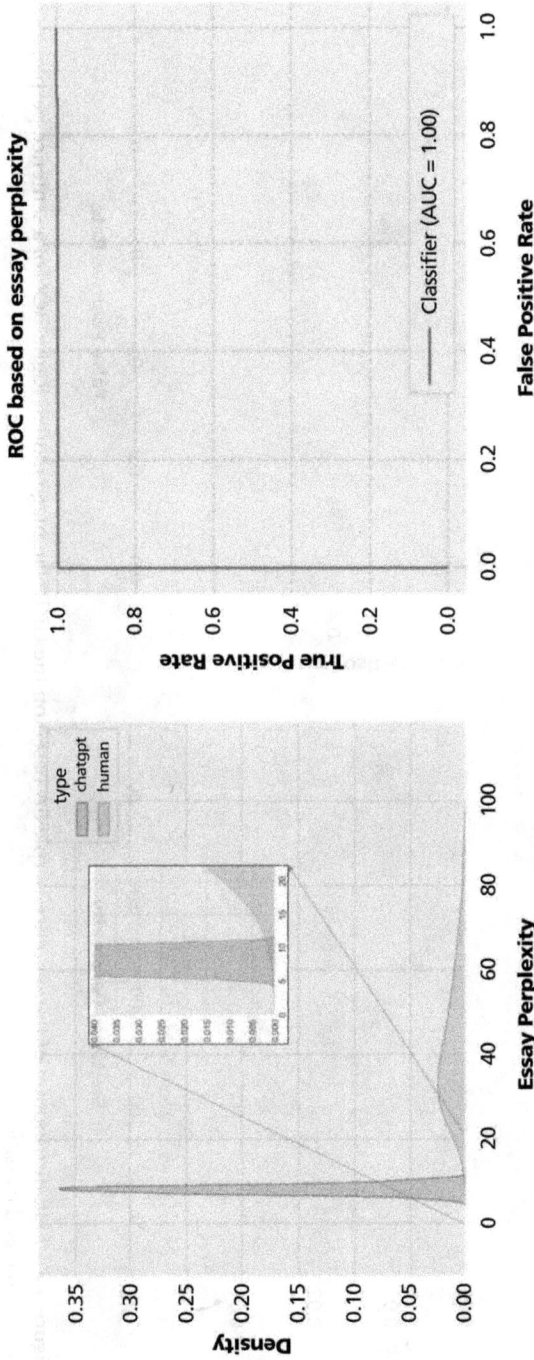

Figure 5.5 Left: distribution of the essay perplexity based on the GPT2 language model. Right: ROC of an essay perplexity threshold-based classifier.

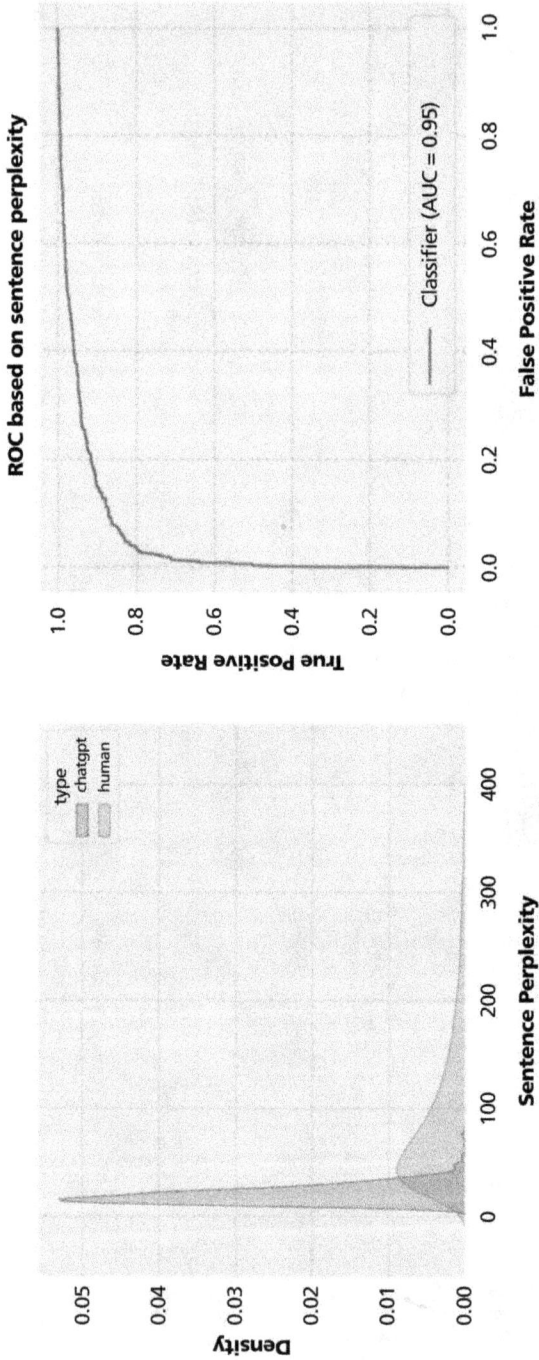

Figure 5.6 Left: distribution of the sentence perplexity based on the GPT2 language model. Right: ROC of a sentence perplexity threshold-based classifier.

2021), and reliable detection of copywriting from draft writing based on keystroke patterns has been shown (Zhang, Hao, & Deane, in preparation). In the following, we will briefly introduce these two lines of research.

A person's writing process under similar writing environments shows unique patterns, which can be used as biometrics to identify the person. Some typical features to characterize the writing process include the number, latency, speed, and total time for specific typing events, initial and repeated backspace events, cut and paste events, and edits that involve jumps from one location to another. The features can also include measures about word edits, typo corrections, and the burst of text production. In addition, summary statistics of the time interval between adjacent letters (digraph) can also be used to characterize the writing process. Readers can refer to (Deane, 2014; Zhang & Deane, 2015) for more discussions of the development of features to characterize the writing process.

To demonstrate that keystroke features can be used to form biometrics to identify persons, we conducted an empirical study by choosing 3,110 repeated test takers (repeaters).We chose two essays from each repeater and created 3,110 repeater essay pairs. We also created 3,110 non-repeater essay pairs as a control by randomly pairing the essays from two non- repeaters. We extracted a set of writing process features for each essay based on the corresponding keystroke logs. Using the repeater essay pairs, we can also check how well the keystroke features are correlated in the two essays by the same test taker. Some highly correlated features are shown in Table 5.1.

Based on these keystroke features, one could develop a classifier to detect whether an essay pair is from the same or a different person. To do this, for each essay pair, we created a distance feature vector by calculating the Euclidean distance between the same keystroke features from each essay in the essay pair. This way, the problem becomes a typical supervised machine-learning task. After comparing different algorithms, we found that the Gradient Boosting Machine (Friedman, 2001) works best for our data. The resulting classifier achieved performance with an equal error rate of 4.7%. This finding provides empirical evidence that keystroke patterns in writing tests could be used as a complementary biometric measure, adding an additional security layer. For more details on this study, we refer readers to our research paper (Choi et al., 2021).

Another important application of keystroke analytics in test security is to detect copywriting from draft writing. The cognitive process of draft writing involves four subprocesses, proposer, translator, transcriber, and evaluator (Hayes, 2012). Figure 5.7 shows a diagram of the four cognitive subprocesses and their meanings. Features from the keystroke process data can be mapped to these cognitive subprocesses(Deane et al., 2018;Zhang& Deane, 2015). For example, the initial pause before writing corresponds to the proposer subprocess.

TABLE 5.1 Highly Correlated Keystroke Features From the Same Test Taker

Feature name	Definition	Within-person correlation
inword_logIKI_median*	Median duration of in-word keystrokes, measured in log milliseconds	0.95
inword_logIKI_mean	Mean duration of in-word keystrokes in log milliseconds	0.95
wordinitiaUogIKI_median•	Median duration of word-initial keystrokes in log miUiseconds	0.92
append_interword_interval_logIKIs_mean	The mean log interkey intervals for keystrokes that add white space between words	0.92
wordinitialJogIKI_mean	Mean duration of word-initial keystrokes in log milliseconds	0.92
append_interword_intervalJogIKis_median•	The median log interkey interval for keystrokes that add white space between words	0.91
append_interword_intervaJ_speed_median•	The speed of keystrokes that add white space between words, measured in characters per second	0.91
wordinitial_char_per_sec_median•	Median speed of typing the first character of a word, in characters per second	0.91
iki400_Append8urst_len_mean	Mean length in characters of bursts of append keystrokes where no pause is greater than 400 milliseconds	0.91
iki400_AllActionBurst_len_mean	Mean length in characters of bursts where all keystrokes count as part of the burst, and bursts end on pauses longer than 400 milliseconds	0.90
initial_backspace_char_per_sec_median•	The median speed of the first in a series of backspace actions, measured in characters per second	0.90
iki200_AppendBurst_len_mean	Mean length in characters of bursts of append keystrokes where no pause is longer than 200 milliseconds	0.90
initial_backspaceJogIKI_median'"	The median log interkey interval for backspace actions that appear first in a series of backspace actions	0.89

Source: Adapted from Choi et al., 2021

Monitoring the process towards the goals

Evaluator

Proposer	Translator	Transcriber
Idea generation and planning	Translating ideas to words/sentences	Motor and orthographic execution

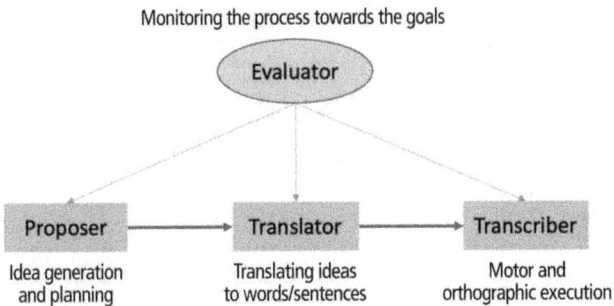

Figure 5.7   The cognitive process of writing based on Hayes, 2012.

On the other hand, in copywriting, where a test taker copies some existing texts and types them to respond to the writing items, the cognitive process is different. For example, the proposer and translator subprocesses could be completely obsolete, and the evaluator subprocess will be different accordingly. The different cognitive processes could leave their traces in the keystroke process data logs.

To verify this, an empirical study has been conducted. About 200 8th graders were recruited to take two writing tasks: a 30-minute copy-typing task and a 30-minute draft writing task. This is a typical supervised machine-learning task. Based on the keystroke features, it was found that a Random Forest (Ho, 1995; Breiman, 2001) classifier can detect copy typing with high accuracy. Figure 5.8 shows that the classifier has an almost perfect AUC based on 3-fold cross-validation. For more details of this study, we refer readers to (Zhang, Hao & Deane in preparation).

The above two keystroke-related applications make it clear that writing process data, when properly used, could have important implications for test security. Keystroke data capture the time stamped typing activities, thus providing important information about the process of how texts were developed. This information is not attainable through traditional NLP approaches, and therefore provides a unique handle for detecting AI-generated responses with human revisions.

SUMMARY

Remote testing has become a crucial means of administering high-stakes tests during the COVID-19 pandemic, with its growing popularity and adoption worldwide. Remote testing offers several benefits, such as convenience, accessibility, and flexibility for test-takers. It also presents cost and time savings and easy scalability for test administrators, as the logistic challenges associated with testing centers are significantly reduced. As a result, remote

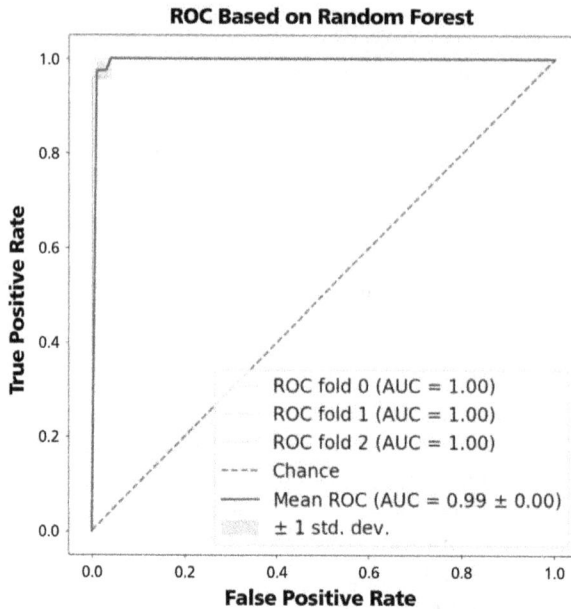

Figure 5.8 ROC of the random forest classifier for detecting copywriting.

testing will likely continue to be an important way of administering high-stakes tests even after the pandemic.

However, remote testing also raises many security concerns, as it is more challenging to maintain security measures of a test when it is taken from a not fully uncontrolled site. In this chapter, with three empirical examples, we have shown that data analytics and AI methods applied to clickstream process data allow us to gain deeper insight into the test-taking process and lead to new methods for detecting anomalies and suspicious behaviors that may indicate cheating. This line of research is indispensable for securing remote testing and should represent an important future direction of test security research.

ACKNOWLEDGMENT

This work was funded by ETS Research Allocation and Test Security Initiative.

REFERENCE

Attali, Y., & Burstein, J. (2006). Automated essay scoring with e-rater® V.2. *The Journal of Technology, Learning and Assessment, 4*(3).

Bradley, A. P. (1997). The use of the area under the ROC curve in the evaluation of machine learning algorithms. *Pattern Recognition, 30*(7), 1145–1159.

Breiman, L. (2001). Random forests. *Machine Learning, 45*(1), 5–32.

Choi, I., Hao, J., Deane, P., & Zhang, M. (2021). Benchmark keystroke biometrics accuracy from high-stakes writing tasks. *ETS Research Report Series, 2021*(1), 1–13.

Cizek, G. J., & Wollack, J. A. (Eds.). (2017). *Handbook of quantitative methods for detecting cheating on tests.* Routledge.

Crothers, E. et al. (2022). Machine generated text: A comprehensive survey of threat models and detection methods. ArXiv abs/2210.07321

Deane, P. (2014). Using writing process and product features to assess writing quality and explore how those features relate to other literacy tasks. ETS Research Report Series, 2014(1), 1–23.

Deane, P, Steck, F., Roth, A., Lewis, M., Litz, A., Richter, T., & Goswami, V. (2018). *Behavioral differences between retyping, drafting, and editing: A writing process analysis.* ETS Research Memorandum, RM-18-06.

ETS News. (2020, March). https://news.ets.org/press-releases/ets-introduces-at-home-solution-for-toefl-ibt-test-and-gre-general-test-amid-coronavirus-pandemic/

Friedman, J. H. (2001). Greedy function approximation: A gradient boosting machine. *Annals of Statistics,* 1189–1232.

Haberman, S. J., & Lee, Y. H. (2017). A statistical procedure for testing unusually frequent exactly matching responses and nearly matching responses. *ETS Research Report Series, 2017*(1), 1–9.

Hayes, J. R. (2012). Modeling and remodeling writing. *Written Communication, 29*(3), 369–388.

Hao, J. (2023). *Detecting ChatGPT-generated essays for high-stakes applications: What you should keep in mind.* LinkedIn. Retrieved February 10, 2023 from https://www.linkedin.com/pulse/detecting-chatgpt-generated-essays-high-stakes-applications-hao

Hao, J. (November 2022). *AI and data analytics approaches to address test security issues from remotely proctored tests.* Symposium at the Conference on Test Security, Princeton, NJ.

Hao, J. & Li, C., (2021). *Using AI and process data to detect remote desktop access in remotely proctored tests.* ETS Statistical Report, SR-2021-025

Hao, J., Fauss, M., & Yan, D. (n.d.). *Dynamic ChatGPT detector.* (Manuscript in preparation.

Ho, T. K. (1995, August). Random decision forests. In *Proceedings of 3rd international conference on document analysis and recognition* (Vol. 1, pp. 278–282). IEEE.

Kingston, N., & Clark, A. (Eds.). (2014). *Test fraud: Statistical detection and methodology.* Routledge.

Lee, Y. H., & von Davier, A. A. (2013). Monitoring scale scores over time via quality control charts, model-based approaches, and time series techniques. *Psychometrika, 78,* 557–575.

Lee, Y. H., & Lewis, C. (2021). Monitoring item performance with CUSUM statistics in continuous testing. *Journal of Educational and Behavioral Statistics, 46*(5), 611–648.

Liu, Y., Ott, M., Goyal, N., Du, J., Joshi, M., Chen, D.,..., & Stoyanov, V. (2019). *Roberta: A robustly optimized BERT pretraining approach.* arXiv preprint arXiv:1907.11692.21

Man, K., Harring, J. R., Ouyang, Y., & Thomas, S. L. (2018). Response time based nonparametric Kullback–Leibler divergence measure for detecting aberrant test-taking behavior. *International Journal of Testing, 19*, 1–23.

Man, K., Harring, J. R., & Sinharay, S. (2019). Use of data mining methods to detect test fraud. *Journal of Educational Measurement, 56*(2), 251–279.

Meijer, R. R., & Sotaridona, L. (2006). *Detection of advance item knowledge using response times in computer adaptive testing.* Law School Admission Council.

Mao, L. (2019). *Entropy, perplexity and its applications.* Lei Mao's Log Book

Novak, J., Choi, I., Hao, J., & Li, C., (October 2022), *AutoESD: An automated solution to detect copied essays.* Presentation given at the Conference on Test Security, Princeton, NJ.

Primoli, V., Liassou, D., Bishop, N. S., & Nhouyvanisvong, A. (2011, April). *Erasure-descriptive statistics and covariates.* Paper presented at the annual meeting of the National Councilon Measurement in Education, New Orleans, LA.

Sinharay, S., Duong, M. Q., & Wood, S. W. (2017). A new statistic for detection of aberrant answer changes. *Journal of Educational Measurement, 54*(2), 200–217.

Sinharay, S., & Johnson, M. S. (2017). Three new methods for analysis of answer changes. *Educational and Psychological Measurement, 77*(1), 54–81.

Skorupski, W. P., & Egan, K. (2011, April). *Detecting cheating through the use of hierarchical growth models.* Paper presented a the annual meeting of the National Council on Measurement in Education, New Orleans, LA.

Slashdot. (2023). *Best AI content detection tools.* Retrieved February 10, 2023 from https://slashdot.org/software/ai-content-detection

Sotaridona, L. S., & Meijer, R. R. (2003). Two new statistics to detect answer copying. *Journal of Educational Measurement, 40*(1), 53–69.

TOEFL Report. (2005). *Test and score data summary for TOEFL computer-based and paper-based tests.* https://www.ets.org/Media/Research/pdf/TOEFL-SUM-0506-CBT.pdf

Tian, E. (2023). *GPT Zero.* Retrieved February 10, 2023 from https://gptzero.me

van der Linden, W. J., & Guo, F. (2008). Bayesian procedures for identifying aberrant response-time patterns in adaptive testing. *Psychometrika, 73*, 365–384.

van der Linden, W. J., & Jeon, M. (2012). Modeling answer changes on test items. *Journalof Educational and Behavioral Statistics, 37*(1), 180–199.

von Davier, A. A., Mislevy, R. J., & Hao, J. (Eds.). (2022). *Computational psychometrics: New methodologies for a newgeneration of digital learning and assessment: With examples in R and Python.* Springer Nature.

Walker, S. M. (2002). *Biometric selection: Body parts online.* SANS Institute Reading Room.

Wollack, J. A. (1997). A nominal response model approach for detecting answer copying. *Applied Psychological Measurement, 21*, 307–320.

Wollack, J. A., & Fremer, J. J. (Eds.). (2013). *Handbook of test security.* Routledge.

Wollack, J. A., & Eckerly, C. (2017). Detecting test tampering at the group level. In G. J. Cizek & J. A. Wollack (Eds.), *Handbook of quantitative methods for detecting cheating on tests* (pp. 214–231). Routledge.

Wollack, J. A., Cohen, A. S., & Eckerly, C. A. (2015). Detecting test tampering using item response theory. *Educational and Psychological Measurement, 75,* 931–953.

Yan, D., Fauss, M., Cui, W., & Hao, J. (October, 2022). *Detection of AI-generated essays.* Presentation given at the Conference on Test Security, Princeton, NJ.

Yan, D., Fauss, M., Hao, J., & Cui, W. (2023), Detection of AI-generated essays in writing assessment. *Psychological Test and Assessment Modeling, 65*(1).

Zhang, M., & Deane, P. (2015). Process features in writing: Internal structure and incremental value over product features. *ETS Research Report Series, 2015*(2), 1–12.

Zhang, M., Deane, P., & Hao, J. (October, 2022). *Detection of retyping vs. drafting through AI-based methods based on keystroke process data.* Presentation given at the Conference on Test Security, Princeton, NJ.

CHAPTER 6

USING LANGUAGE MODELS TO DETECT ALARMING STUDENT RESPONSES

Chirstopher Ormerod
Cambium Assessment

Milan Patel
Cambium Assessment

Harry Wang
Cambium Assessment

ABSTRACT

This chapter details the advances made to a system that uses artificial intelligence to identify alarming student responses. This system is built into our assessment platform to assess whether a student's response indicates they are a threat to themselves or others. Such responses may include details concerning threats of violence, severe depression, suicide risks, and descriptions of abuse. Driven by advances in natural language processing, the latest model is a fine-tuned language model trained on a large corpus consisting of student

Machine Learning, Natural Language Processing, and Psychometrics, pages 133–146
Copyright © 2024 by Information Age Publishing
www.infoagepub.com

responses and supplementary texts. We demonstrate that the use of a language model delivers a substantial improvement in accuracy over the previous iterations of this system.

Automated Text Scoring (ATS) refers to using artificial intelligence (AI) to approximate the assessment of constructed text responses. Despite its potential for reducing costs, ensuring consistent scores, and minimizing bias, there are still very real and valid concerns about the complete removal of human oversight from the scoring process. In particular, this chapter concerns instances where the constructed response suggests that the student poses a risk to themselves or others. These are situations where it is necessary for a person to intervene to ensure the safety of everyone in the school community. We refer to responses of this nature as an Alarming Student Response (ASR), which may include threats of violence, severe depression, suicide risks, and descriptions of abuse (Burkhardt, Lottridge, & Woolf, 2021). This program is incredibly important, especially given the regularity and severity of school shootings.

While some testing agencies ensure that all responses are reviewed by a person to detect ASRs, screening for these types of responses can be very time-consuming, especially when millions of responses are received daily. Furthermore, the concerning situations associated with these responses can be time-sensitive. This study presents the advancements made to our human-AI hybrid system in which the same AI used in ATS systems are used to prioritize a small collection of responses for human review. By integrating AI into the detection of ASRs, the time required to provide an appropriate response can be significantly reduced. The program in place, and the infrastructure and protocols around this piece of AI, aim to provide the fastest possible response to life-threatening situations.

We typically categorize ATS into two main classes: Automated Essay Scoring (AES) and Automated Short Answer Scoring (ASAS). The development of AES can be traced back to the 1960s when researchers started exploring the use of computers to analyze and evaluate natural language. The first AES system, Project Essay Grade (PEG), was developed in 1966 by Ellis Page and used a set of rules to analyze the structure and content of an essay (Page, 2003). The PEG system is based on a concept known as Bag-of-Words (BoW), which uses the frequencies of keywords in addition to handcrafted features. A BoW model was the first instance of ATS methods used to detect ASRs.

It is well known that frequency-based approaches, such as BoW, can be very brittle when handling ASAS. This is why reliable systems for ASAS were developed much later (Leacock & Chodorow, 2003). Over the years, researchers have refined the algorithms and techniques used in AES and ASAS. With the increasing sophistication of natural language processing (NLP) researchers began to use machine learning techniques such as neural networks (Dong, Zhang, & Yang, 2017; Taghipour & Ng, 2016). In 2018, a systematic study was conducted on the effectiveness of recurrent neural network architectures in the detection of ASRs (Ormerod & Harris, 2018). The study considered two main recurrent neural network (RNN) architectures: Long-Short-Term Memory (LSTM) networks (Hochreiter & Schmidhuber, 1997) and Gated Recurrent Units (Cho et al., 2014) with and without attention (Bahdanau et al., 2016). As a result of the study by Ormerod and Harris (2018), the BoW model used to detect ASRs was replaced with a two-layer bidirectional LSTM with attention.

More recently, the field has embraced the use of language models in both AES (Ormerod, Malhotra, & Jafari, 2021; Uto & Uchida, 2020) and ASAS (Ormerod, 2022; Ormerod et al., 2022). It stands to reason that the detection of ASRs could greatly benefit from language models. This chapter demonstrates significant improvements from using language models to detect ASRs over previous methods.

This chapter is organized into the following sections: we present the data and give a brief overview of how the model works, and how we train it to detect ASRs in Section 2. In Section 3 we detail the improvements over two baselines used in previous generations of the program.

METHOD

To understand the context of the model, we give a brief overview of how the model fits into the broader system used to detect ASRs. We then consider the data used to train and validate the model, we then consider the model itself, why we chose it, and how it was trained.

The System

Given the nature of the problem, it is not reasonable to expect that a machine-learning model is solely responsible for the detection of alarming student responses. The model that detects alarming student responses is part of a larger program that is built into an online assessment program (Ormerod & Harris, 2018). When a student submits a response, our system divides the response into multiple fragments, each of which is processed by the model, which classifies the response as either a normal student response or a response that should be routed to another system for human review. During the 2018–2019 school year, this system processed almost 82 million fragments, which, during the peak testing season can reach up to 7 million responses a day. This means that efficiency is a key concern. The

TABLE 6.1 A Rubric for the Detection of ASRs		
Category	Details	Examples
Harm to Self	Suicidal thoughts or actions Self-harming thoughts or actions Eating Disorder Drug Use	I wanna kill myself I cut a lot
Harm to Another	Threat or admission of violence Threat of sexual assault Threatening hate speech	I hit my girlfriend All (PC*) must die I want a sniper rifle
Harm from another	Report of abuse Report of sexual assault Bullying	My dad beats me I get bullied
Severe depression and/or Trauma	Ongoing or unresolved	Please kill me I want to die I wish I was dead
Specific serious request for help	Not test related	I hate my life, please help Help me or kill me

Note: PC = Protected class

faster the system can process responses, the faster the human review can be completed, and ultimately, the faster human intervention can take place.

A trained team of reviewers is responsible for reading the response and determining whether the response is a true ASR or simply a false positive. A full rubric for how they are assessed was featured in Burkhardt, Lottridge, and Woolf (2021). Table 6.1 outlines various diagnostic criteria used to ascertain whether a response should be categorized as an ASR. While these criteria may be used to delineate between classes of ASR, the team of reviewers are instructed to simply treat this as a binary classification task. Once a response is deemed to be an ASR, the response and any identifying information are sent via a secure platform to the appropriate authorities.

There are some responses that may be genuine ASRs that are not correctly classified by the model, however, depending on where and how the response was entered, those responses are also scored by hand-scorers and are subjected to a set of protocols in case they are alarming in nature.

Data

For any modeling to be effective, it is crucial that the data is carefully considered and appropriate for the problem at hand. We use an updated version of the corpus that was used in Ormerod and Harris (2018). The system in place assesses texts from various sources, such as short answers, essay

TABLE 6.2 Summary of the Training Data				
Category		ASR	Normal	Total
Training	Student	20,409	1,214,381	1,234,790
	Supplementary	5,476	4,122	9,598
	Total	25,885	1,218,503	1,244,388

responses, and comments made by students. We estimate that true ASRs are approximately 0.012% of all responses (Ormerod & Harris, 2018), which creates an imbalanced and difficult classification problem. To address this issue, we supplement actual ASRs with responses from a diverse set of open online forums and other texts that are similar to student responses. By including this supplementary data, our dataset heavily oversamples the ASRs, resulting in approximately 2.08% of all responses being ASRs in our training set, which is still about 100 times the frequency that they appear in production. While this percentage is still very small, and issues arising from class imbalance are still present, the resulting classification problem is more manageable. An outline of this data is detailed in Table 6.2.

In this project, we do not adhere to standard machine learning practices for segmenting our data into different splits because our objective is not to maximize accuracy. Rather, in the operational setting, the engine must classify a conservatively defined fixed percentage of the overall population for review. In practice, our aim is to increase the number of true positives within that fixed percentage even if it means that we have a very large number of false positives. As a result, the model validation process is very different. For a given response, we use the model's output probability as a measure of the severity of the response and establish thresholds that align with the fixed percentages.

Our validation sample consists of a set of one thousand ASRs that have been reviewed by human experts. Using the threshold data, an associated cutoff value, and the percentage of responses that we can review, we aim to determine the number of ASRs that will be correctly classified by the model as being for review. The percentage of correctly classified ASRs from the validation sample is our measure of the effectiveness of the model for that percentage. Typically we want to know the effectiveness of the model for a number of viable percentage values, which informs the decision regarding what percentage of all responses we should review.

Previous Benchmarks

The BoW model is based on the term-frequency inverse-document-frequency (tf-idf) matrix. Suppose we have a set of training data, D, which contains words from a vocabulary, V. We can summarize the word-frequency information in D in a matrix, $\mathbf{X} = (x_{v,d})$, where $d \in D$ and $v \in V$. We define the term frequency matrix as

$$tf(v, d) = \frac{x_{v,d}}{\Sigma_u x_{u,d}} \tag{6.1}$$

which encodes the proportions of each word in the document. The other component is the inverse document frequency term, given by

$$idf(v) = \log \frac{|D|}{|\{d \in D : v \in D\}|}. \tag{6.2}$$

Together, the tf-idf matrix is given by

$$Tv, d = tf(v, d) \cdot idf(v). \tag{6.3}$$

This matrix still has far too many rows for a meaningful analysis, so what is often done is we perform a latent semantic analysis (LSA), where a fixed number of dominant eigenvectors of the tf-idf matrix summarizes the key features of the space. By discarding all but the fixed number of dominant eigenvectors, we obtain a transformation from the set of documents to some fixed dimensional vector space. The classification pipeline that uses this vector space as the input into a traditional logistic regression is called a Bag-of-Words classifier. What this approach operates on is a collection of important words in the student response, which does not capture the true semantics of the response. We trained a BoW model using 500 eigenvectors on the training data for this study.

The other classifier, a recurrent neural network, is based on the Long-Short-Term-Memory (LSTM) unit (Hochreiter & Schmidhuber, 1997). Firstly, all words are mapped to a vector space via an embedding, such as the GloVe embedding (Pennington, Socher, & Manning, 2014), and then are sequentially used as input into the recurrent neural network. The reason for using a pretrained embeddings, like the GloVe embedding, is that they have accurate embeddings for words not necessarily found in our training set since they are typically trained on much larger corpora of text. Within the neural network, then the input of a recurrent unit is a word vector and the memory state from the previous iteration where the initial memory state is zero. The memory state within a recurrent neural network allows information to persist and be used in any final classification. We use the final output of the LSTM as input into a linear classifier, whose outputs are interpreted as log probabilities for a classification. Figure 6.1 demonstrates the flowchart of how RNN works. When we unfold an RNN, we express it as

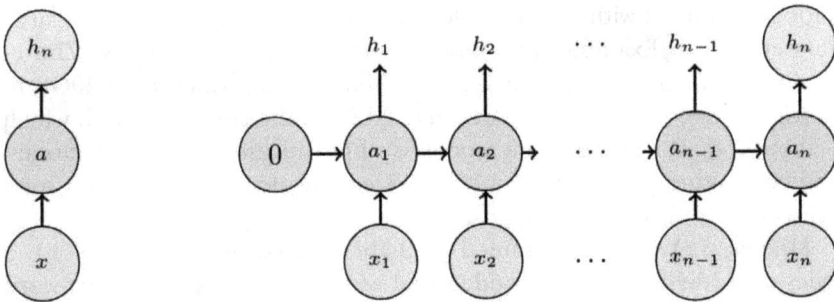

Figure 6.1   The flowchart of how RNN works.

a sequence of cells each accepting, as input, an element of the sequence. The output of the RNN is the output of the last state.

The first modification of the basic RNN architecture is to use the states of the RNN as input into another layer of recurrent units. This practice is known as stacking RNNs (Hochreiter & Schmidhuber, 1997). A second modification is to segment the recurrent units into two groups; one in which we use the sequence of inputs and the other in which we use the reversed sequence. For obvious reasons, the resulting structure is called a bidirectional RNN. Lastly, we can subject the outputs of the RNN to an attention mechanism (Bahdanau et al., 2016), which is a way we can appropriately focus on important aspects of the input to classification and disregard those aspects that are not as important. All these modifications to the basic RNN structure are beneficial to many downstream tasks. An attempt to quantify the benefit of these modifications to the detection of ASRs appears in Ormerod and Harris (2018). We used the new training sample to train a version of the RNN used in Ormerod and Harris (2018). This RNN is a bidirectional two-layer LSTM model with 512 hidden units (in each direction) with attention for this study.

Modeling Details

The introduction of transformer-based language models has sparked a revolution in natural language processing. Among the first of these models was the GPT model (Radford et al., 2018) and the BERT model (Devlin et al., 2019). These models made waves by establishing new state-of-the-art benchmarks on a standard set of tasks designed to push the limits of natural language processing models (Wang et al., 2019). The underlying premise is that one can improve downstream tasks on supervised data, where the corpora are limited in size, by pretraining the model on unsupervised data, where the corpora can be as large as one needs. One uses pretraining to endow the model with a basic understanding of language based on a large dataset of text. Examples of datasets used are the Book Corpus (Zhu et al., 2015), which is about 4.5GB, Wikipedia dumps, which have 40GB in English alone, and the C4 dataset derived from the common crawl, which is about 750GB. Training such models is a huge investment of time, money, and computing power, which ultimately equates to a sizable carbon footprint (Luccioni, Viguier, & Ligozat, 2022).

Models are typically pretrained on these huge corpora to be one of two types of models: generative models that are trained to perform next-word prediction, like GPT (Radford et al.), or masked models that are trained to predict masked words, like BERT (Devlin et al., 2019). There are some variations on this, such as the adding sentence ordering to the loss function, or adversarial training mechanisms like the Efficiently Learning an Encoder that Classifies Token Replacements Accurately (ELECTRA) model (Clark et al., 2020) or DeBERTa (He, Gao, & Chen, 2021), however, the vast majority of language models available in standard libraries are masked-word models. These models are all variations of the same transformer architecture described in Vaswani et al. (2017). The transformer architecture, presented in Figure 6.2, contains two components; an encoder and a decoder. The encoder on the left of Figure 6.2, take the text as input through N layers of

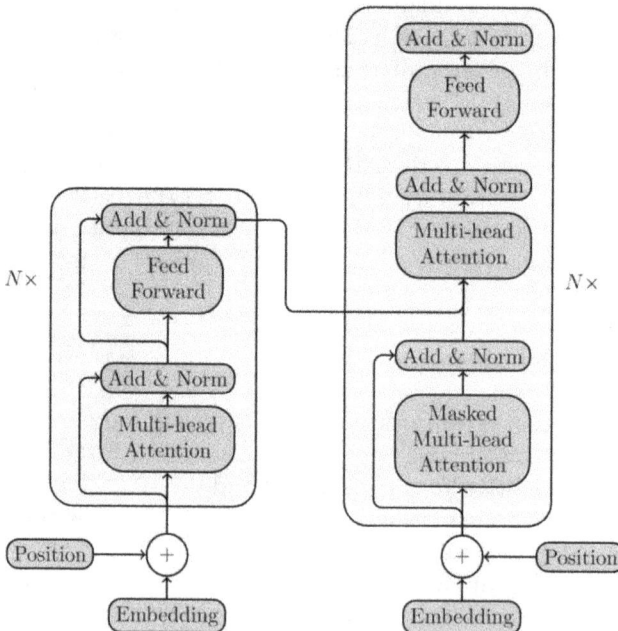

Figure 6.2 The architecture of transformer-based model.

transformer units to produce a finite dimensional representation of the input. This finite dimensional representation is then mapped to textual output using the decoder on the right of Figure 6.2. The decoder uses N layers of transformers that are slightly different from those used in the encoder.

At the heart of the transformer-based model is the idea of an attention mechanism. From a mathematical perspective, we define a query matrix, $\mathbf{Q}$, a key matrix, $\mathbf{K}$ and a value matrix, $\mathbf{V}$, which are all normalized linear transformations of the input matrix. Attention is defined as

$$Attention(\mathbf{Q},\mathbf{K},\mathbf{V}) = softmax\left(\frac{\mathbf{Q}\mathbf{K}^{T}}{\sqrt{d}}\right)\mathbf{V} \tag{6.4}$$

where d is the dimension of the query and key values. The softmax component of Equation 6.4 is referred to as the attention matrix. The multi-headed attention that features in Figure 6.2 operates on a decomposition of the input space into a disjoint union of subspaces and computes attention as it applies to each subspace (Devlin et al., 2019).

Intuitively, attention and multi-headed attention are mechanisms that enable a model to selectively focus on certain parts of the input data while disregarding others. This mechanism is inspired by how humans selectively attend to relevant information and ignore irrelevant information. In neural networks, attention works by assigning weights to different parts of the input data, which indicates how important each part is to the training task. These weights are learned during the training process. During inference, the attention weights are used to compute a weighted sum of the input features, where the weights reflect the relevance of each feature for the task. This enables the model to selectively attend to the most informative features, which can improve its performance on the task. Self-attention is a key component of the Transformer architecture, which allows the model to capture long-range dependencies and contextual information within a sequence of input tokens, such as words in a sentence. In a transformer-based language model, multiple layers of self-attention are used on the entire sequence of input tokens at once, rather than attending to a fixed-size window of tokens as in traditional recurrent neural networks.

The model we use for this task is a small and very efficient language model based on the ELECTA architecture (Clark et al., 2020). The model follows a very similar architecture to the base BERT model where the hidden size, the feed-forward layer, and the number of attention heads are a third of those found in the base BERT model. Secondly, the small ELECTRA model has a much smaller embedding facilitated by a linear layer between the embedding and the transformer layers. The more substantial change is the adversarial training scheme. The model is part of a pair of models, one trained to generate masked tokens, like BERT, and the other trained to distinguish between generated and original tokens.

In classification tasks, such as the Corpus of Linguistic Acceptability (CoLA; Warstadt, Singh, & Bowman, 2019) and the Stanford Sentiment Treebank (SST; Socher et al., 2013), the small ELECTRA model delivers strong performance despite its small size. In fact, the small ELECTRA model has a better performance on the Kaggle Automated Student Assessment Prize essay dataset (Shermis, 2014; Ormerod, Malhotra, & Jafari, 2021) and the Short Answer dataset (Shermis, 2015; Ormerod, 2022). Among the collection of all pretrained language models available using standard libraries (Wolf et al., 2020), very few models are as computationally efficient while still delivering strong performance in classification tasks in the GLUE benchmark. Other tasks in the GLUE benchmark (Wang et al., 2018) include the Microsoft Research Paraphrase Corpus (MRPC), the Semantic Textual Similarity (STS) Benchmark, the Quora Question Pairs (QQP) dataset, the Multi-Genre Natural Language Inference (MNLI) Corpus, the Stanford Question-Answering Natural Language Inference (QNLI) dataset, and the Recognizing Textual Entailment (RTE) dataset. A comparison of the previously reported results of the GLUE benchmark for a small collection of models relevant to this study are presented in Table 6.3.

After choosing a model, the next step is to apply it. ELECTRA has input limits, and the number of operations required to compute attention grows quadratically with length. As a result, most models are limited to 512 tokens. We can train the engine on segments of 256 sub-word tokens to get around this, where ASRs are given a label of 1 and normal text is given a label of 0. In this way, we can interpret the model's output for a fragment as a measure of the level of concern of the response.

Specific references to self-harm or threats made to other teachers do not necessarily require long-term dependencies in the same way that an essay might. This is one of the key observations regarding ASRs. We can use this to our advantage by training the engine on segments of 256 sub-word tokens. This is because what typically makes ASRs alarming is isolated to a few sentences.

We fine-tuned the pretrained ELECTRA model on our labeled text using the Adam optimizer (Kingma & Ba, 2014) with a weight decay mechanism

TABLE 6.3	Baseline Performance on the GLUE Task Test Sets								
	Params	CoLA	SST	MRPC	STS	QQP	MNLI	QNLI	RTE	Avg
BiLSTM+Attn		15.7	85.8	68.5	59.3	83.5	74.2	77.2	51.9	63.9
GPT	117M	45.4	91.3	75.7	80.0	88.5	82.1	88.1	56.0	75.9
BERT (base)	110M	52.1	93.5	84.8	85.8	89.2	84.6	90.5	66.4	80.9
ELECTRA	13M	54.6	89.1	83.7	80.3	88.0	79.7	87.7	60.8	78.0

(Loshchilov & Hutter, 2019), a learning rate of 2.5×10–5, a batch size of 32, and a linear learning rate scheduler. Given the size of the data, we trained for 2 epochs on a T4 graphics card. At inference, we divide any fragment into segments of length 256 with an overlap of 32 sub-word tokens. The final score is the maximum model output over all the segments. We combine this with the Open Neural Network Exchange (ONNX), which is an optimized execution platform. With the advancements in GPU technology, and the availability of standard libraries supported by ONNX, our system is able to classify all responses even with heavy loads within 1–4 hours, whereas larger systems like BERT might take approximately 3 times longer on equivalent hardware with comparable efficacy.

RESULTS

To evaluate the results, recall that our measure of efficacy is the percentage of ASRs in the validation sample that would be sent for review if some fixed percentage of all responses are sent for review. If we denote the efficacy by E, then E is a function of the fixed percentage, which we denote p. Table 6.4 contains the efficacy values, $E(p)$, for the BoW, the bidirectional LSTM with attention, and our latest ELECTRA model at values of p that make sense from an operational standpoint.

We can interpret the values in Table 6.4 in terms of the number of ASRs not detected by the system for each model used in this study. For typical values used in production, such as $p = 0.3\%$, the percentage of ASRs not detected goes from 20% to 4.9% to 1.3%. This trend is similar for other p values, indicating a reduction by a multiplicative factor of between 3 and 4 for each successive iteration of this program for typical values used in production.

Figure 6.3 is a graphical representation of the efficacy values in Table 6.4 as a continuous function of the percentage, p (on a logarithmic scale). The horizontal lines in Figure 6.3 give us an indication of what reductions in p values are possible while keeping the efficacy constant. We see that the

TABLE 6.4 The Efficacy Values of the Three Different Systems

Model	Percentages						
	0.05%	0.1%	0.3%	0.5%	1%	2%	4%
Bow + LSA + Logistic Regression	61.3%	69.8%	80.0%	83.7%	88.0%	91.5%	94.1%
Bidirectional LSTM + Attention	92.2%	93.6%	95.1%	96.6%	96.9%	97.4%	98.0%
ELECTA (small)	96.3%	97.6%	98.7%	99.2%	99.6%	99.9%	99.9%

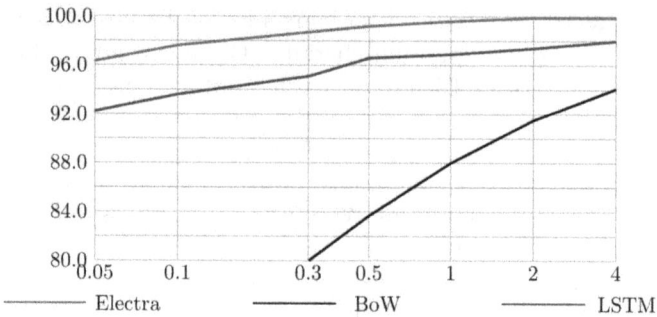

Figure 6.3   The approximate percentage of ASRs caught against the logarithm of the approximate percent of responses flagged.

ELECTRA model has approximately the same efficacy at $p = 0.1\%$ as the bidirectional LSTM with attention at $p = 2\%$. Furthermore, the bidirectional LSTM has the same efficacy at $p = 0.1\%$ as the BoW at 2%. This figure makes it clear that each successive iteration of this program allows us to reduce the number of responses by a factor of 20 while keeping the same efficacy.

DISCUSSION

In this chapter, we shown that language models provide a substantial improvement over previously applied methods to a real-world problem that arises in automated scoring. The use of language models allowed for a significant decrease the number of fragments that required review while increasing the number of verified ASRs detected by the system. Decreasing the number of fragments that are required to be reviewed is not about decreasing costs, it is about significant reductions in the number of false positives, which reduces the amount of time required to review serious and critical threats to the safety of students. Keeping the percentage low, while maintaining a certain efficacy, and focusing on efficient models is a way of ensuring that the appropriate authorities are made aware of these life-threatening situations in a timely manner.

The current system that identifies ASRs is based on a binary classification and does not distinguish between the various types of ASRs detailed in this chapter. Certain categories of responses mandate more urgent intervention compared to others, necessitating research into methods to discern which responses require expedited review. As the current dataset does not discriminate between the classes of ASRs, any system engineered to distinguish these classes would need to leverage unsupervised methods. This is a possible direction for future research.

REFERENCES

Bahdanau, D., Cho, K., & Bengio, Y. (2016). *Neural machine translation by jointly learning to align and translate.* arXiv preprint arXiv:1409.0473

Burkhardt, A., Lottridge, S., & Woolf, S. (2021). A rubric for the detection of students in crisis. *Educational Measurement: Issues and Practice, 40*(2), 72–80.

Cho, K., van Merriënboer, B., Gulcehre, C., Bahdanau, D., Bougares, F., Schwenk, H., & Bengio, Y. (2014). *Learning phrase representations using RNN encoder-decoder for statistical machine translation.* arXiv preprint arXiv:1406.1078

Clark, K., Luong, M. T., Le, Q. V., & Manning, C. D. (2020). *ELECTRA: Pre-training text encoders as discriminators rather than generators.* arXiv preprint arXiv:2003.10555

Devlin, J., Chang, M. W., Lee, K., & Toutanova, K. (2019). *BERT: Pre-training of deep bidirectional transformers for language understanding.* arXiv preprint arXiv:1810.04805

Dong, F., Zhang, Y., & Yang, J. (2017, August). Attention-based recurrent convolutional neural network for automatic essay scoring. In *Proceedings of the 21st Conference on Computational Natural Language Learning (CoNLL 2017),* 153–162.

He, P., Gao, J., & Chen, W. (2021). *DeBERTaV3: Improving DeBERTa using ELECTRA-style pre-training with gradient-disentangled embedding sharing.* arXiv preprint arXiv:2111.09543

Hochreiter, S., & Schmidhuber, J. (1997). Long short-term memory. *Neural computation, 9*(8), 1735–1780.

Leacock, C., & Chodorow, M. (2003). C-rater: Automated scoring of short-answer questions. *Computers and the Humanities, 37*(4), 389–405.

Loshchilov, I., & Hutter, F. (2019). *Decoupled weight decay regularization.* arXiv preprint arXiv:1711.05101

Luccioni, A. S., Viguier, S., & Ligozat, A. L. (2022). *Estimating the carbon footprint of BLOOM, a 176B parameter language model.* arXiv e-prints, arXiv-2211

Ormerod, C. (2022). *Short-answer scoring with ensembles of pretrained language models.* arXiv preprint arXiv:2202.11558

Ormerod, C., Lottridge, S., Harris, A. E., Patel, M., van Wamelen, P., Kodeswaran, B., Woolf, S., & Young, M. (2022). Automated short answer scoring using an ensemble of neural networks and latent semantic analysis classifiers. *International Journal of Artificial Intelligence in Education, 33,* 467–496.

Ormerod, C. M., & Harris, A. E. (2018). *Neural network approach to classifying alarming student responses to online assessment.* arXiv preprint arXiv:1809.08899

Ormerod, C. M., Malhotra, A., & Jafari, A. (2021). *Automated essay scoring using efficient transformer-based language models.* arXiv preprint arXiv:2102.13136

Page, E. B. (2003). Project essay grade: PEG. In *Automated essay scoring: A cross-disciplinary perspective* (pp. 43–54). Lawrence Erlbaum Associates.

Pennington, J., Socher, R., & Manning, C. (2014, October). GloVe: Global vectors for word representation. In *Proceedings of the 2014 conference on empirical methods in natural language processing (EMNLP),* 1532–1543.

Radford, A., Narasimhan, K., Salimans, T., & Sutskever, I. (2018). *Improving language understanding by generative pre-training.*

Shermis, M. D. (2014). State-of-the-art automated essay scoring: Competition, results, and future directions from a United States demonstration. *Assessing Writing, 20,* 53–76.

Shermis, M. D. (2015). Contrasting state-of-the-art in the machine scoring of short-form constructed responses. *Educational Assessment, 20*(1), 46–65.

Socher, R., Perelygin, A., Wu, J. Y., Chuang, J., Manning, C. D., Ng, A. Y., & Potts, C. (2013). Recursive deep models for semantic compositionality over a sentiment treebank. In *Proceedings of the 2013 Conference on Empirical Methods in Natural Language Processing,* pp. 1631–1642.

Taghipour, K., & Ng, H. T. (2016, November). A neural approach to automated essay scoring. In *Proceedings of the 2016 Conference on Empirical Methods in Natural Language Processing,* pp. 1882–1891.

Uto, M., & Uchida, Y. (2020, June). Automated short-answer grading using deep neural networks and item response theory. In *International Conference on Artificial Intelligence in Education* (pp. 198–212). Springer.

Vaswani, A., Shazeer, N., Parmar, N., Uszkoreit, J., Jones, L., Gomez, A. N., . . . & Polosukhin, I. (2017). Attention is all you need. *Advances in neural information processing systems, 30.*

Wang, A., Singh, A., Michael, J., Hill, F., Levy, O., & Bowman, S. R. (2019). *GLUE: A multi-task benchmark and analysis platform for natural language understanding.* arXiv preprint arXiv:1804.07461

Warstadt, A., Singh, A., & Bowman, S. R. (2019). *Neural network acceptability judgments.* arXiv preprint arXiv:1805.12471

Wolf, T., Debut, L., Sanh, V., Chaumond, J., Delangue, C., Moi, A., . . . & Rush, A. M. (2020). *HuggingFace's transformers: State-of-the-art natural language processing.* arXiv preprint arXiv:1910.03771

Zhu, Y., Kiros, R., Zemel, R., Salakhutdinov, R., Urtasun, R., Torralba, A., & Fidler, S. (2015). *Aligning books and movies: Towards story-like visual explanations by watching movies and reading books.* arXiv preprint arXiv:1506.06724

CHAPTER 7

EPIC ANALYSIS

Evaluating Phrases in Context to Better Understand AI Scoring of Essays

Steven Tang
eMetric LLC

This report motivates, describes, and shows examples of EPIC Analysis, a technique designed to interpret Large Language Model scoring output used in essay scoring contexts. The technique highlights the most impactful regions of a text response according to a trained AI scoring model. EPIC Analysis is intended to help interpret how an AI scoring model is parsing text responses in testing contexts.

LARGE LANGUAGE MODELS

Large Language Models (LLMs) have powerful capability in summarizing, classifying, and generating language and text. Some notable LLMs include BERT (Devlin, Chang, Lee, & Toutanova, 2019), Longformer (Beltagy, Peters, & Cohan, 2020), and GPT4 (OpenAI, 2023). AI-based understanding of

Machine Learning, Natural Language Processing, and Psychometrics, pages 147–158
Copyright © 2024 by Information Age Publishing
www.infoagepub.com
147

language serves many purposes for a wide variety of stakeholders. In education, one potentially valuable application is the scoring of student responses to writing-based tests and test questions. Additionally, it is possible for increasingly sophisticated AI to give feedback about written responses, a potentially huge domain where AI can have positive impacts in the education field.

A key feature of LLMs is that they are pre-trained to predict language. This pre-training allows for a strong base level of semantic, syntactic, and world knowledge to be embedded within the model itself. After pre-training, LLMs can be further trained or fine-tuned to solve specific tasks, such as scoring an open-ended test question. Fine-tuning utilizes labeled human-scored response data; the LLM iteratively learns a correspondence between its pre-trained linguistic knowledge and the provided human-scores for the particular test question. For some test questions, it might be critically important to get a key set of facts correct. For other test questions, tone and grammar might be more important.

Interpreting the Output of LLMs

Interpreting the output of LLMs is an area of research with a very large scope. One prominent approach towards interpreting machine learning model output in general is implemented through the SHAP (Lundberg & Lee, 2017) programming package. SHAP is short for Shapley Additive Explanations and takes a game theoretic approach (Casajus, 2009) to explain the output of any machine learning model. In this report, the SHAP programming package is used to compute the underlying partial credit scores in each text response.

Other interpretation techniques exist, such as Local Interpretable Model-agnostic Explanations (LIME) (Ribeiro, Singh, & Guestrin, 2016). Methods like SHAP and LIME attempt to provide nearly generic interpretations of many kinds of models. There are additionally thousands of other research articles aimed at interpreting the outputs of LLMs. Rogers, Kovaleva, and Rumshisky (2020) surveyed over 150 research papers that explored one or more facets of LLM output and interpretation, serving as an excellent starting point to further explore the research domain related to better interpreting LLM outputs.

EPIC Analysis—A Heatmap of Successful Writing

Based on prior research, it has been noted that LLMs can be equal to or better than other computer-based scoring methods according to metrics like Exact Agreement and QWK. This is not surprising given the widespread capabilities that LLMs have shown across many domains. The appendix section of this report shows agreement metrics between our AI rater and human raters for the specific writing prompt used in this report.

When it comes to high-stakes applications, the issue of AI alignment is often brought forward. AI Alignment describes the general goal "to make AI systems behave in line with human intentions and values" (Ji et al., 2023). Put another way, when utilizing AI scoring for higher stakes scenarios, it becomes increasingly important to focus on the justifiability and defensibility of using the AI model as part of the scoring procedure. With this context in mind, we introduce our EPIC Analysis Heatmap procedure.

In medicine, AI image recognition might automatically detect a disease based on an X-ray image. However, such detection becomes more impactful if the AI can highlight which region of the image is most responsible or contributory towards the model's decision to trigger a positive result. This highlighting can be analyzed and confirmed/refuted later by a human radiologist, allowing for the AI to be used harmoniously and safely to help predict impactful and important outcomes. Analogously, EPIC Analysis can be utilized to provide a chain of diagnostic evidence that helps to explain AI model outputs when applied in open ended response scoring scenarios.

An EPIC Heatmap is essentially a highlighted version of a student's original response, where different shades of highlighting correspond to differing levels of writing quality as assessed by the AI model. This highlighting corresponds to the AI's valuation of the writing for that response, providing a baseline interpretation of how and why an AI is arriving at its output score. A moderator can then utilize and interpret the heatmap to determine whether the AI model's results are valid, especially useful when scoring discrepancies between multiple raters arises.

Imagine a scoring scenario where there are tens of thousands of student responses, and each response has two human-rater scores as well as an AI score. First, EPIC Analysis utilizes the AI model to generate easy-to-interpret heatmaps for each response. With these heatmaps, it becomes possible to better decipher why certain responses are receiving higher scores according to the AI model, an invaluable source of feedback for the scoring program. Additionally, when a human score and an AI score disagree, a moderator could consult the heatmap to quickly get a sense of the "scoring rationale" behind the AI model's output for that response, allowing for a more informed judgment to be made in resolving the discrepancy between scores. With these two use-cases in mind, EPIC Analysis can be seen as a valuable secondary tool that enhances the use and defensibility of integrating LLM-based AI procedures that score complex writing tasks for both low and higher stake scenarios.

Breakdown of EPIC Analysis

EPIC Analysis can be summarized in three steps:

1. Fine-tune a Large Language Model to be able to score written responses for a test question.
2. Generate Adjusted Owen Values for each phrase within each response based on the AI model.
3. Generate a colorful and visual heatmap based on the Adjusted Owen Values.

For Step 1, a pre-trained LLM is trained to score a particular test question. This training could require, for example, 1000 responses that are already scored by a human rater. Using this training set of data, the LLM learns to distinguish between different score points based on the elements of language present in each response. The kinds of dimensions of language that LLMs can leverage are impressively vast and are growing continuously. A full discussion of LLMs is outside the scope of this report, but in short, LLMs have been theorized to have Syntactic Knowledge, Semantic Knowledge, and World Knowledge. A deep dive into the world of LLMs can start with a primer with BERTology by Rogers, Kovaleva, and Rumshisky (2020), which introduces and motivates LLM technology before discussing a survey overview of 150 studies related to LLM results.

Once an LLM is trained to be able to score a specific test question, we can refer to that LLM as the AI Model. This AI model is now capable of producing scores for new student responses. However, that's all the output we currently get: the score. This final score can be thought of as a "holistic" score, considering the entirety of the response. However, it is often the case that there are key phrases or key elements within a response that strongly sway a response towards higher or lower scores.

Step 2 in EPIC Analysis identifies these key phrases by using an Owen Value computation algorithm to effectively assign a partial credit value to each key phrase within a response. The Owen Value computation is a widely used method to assign partial credit, especially to text-based responses. See (Wagner, 2022) for a comprehensible deep dive into this approach. Owen Values are a form of partial credit assignment that is linearly additive on the same scale as the actual scoring rubric. A final adjustment step is taken following Owen Value computation. The goal of adjusting the Owen Values is to ensure that each Adjusted Owen Value has the same overall meaning between responses. An Adjusted Owen Value of +0.5, for example, has the same interpretation across all responses.

In other words, at the end of Step 2, each phrase within each response has been assigned an Adjusted Owen Value (AOV). AOVs are numbers that represent partial credit values on the same scale as the scoring rubric for the writing task at hand. The sum of all AOVs for a response will total to the AI model's holistic score output for that response.

For an illustration of the AOV calculation and interpretation, consider the phrase:

> ...In addition, airships used hydrogen-a highly flammable gas. An accident could be fatal in a densely populated area like New York City.

With this phrase, the Owen Value computation algorithm breaks this up into 6 smaller phrases:

- "In addition,"
- "airships used hydrogen-a highly"
- "flammable gas."
- "An accident could be"
- "fatal in a densely-"
- "populated area like New York City."

These six particular smaller phrases were chosen based on the Owen Value's algorithmic approach towards assigning partial credit, as detailed in (Wagner, 2022). Each of these smaller phrases is assigned an Owen Value, which represents a linear and additive amount of partial credit that is attributable to each phrase. After technical adjustment, we obtain an Adjusted Owen Value (AOV) for each of these phrases. Here are those AOVs as presented in Table 7.1.

We see AOVs of +.075, +.152, +.182, +.112, +.102, +.106. These can be considered the amount of "score" or "partial credit" that each phrase is partially responsible for. Note the value of +.182 is much larger than the

TABLE 7.1 Adjusted Owen Values for Each Phrase in Example Snippet	
Phrase	**AOV**
"In addition,"	+.075
"airships used hydrogen-a highly"	+.152
"flammable gas."	+.182
"An accident could be"	+.112
"fatal in a densely-"	+.102
"populated area like New York City"	+.106

value of +.075. Clearly, some phrases are responsible for much more credit than others. These 6 phrases are interpreted to be responsible for

$$(.075 + .152 + .182 + .112 + .102 + .106) = .729 \text{ points}$$

For this particular test question, the maximum number of points was 4.0. This snippet was not an entire student response, so the other parts of the response would be responsible for the rest of the credit that this response received from the AI model.

Once AOVs have been generated for every response, Step 3 comes next. Step 3 in EPIC Analysis is to generate visual "heatmaps" of each student response. A heatmap is simply a color-coded version of the original response, where the color-codes correspond to varying levels of AOVs. Our current version of the heatmap has five distinct colors: White, Light Blue, Deep Blue, Light Green, Deep Green. This spectrum of color, going from White -> Blue -> Green, corresponds to increasing AOVs; higher AOVs represent stronger contributions to better scores. Using this color scheme enables rapid identifiability and interpretability for end users. Table 7.2 shows the conversion table for AOV to color code.

Determining which range of AOVs falls into which color-code can be adjusted based on experimentation and use case. For our current implementation of EPIC Analysis, we break the range of AOVs from all responses up into 5 equidistant ranges. Technically, we leave out the bottom and top 2% of AOVs from this range calculation to mitigate the effect of outlier values.

Finally, after all 3 steps are complete, we have now accomplished:

- Each phrase in each response has been assigned a numerical AOV representing attributable partial credit determined by the AI model.
- The range of AOVs has been mapped to a color scheme. Low AOVs are white, medium AOVs are blue, and high AOVs are green.
- Using this color scheme, each response can now be transformed into a color-coded response (a **heatmap**) that instantly shows low, medium, and high performing regions of each response based on the AI model's scoring capabilities.

TABLE 7.2 AOV Ranges for Color Codes		
AOV Range	Text Highlight Color	Interpretation
$.146 < AOV \leq +\infty$		Important Contribution to Higher Scores
$.111 < AOV \leq .146$		
$.075 < AOV \leq .111$		Distinguishing Contribution to Higher Scores
$.040 < AOV \leq .075$		
$-\infty < AOV \leq .040$		Not a Distinguishing Contribution to Higher Scores

- Stakeholders can now use EPIC Analysis to interpret, validate, and understand LLM-based AI modeling applied to open ended response scoring.

ILLUSTRATIVE EXAMPLES OF EPIC ANALYSIS HEATMAPS

In this section, response data from Prompt#6 of the Kaggle Essay Scoring Competition is used (Hamner, Morgan, lynnvandev, Shermis, & Vander Ark, 2012). 1000 essays were randomly selected as a training set for the LLM scoring model, and the remaining 800 essays were run through our EPIC Analysis heatmap procedure based on the trained scoring model. Rater agreement metrics can be found in the Appendix section. Essays were 150 words long on average, possible scores ranged from 0 through 4, and these responses were considered to be "Source Dependent Responses." Students were tasked with responding to the writing prompt: "Based on the excerpt, describe the obstacles the builders of the Empire State Building faced in attempting to allow dirigibles to dock there. Support your answer with relevant and specific information from the excerpt." An excerpt was provided to the students to use.

EXAMPLE 1

DAISY Score	Human1 Score	Human2 Score
2	2	2

EPIC Analysis Heatmap

the obstacles the builders went threw was using hydrogen which is flammable. Another one is the "wind on the top of the building were constintly shifting due to violent air currents." the third one is when the back of the ship would swivel around and around the mooring mast. last but not least the law against airships flying to low over urban areas.

In this first example, we show a response that received 2 out of 4 possible points from all raters, including two human raters as well as our LLM-based scoring model named DAISY.

The EPIC Analysis Heatmap is highlighted according to our coloring scheme. Remember that the color scale goes from White -> Light Blue -> Deep Blue -> Light Green -> Deep Green in order of increasing importance and increasing partial credit.

Take a moment to read through the heatmap and notice which particular phrases achieved blue or green highlighting. This is perhaps the main use case of the EPIC procedure: letting an additional reader or moderator visually see which phrases the AI might deem as more important for scoring purposes. In ideal settings, the additional reader would think "yes, the green highlighting here makes sense. It is clear why this part of the response contributes more to higher scores."

As you read through example heatmaps, try to make judgments about whether the white, blue, and green parts of the heatmap coincide with what you might have determined as important as a human rater.

Looking at the green highlights, "shifting due to violent air currents", "the law against…", and "low over urban areas" were some of the key phrases that most contributed to the score for this response. These concepts clearly respond to the prompt, identifying relevant obstacles that builders faced.

"using hydrogen" and "wind on the top of the building were constantly…" are some examples of the blue highlights. These phrases are interpreted to contribute to a higher score but are generally less important relative to the green highlights.

Finally, some of the text is left in white. This text is interpreted to not necessarily contribute to a higher score, at least on its own. Sometimes, this text could be unnecessary, off-topic, factually inaccurate, or contain grammar and spelling mistakes. Even if a rubric does not necessarily directly penalize certain mistakes, human raters may still factor mistakes into the score, as writing is often rated at least partially holistically.

This was an example of an essay that only received 2 out of 4 possible points. The heatmap showcases the best parts of the student's writing, highlighting the key phrases that best respond to the prompt.

Next, let's look at a heatmap of a higher scoring essay.

EXAMPLE 2

DAISY Score	Human1 Score	Human2 Score
4	4	4

EPIC Analysis Heatmap

While the construction of the Empire State Building was in progress, the builders faced many obstacles in trying to allow dirigibles to dock there. At first, people thought it was going to be wonderful and lead to the "transportation of the future". One obstacle the builders faced was the fact that a large dirigible moored to the roof would have negative effects on the building's frame. "The stress of the dirigibles load and the wind pressure would have to be transmitted all the way to the building's foundation". The builders would have to pay @MONEY1 to fix this problem. Another problem that was present was also the lack of safety. "Most dirigibles from outside of the united states used hydrogen rather than helium, and hydrogen is highly flammable." Also, even if the dirigible were tethered to the mooring mast, the violent winds would cause the back of the ship to swivel around and around the mooring mast." Even if the back of the dirigibles were weighted down with lead, it would not be safe; as the lead would be "dangling high above pedestrians on the street." There was also a law stating that airships could not fly too low above urban areas. Nature itself presented many more problems, such as winds blowing the dirigible onto the "sharp spires of other buildings." As numerous problems became apparent after the building was finished, the idea of dirigibles being the "future of transportation" was dropped.

This example was scored as a 4 by all three raters, which is the highest possible score. When all raters agree on a top score, the response could be considered as one of the highest quality responses.

Once again, take a moment to read or skim through the heatmap to get an overall impression of when phrases are white, blue, or green. In an ideal circumstance, the highlighting should coincide with what a human reader might expect to be important in a response.

In this case, it is apparent that the introduction to the essay was left unhighlighted. In our interpretation, the white highlighting does not necessarily mean the introduction was poorly written, but rather the AI perhaps did not deem it as important as the body and the rest of the response. This shows that white highlighting is not always indicative of poor writing, but instead could indicate text that might "support" the essay but is not the "main focus" or "main thesis" of the response.

Past the introduction, the entire essay is highlighted in blue or green. Seeing exactly which phrases were green highlighted could give a better sense to the moderator of what the AI scoring model deems as the most important phrases towards achieving a high score, such as a 4.

Some of the key deep green highlighted phrases are:

- "the wind pressure would have to be transmitted"
- "from outside the united states used hydrogen rather than helium"
- "the violent winds would"
- "a law stating that airships could not"

From our perspective, these deep green highlighted phrases seem to directly respond and apply to the prompt at hand, giving concrete evidence and supporting statements to describing the obstacles faced by the builders. The rubric states that a 4-scoring response should be "clear, complete, and accurate."

In this case, both the human raters as well as the AI scorer all agreed that this response was a 4. When agreement happens, there may appear to be less "need" to analyze an EPIC Analysis Heatmap. There could still be value, however, in confirming that the AI model is at least scoring the response in a way that aligns with human values. Using the heatmap in this example, a moderator can better understand which aspects of the essay the AI views as the primary reason for assigning a high score of 4. If the highlighting does not make sense to the moderator, then further scrutiny towards the AI approach can be applied by the scoring program.

EXAMPLE 3

DAISY Score	Human1 Score	Human2 Score
2	1	3

EPIC Analysis Heatmap

The obstacles the builders of the Empire State Building faced in attempting to allow dirigibles (Blimps) to dock there was that there were way too many risks that were being taken to make this mast and it was just too dangerous.I think that the mast opposed too many risks because for one it would be flying too low and two, if it caught on fire or was hit by lightning it would explode and people would get seriously hurt, OR the mast could snap off!As @PERSON1 said, "The as yet unsolved problems of mooring air ships to a fixed mast at such a height made it desirable to postpone to a later date the final installation of the landing gear."@CAPS1 @PERSON1 Clavan means is that the fact that there are so many problems with mooring air ships to this "mast" that it just isn't safe to go through with right now!

This response was scored as a 1 and a 3 by the two human readers, indicating "discrepant" scoring where the readers disagreed by 2 score points. DAISY scored in the middle, as a 2.

Responses that have discrepant scoring can be great candidates for moderator review, using the heatmap as insight into how the AI scorer interpreted the response.

Take a moment to skim or read through the heatmap. In this case, since we know that two humans strongly disagreed on the scoring of the response, it becomes increasingly important to focus on the details of each phrase and parse through where credit is deserved or not deserved.

Looking at the deep blue and light green highlights, we see phrases like "if it caught on fire or was hit by lightning it would explode and people would get seriously hurt" and "it just isn't safe to go through with right now!" These phrases seem on-topic and highlight dangers faced by builders according to the prompt and excerpt.

Additionally, the text left unhighlighted in white could also give some clues as to why the AI scored this as a 2 rather than higher. Much of the response is left in white, indicating that these parts of the response are not as directly relevant to answering the prompt comprehensively.

Overall, by reading through which parts of the response are white, blue, or green, a moderator can get a sense of what the AI viewed positively in this response. It does seem reasonable to assign a score of 2, and the highlighting appears to be reasonable.

Finally, the ultimate question: which of the three raters is correct? Is this response a 1, 2, or 3? The final scoring decision ought to be made by a moderator with contextual knowledge of this test question. However, discrepancies in scoring do happen relatively frequently, and moderators need to make judgment calls to give a final score. EPIC Analysis Heatmaps can provide a quick, visual starting point to provide some perspective for how the AI may be valuing different parts of the response.

IMPLICATIONS AND FURTHER STEPS

LLMs are part of an exciting wave of new developments in the field of AI-based understanding of language. These models have the potential to improve language learning, improve automated feedback at scale for writing tasks, and provide personalized interactions in novel ways especially in educational contexts.

In this report, a walkthrough of the EPIC Analysis procedure was provided. Using heatmaps, scoring teams can interpret, analyze, and leverage outputs from LLM scoring models for open ended tasks. Three example heatmaps were provided, showcasing applications to a variety of potential situations that could arise during a scoring session.

Several implications can be drawn from the examples shown in this report. Firstly, EPIC Analysis heatmaps seem to clearly highlight key phrases and key answers within responses. Secondly, context of the overall response mattered in the highlighting. Thirdly, when a heatmap showed a lack of highlighting (white color), there can be deficiencies in the writing, with writing that seemed off-topic, incorrect, or showcasing grammatical errors. Fourth, it is important to note that such contextual interpretations would be nearly impossible with traditional or older methods of processing language. The general architecture of modern LLMs relies on context to process and understand language, enabling a secondary tool like our EPIC Analysis procedure to highlight that contextual nature.

Overall, the introduction of LLM technology is still in its relative infancy. There are many possible applications as LLMs and other AI technologies continue to mature over time. Regarding next steps, we hope to gather procedural feedback from interested partners to make iterative improvements, identify potential use-case scenarios and applications related to open-ended-response scoring settings, and continue to generate reports that document the results and progression of the novel EPIC Analysis procedure.

APPENDIX
AI Scoring Metrics Compared to Humans

TABLE A1 Model Metrics on Empire Building Test Set (*N* = 800)				
Raters	QWK	Exact Agree	Adjacent Agree	Off-by-2 or more
Human1—Human2	.807	.646	.990	.010
Human1—DAISY	.806	.640	.995	.005
Human2—DAISY	.801	.633	.994	.006

REFERENCES

Beltagy, I., Peters, M. E., & Cohan, A. (2020). *Longformer: The long-document transformer.* https://arxiv.org/abs/2004.05150

Casajus, A. (2009, December). *The shapley value, the owen value, and the veil of ignorance.* Retrieved from https://www.researchgate.net/publication/46510645_The_shapley_value_the_owen_value_and_the_veil_of_ignorance

Devlin, J., Chang, M.-W., Lee, K., & Toutanova, K. (2019). *BERT: Pre-training of deep bidirectional transformers for language understanding.* https://arxiv.org/pdf/1810.04805.pdf

Hamner, B., Morgan, J., lynnvandev, Shermis, M., & Vander Ark, T. (2012). *The Hewlett Foundation: Automated essay scoring. Kaggle.* Retrieved from https://kaggle.com/competitions/asap-aes

Ji, J., Qiu, T., Chen, B., Zhang, B., Lou, H., Wang, K., . . . Gao, W. (2023). *AI alignment: A comprehensive survey.* Retrieved from https://arxiv.org/abs/2310.19852

Lundberg, S. M., & Lee, S.-I. (2017). A unified approach to interpreting model predictions. *NIPS,* 4765–4774.

OpenAI. (2023). *GPT-4 technical report.* Retrieved from https://arxiv.org/abs/2303.08774

Ribeiro, M. T., Singh, S., & Guestrin, C. (2016). "Why should I trust you?" Explaining the predictions of any classifier. *22nd ACM SIGKDD International Conference on Knowledge Discovery and Data Mining,* 1135–1144.

Rogers, A., Kovaleva, O., & Rumshisky, A. (2020). A primer in BERTology: What we know about how BERT works. *Transactions of the Association for Computational Linguistics,* 842–866. Retrieved from https://direct.mit.edu/tacl/article/doi/10.1162/tacl_a_00349/96482/A-Primer-in-BERTology-What-We-Know-About-How-BERT

Wagner, L. (2022). *Shap's partition explainer for language models.* Retrieved from https://towardsdatascience.com/shaps-partition-explainer-for-language-models-ec2e7a6c1b77

CHAPTER 8

FULLY DATA-DRIVEN COMPUTERIZED ADAPTIVE TESTING

Aritra Ghosh
University of Massachusetts Amherst

Wanyong Feng
University of Massachusetts Amherst

Stephen Sireci
University of Massachusetts Amherst

Andrew Lan
University of Massachusetts Amherst

ABSTRACT

Computerized adaptive testing (CAT) leads to personalized tests/assessments with reducing test length by adaptively selecting the next most informative question/item for each student, given their responses to previous questions. Existing CAT methods use item response theory (IRT) based models to

---

Machine Learning, Natural Language Processing, and Psychometrics, pages 159–175
Copyright © 2024 by Information Age Publishing
www.infoagepub.com
All rights of reproduction in any form reserved.

relate students' abilities to their responses to questions and static question selection algorithms designed to reduce the ability estimation error as quickly as possible; therefore, these algorithms cannot improve by learning from large-scale student response data. In this chapter, we propose BOBCAT, a Bilevel Optimization-Based framework for CAT to directly learn a data-driven question selection algorithm from training data. BOBCAT is agnostic to the underlying student response model and is computationally efficient during the adaptive testing process.

Additionally, we also use a constrained version of BOBCAT to balance test accuracy and question exposure and test overlap rates. Through extensive experiments on several real-world student response datasets, we show that BOBCAT outperforms existing CAT methods (sometimes significantly) when large-scale training data is available.

One important feature of computerized/online learning platforms is computerized adaptive testing (CAT), which refers to tests that can accurately measure the ability/knowledge of a student/test taker using few questions/ items, by using an algorithm to adaptively select the next question for each student given their response to previous questions (Luecht & Sireci, 2011; van der Linden & Glas, 2000). An accurate and efficient estimate of a student's knowledge levels helps computerized learning platforms to deliver personalized learning experiences for every learner. A CAT system generally consists of the following components: an underlying psychometric model that links the question's features and the student's features to their response to the question, a bank of questions with features learned from prior data, and an algorithm that selects the next question for each student from the question bank and decides when to stop the test; see (Han, 2018) for an overview. Most commonly used response models in CAT systems are item response theory (IRT) models, with their simplest form (1PL) given by

$$p(Y_{i,j} = 1) = \sigma(\theta_i - b_j), \tag{8.1}$$

where $Y_{i,j}$ is student i's binary-valued response to question j, where 1 denotes a correct answer, $\sigma(\cdot)$ is the sigmoid/logistic function, and $\theta_i \in \mathbb{R}$ and $b_j \in \mathbb{R}$ are scalars corresponding to the student's ability and the question's difficulty, respectively (Lord, 1980; Rasch, 1993). More complex IRT models use additional question features such as the scale and guessing parameters or use multidimensional student features, i.e., their knowledge levels on multiple skills (Reckase, 2009).

Most commonly used question selection algorithms in CAT systems select the most informative question that minimizes the student feature measurement error; see (van der Linden & Pashley, 2009) for an overview and (Ueno & Miyazawa, 2019, 2022; Vats, Lan, Studer, & Baraniuk, 2016; Vats,

Studer, Lan, Carin, & Baraniuk, 2013) for examples. Specifically, in each step of the adaptive testing process (indexed by t) for
student i, they select the next question as

$$j_i^{(t)} = \text{argmax}_{j \in \Omega_i^{(t)}} I_j(\hat{\theta}_i^{(t-1)}), \tag{8.2}$$

where $\Omega_i^{(t)}$ is the set of available questions to select for this student at time step t (the selected question at each time step is removed afterwards), $\hat{\theta}_i^{(t-1)}$ is the current estimate of student's ability parameter given previous responses $Y_{i,j_i^{(1)}}, \ldots, Y_{i,j_i^{(t-1)}}$, and $I_j(\cdot)$ the informativeness of question j. In the context of 1PL IRT models, most informativeness metrics will select the question with difficulty closest to the current estimate of the student's ability, i.e., selecting the question that the student's probability of answering correctly is closest to 50%. This criterion coincides with uncertainty sampling (Lewis & Gale, 1994) for binary classification, a commonly used method in active learning (Settles, 2012; Settles, T. LaFlair, & Hagiwara, 2020).

Despite the effectiveness of existing CAT methods, two limitations hinder their further improvement. First, most question selection algorithms are specifically designed for IRT models (Equation 8.1). The *highly structured* nature of IRT models enables theoretical characterization of question informativeness but limits their ability to capture complex student-question interactions compared to more flexible, deep neural network-based models (Cheng et al., 2019; F. Wang et al., 2020). This limitation is evident on large-scale student response datasets (often with millions of responses) that have been made available (Choi et al., 2020; Z. Wang et al., 2020). Second, most existing question selection algorithms are *static* since they require a predefined informativeness metric (Equation 8.2); they can only use large-scale student response data to improve the underlying IRT model (e.g., calibrating question difficulty parameters) but not the question selection algorithm. Therefore, they will not significantly improve over time as more students take tests. Recently, there are ideas on using reinforcement learning to learn question selection algorithms (Li, Xu, Zhang, & Chang, 2020; Nurakhmetov, 2019); however, these methods have not been validated on real data. Following our work, others have developed data-driven CAT methods as well (Zhuang et al., 2022).

CONTRIBUTIONS

We propose BOBCAT, a Bilevel Optimization-Based framework for Computerized Adaptive Testing; see (Ghosh & Lan, 2021) and (Feng, Ghosh, Sireci, & Lan, 2023). BOBCAT is based on the key observation that the ultimate goal of CAT is to reduce test length. Therefore, estimating student ability parameters is a *proxy* of the real objective: *predicting a student's responses to all questions on a long test that cannot be feasibly administered.* We make three key contributions:

First, we recast CAT as a bilevel optimization problem (Franceschi, Frasconi, Salzo, Grazzi, & Pontil, 2018) in the meta learning (Finn, Abbeel, & Levine, 2017) setup: in the *outer-level* optimization problem, we learn both the response model parameters and a data-driven question selection algorithm by *explicitly* maximizing the predictive likelihood of student responses in a held-out *meta* question set. In the *inner-level* optimization problem, we adapt the outer-level response model to each student by maximizing the predicted likelihood of their responses in an observed *training* question set. This bilevel optimization framework directly learns an effective and efficient question selection algorithm through the training-meta setup. Moreover, BOBCAT is agnostic to the underlying response model, compatible with both IRT models and deep neural network-based models; Once learned, the question selection algorithm selects the next question from past question responses directly, without requiring the student parameters to be repeatedly estimated in real time. To train BOBCAT, we employ an effective method to estimate the gradient w.r.t. the question selection algorithm parameters in the bilevel optimization problem.

Second, we introduce a constrained version of BOBCAT (C-BOBCAT) that can trade off test accuracy for question exposure and test overlap rates. C-BOBCAT (a) uses a stochastic question selection algorithm instead of a deterministic one and (b) adds a penalty term to BOBCAT's optimization objective to promote the learned question selection algorithm to select diverse questions across different students.

Third, we verify the effectiveness of BOBCAT through extensive quantitative and qualitative experiments on five large-scale, real-world student response datasets. We observe that the learned data-driven question selection algorithms outperform existing CAT algorithms at reducing test length, requiring 50% less questions to reach the same predictive accuracy on meta question set in some cases; this improvement is generally more significant on larger datasets.[1]

THE BOBCAT FRAMEWORK

We now detail the BOBCAT framework for a fixed-length test setting, visualized in Figure 8.1. Let N and Q denote the number of students and questions in the student response dataset we use to train BOBCAT, respectively. For a single student i, we sequentially select a total of $n\left(\ll |\Omega_i^{(1)}|\right)$ questions, $\left\{ j_i^{(1)}, \ldots, j_i^{(n)} \right\}$, observe their responses, and predict their response on a held-out set of meta questions, Γ_i; $\Omega_i^{(1)}$ denotes the initial set of available

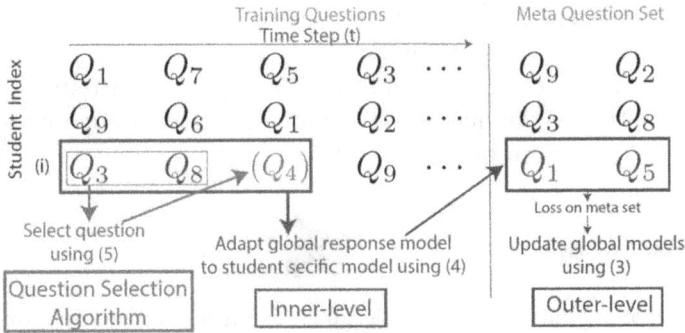

Figure 8.1 Overview of the BOBCAT framework.

questions and $\Omega_i^{(1)} \cap \Gamma_i = \varnothing$. The training and meta question sets are randomly selected and not the same for each student in the dataset. We solve the following bilevel optimization problem (Franceschi et al., 2018; Rajeswaran, Finn, Kakade, & Levine, 2019):

$$\underset{\gamma,\phi}{\text{minimize}}\,\frac{1}{N}\sum_{i=1}^{N}\sum_{j\in\Gamma_i}\ell\big(Y_{i,j},g(j;\theta_i^*)\big):=\frac{1}{N}\sum_{i=1}^{N}\mathcal{L}(\theta_i^*,\Gamma_i) \qquad (8.3)$$

$$\text{s.t. } \theta_i^* = \underset{\theta_i}{\text{argmin}}\sum_{t=1}^{n}\ell\Big(Y_{i,j_i^{(t)}},g(j_i^{(t)};\theta_i)\Big)+\mathcal{R}(\gamma,\theta_i):=\mathcal{L}'(\theta_i) \qquad (8.4)$$

$$\text{where } j_i^{(t)} \sim \Pi(Y_{i,j_i^{(1)}},\dots,Y_{i,j_i^{(t-1)}};\phi)\in\Omega_i^{(t)}. \qquad (8.5)$$

Here, γ and ϕ are the *global* response model and question selection algorithm parameters, respectively. $g(\cdot)$ is the response model, which takes as input the index of the question of interest, j, and uses the *local* parameter specific to student i, θ_i^*, to output the prediction of the student's likelihood of responding to the question correctly. $\Pi(\cdot)$ is the question selection algorithm, which takes as input the student's previous responses and outputs the index of the next selected question.

The outer-level optimization problem minimizes the binary cross-entropy loss, $\ell(\cdot)$, on the *meta* question sets across all students to learn both the global response model and the question selection algorithm; $\mathcal{L}(\cdot)$ corresponds to the sum of this loss over questions each student responded to in the meta question set. The inner-level optimization problem minimizes $\mathcal{L}'(\cdot)$, the cross-entropy loss on a small number of questions selected for each student on the *training* question set to adapt the global response model to each local student, resulting in a student-specific parameter θ_i^*;

$\mathcal{R}(\gamma, \theta_i)$ is a regularization term that penalizes large deviations of the local parameters from their global values. Note that θ_i^* is a function of the global parameters γ and ϕ, reflected through both the regularization term in (Equation 8.4) and the question selection algorithm through questions it selects for this student in (Equation 8.5).

Response Model

The response model $g(\cdot)$ can be taken as either IRT models or neural network-based models. In the case of IRT models, the global parameters γ corresponds to the combination of the question difficulties and the student ability prior. We adapt these parameters to each local student through their responses to selected questions in the inner-level optimization problem. In our experiments, we only use the global student ability as the prior mean of each local student's ability estimate and keep the question difficulties fixed in the inner-level optimization problem, following the typical setup in real-world CAT systems. In the case of neural network-based models, the parameters are usually not associated with any specific meaning; following standard practices in meta-learning (Lee, Maji, Ravichandran, & Soatto, 2019), we fix part of the network (e.g., all weights and biases, which one can regard as a nonlinear version of question difficulties) and optimize the rest of the network (e.g., the input vector, which one can regard as student abilities) in the inner-level optimization problem.

Question Selection Algorithm

The question selection algorithm $\Pi(\cdot)$ can be either deterministic or probabilistic, i.e., it either outputs a single selected question or a probability distribution over available questions. We define the input *state* vector to the question selection algorithm at step t as $\mathbf{x}_i^{(t)} \in \{-1, 0, 1\}^Q$, where an entry of -1 denotes an incorrect response to a past selected question, 1 denotes a correct response, while 0 denotes questions that have not been selected. We do not include the time step at which a question is selected in the state vector since in CAT settings, the student's true ability is assumed to be static during the testing process while an estimate is being updated. Although any differentiable model architecture can be used for the question selection algorithm, we use the multi-layer perceptron model that is invariant to question ordering. For probabilistic question selection algorithms, we select a question by sampling from the output distribution $j_i^{(t)} \sim \Pi(\mathbf{x}_i^{(t)}, \Omega_i^{(t)}; \phi)$.

Optimization and Computational Complexity

We use gradient descent (GD) to solve both the inner and outer optimization problems. Compute the gradient w.r.t. the question selection algorithms parameters, ϕ, is hard due to the discrete nature of the question selections, $j_i^{(1:n)}$. Therefore, we introduce two methods to estimate this gradient, an unbiased one based on policy gradients (Williams, 1992) and a biased one based on influence function scores (Koh & Liang, 2017). See (Ghosh & Lan, 2021) for details on the training algorithm for BOBCAT.

At training time, we need to solve the full BOBCAT bilevel optimization problem, which is computationally intensive on large datasets. However, at test time, when we need to select the next question for each student, we only need to use their past responses as input to the learned question selection algorithm $\Pi(\cdot;\phi)$ to get the selected question as output; this operation is more computationally efficient than existing CAT methods that require updates to the student's ability estimate after every question.

Constrained BOBCAT

One potential problem with BOBCAT is that since it is fully data-driven, it may be biased to learn question selection algorithms that lead to poor test security, i.e., selecting a few highly informative questions and thus exhibiting high question exposure and test overlap rates. To address this issue, we also introduce a constrained version of BOBCAT (C-BOBCAT). We turn BOBCAT's underlying question selection algorithm from deterministic to stochastic, which injects some randomness into the questions selected for each student. We transform the original categorical question selection distribution to the Gumbel-Softmax distribution (Jang, Gu, & Poole, 2017) with a fixed temperature hyperparameter. Moreover, since the entropy of a distribution increases as the distribution approaches the uniform distribution, maximizing the entropy of the categorical question selection distribution

can further encourage the learned question selection algorithm to select a diverse set of questions for each student. We add the negative summation of the entropy of categorical question selection distributions of all selected questions for each student to the outer level optimization function to create the new outer level function. During the training process, the model needs to maximize the combination of both prediction accuracy on the held-out meta data and the uncertainty of the question selection algorithm, which is reflected in the entropy regularization term. We use a hyperparameter λ to balance the two terms: when $\lambda = 0$, the problem reduces to the original BOBCAT bi-level optimization problem; when $\lambda = \infty$, the solution to the problem is a question selection algorithm that selects each question with equal probability, i.e., the entropy is maximized when the question selection distribution is uniform distribution.

EXPERIMENTS

We now detail both quantitative and qualitative experiments we conducted on numerous real-world student response datasets to validate BOBCAT's effectiveness.

Datasets, Training, Testing and Evaluation Metric

We use five publicly available benchmark datasets: EdNet,[2] Junyi,[3] Eedi-1, Eedi-2,[4] and ASSISTments[5] to validate BOBCAT; see (Ghosh & Lan, 2021) for details. We perform 5-fold cross validation for all datasets; for each fold, we use 60%–20%–20% *students* for training, validation, and testing, respectively. For each fold, we use the validation students to perform early stopping and tune the parameters for every method. For BOBCAT, we partition the questions responded to by each student into the training ($\Omega_i^{(1)}$, 80%) and meta (Γ_i, 20%) question sets. To prevent overfitting, we randomly generate these partitions in each training epoch. We use both Accuracy and the area under the receiver operating characteristics curve (AUC) as metrics to evaluate the performance of all methods on predicting binary-valued student responses on the meta set Γ_i. We implement all methods in PyTorch and run our experiments in a NVIDIA TitanX/1080Ti GPU.

Methods and Baselines

For existing CAT methods, we use IRT-Active, the uncertainty sampling-based (Lewis & Gale, 1994) active learning question selection algorithm, which selects the next question with difficulty closest to a student's current ability estimate, as a baseline (Settles et al., 2020). This method coincides with the question information-based CAT methods under the 1PL IRT model. We also use an additional baseline that selects the next question randomly, which we dub IRT-Random. For BOBCAT, we consider the cases of using IRT models (which we dub as BiIRT) and neural networks (which we dub as BiNN) as the response model. For both BiIRT and BiNN, we use four question selection algorithms: in addition to the -Active and -Random algorithms above, we also use learned algorithms with the -Unbiased gradient and the approximate (-Approx) gradient on the question selection algorithm parameters ϕ.

Networks and Hyper-parameters

We train IRT models using logistic regression with l_2-norm regularization. For IRT-Active, we compute the student's current ability estimate with l_2-norm regularization to penalize deviation from the mean student ability parameter. For BiNN, we use a two-layer, fully connected network (with 256 hidden nodes, ReLU nonlinearity, 20% dropout rate, and a final sigmoid output layer; Goodfellow, Bengio, & Courville, 2016) as the response model, with a student-specific, 256-dimensional ability vector as input. We use another fully-connected network (with two hidden layers, 256 hidden nodes, Tanh nonlinearity, and a final softmax output layer) (Goodfellow et al., 2016) as the question selection algorithm. For BiNN/IRT-Unbiased, we use another fully-connected critic network (two hidden layers, 256 hidden nodes, Tanh nonlinearity) in addition to the question selection actor network. For BiIRT and BiNN, we learn the global response model parameters γ and question selection algorithm parameters ϕ using the Adam optimizer (Kingma & Ba, 2015) and learn the response parameters adapted to each student (in the inner-level optimization problem) using the SGD optimizer (Goodfellow et al., 2016). For all methods, we select $n \in \{1, 3, 5, 10\}$ questions for each student.

RESULTS AND DISCUSSION

In Table 8.1, we list the mean accuracy numbers across all folds for selected BOBCAT variants and IRT-Active on all datasets; in Table 8.2, we do the same using the AUC metric. For full results, see (Ghosh & Lan, 2021). Using a neural network-based response model, BiNN-Approx outperforms other methods in most cases. Using an IRT response model, BiIRT-Approx performs similarly to BiNN-Approx and outperforms other methods. All BOBCAT variants significantly outperform IRT-Active, which uses a static question selection algorithm. On the ASSISTments dataset, the smallest of the five, BiIRT-Approx outperforms BiNN-Approx, which overfits. These results show that (a) BOBCAT improves existing CAT methods by explicitly learning a question selection algorithm from data, where the improvement is more obvious on larger datasets, and (b) since BOBCAT is agnostic to the underlying response model, one can freely choose either IRT models when training data is limited or neural network-based models when there is plenty of training data.

TABLE 8.1   Average Predictive Accuracy on the Meta Question Set Across Folds on All Datasets

Dataset	n	IRT-Active	BiIRT-Active	BiIRT-Unbiased	BiIRT-Approx	BiNN-Approx
EdNet	1	70.08	70.92	71.12	**71.22**	**71.22**
	3	70.63	71.16	71.30	71.72	**71.82**
	5	71.03	71.37	71.45	71.95	**72.17**
	10	71.62	71.75	71.79	72.33	**72.55**
Junyi	1	74.52	74.93	74.97	**75.11**	75.10
	3	75.19	75.48	75.53	75.76	**75.83**
	5	75.64	75.79	75.75	76.11	**76.19**
	10	76.27	76.28	76.19	76.49	**76.62**
Eedi-1	1	66.92	68.22	68.61	**68.82**	68.78
	3	68.79	69.45	69.81	70.30	**70.45**
	5	70.15	70.28	70.47	70.93	**71.37**
	10	71.72	71.45	71.57	72.00	**72.33**
Eedi-2	1	63.75	64.83	65.22	65.30	**65.65**
	3	65.25	66.42	67.09	67.23	**67.79**
	5	66.41	67.35	67.91	68.23	**68.82**
	10	68.04	68.99	68.84	69.47	**70.04**
ASSISTments	1	66.19	68.69	69.03	**69.17**	68.00
	3	68.75	69.54	69.78	**70.21**	68.73
	5	69.87	69.79	70.30	**70.41**	69.03
	10	71.04	70.66	**71.17**	71.14	69.75

Note: Best methods are shown in **bold** font. For standard deviations and results on all methods, see (Ghosh & Lan, 2021).

In Figure 8.2, we use a series of plots as ablation studies to present a more detailed comparison between different methods; here, we include random question selection as a bottom line. In the first column, we plot the mean and the standard deviation of accuracy for IRT-Random, IRT-Active, BiIRT-Random, and BiIRT-Active versus the number of questions selected. On the Eedi-1 dataset, BiIRT-Active performs better than IRT-Active on smaller n but performs slightly worse for $n = 10$. On the ASSISTments dataset, we observe a high standard deviation for larger n; nevertheless, BiIRT variants outperform IRT counterparts. On all other datasets, the BiIRT methods outperform their IRT counterparts significantly. To reach the same accuracy, on the EdNet, Eedi-2, and Junyi datasets, BiIRT-Active requires ~30% less questions compared to IRT-Active. This head-to-head comparison using IRT as the underlying response model demonstrates the

TABLE 8.2   Average AUC on the Meta Question Set Across Folds on All Datasets

Dataset	n	IRT-Active	BiIRT-Active	BiIRT-Unbiased	BiIRT-Approx	BiNN-Approx
EdNet	1	73.58	73.82	74.14	74.34	**74.41**
	3	74.14	74.21	74.49	75.26	**75.43**
	5	74.60	74.56	74.77	75.68	**76.07**
	10	76.35	75.21	75.39	76.35	**76.74**
Junyi	1	74.92	75.53	75.67	**75.91**	75.90
	3	76.06	76.52	76.71	77.11	**77.16**
	5	76.82	77.07	77.07	77.69	**77.80**
	10	77.95	77.95	77.86	78.45	**78.60**
Eedi-1	1	68.02	70.22	70.95	**71.34**	71.33
	3	71.63	72.47	73.26	74.21	**74.44**
	5	73.69	73.97	74.54	75.47	**76.00**
	10	76.12	75.90	76.34	77.07	**77.51**
Eedi-2	1	69.00	70.15	70.64	70.81	**71.24**
	3	71.11	72.18	73.11	73.37	**73.88**
	5	72.42	73.21	74.19	74.55	**75.20**
	10	74.36	75.17	75.37	75.96	**76.63**
ASSISTments	1	69.14	70.55	71.00	**71.33**	70.12
	3	71.17	71.60	72.35	**73.16**	71.57
	5	72.26	71.65	73.10	**73.71**	72.14
	10	73.62	72.52	74.38	**74.66**	73.59

Note: Best methods are shown in **bold** font.

power of bilevel optimization; even using static question selection algorithms, explicitly maximizing the predictive accuracy on a meta question set results in better performance, although the performance gain may not be significant.

In the second column, we compare different BOBCAT variants using the same underlying neural network-based response model. We observe that on all datasets, BiNN-Approx significantly outperforms other methods, reaching the same accuracy as BiNN-Active with 50%–75% less questions. This performance gain is more significant on larger datasets. It also significantly outperforms the unbiased gradient estimate, reaching the same accuracy with 10%–70% less questions. BiNN-Unbiased significantly outperforms BiNN-Active for smaller n but not for large n; we believe the large variance of the unbiased gradient might be the reason for this behavior. This head-to-head comparison shows that our approximate gradient

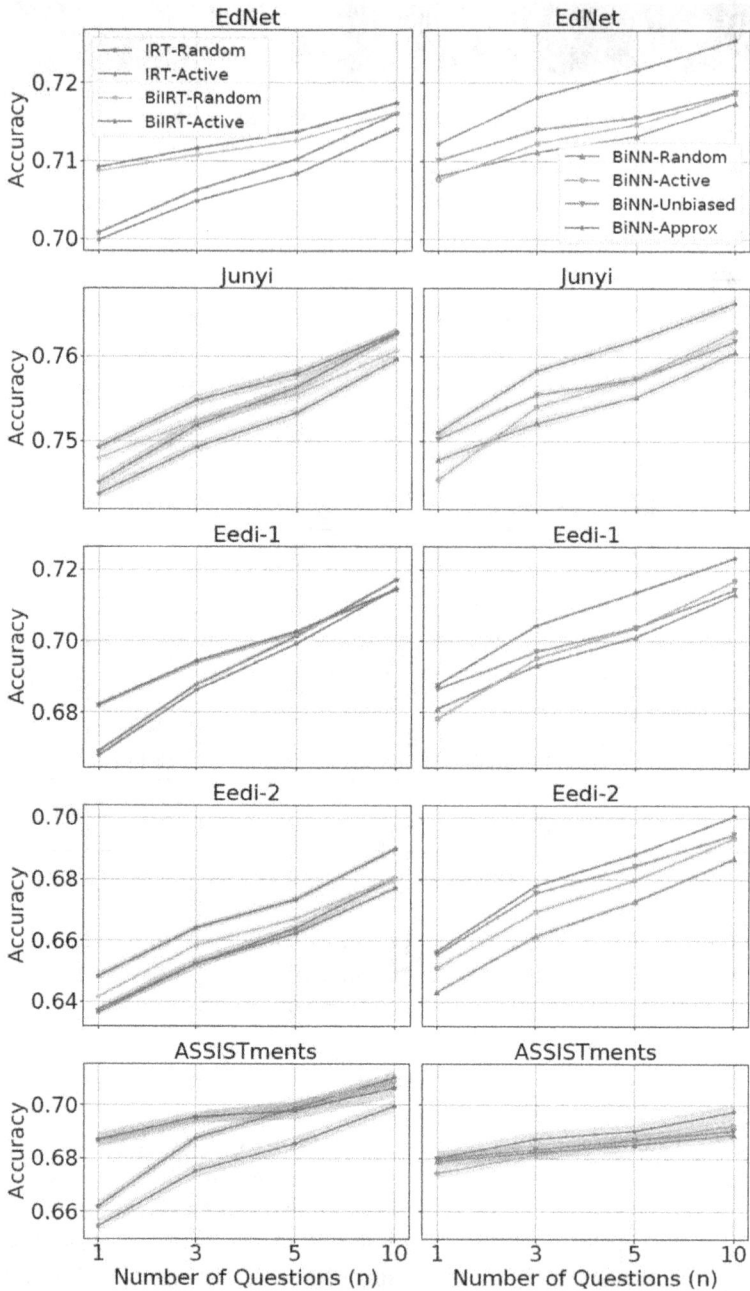

Figure 8.2 Average accuracy (dark lines) and 5-fold standard deviation (light fill lines) on all datasets. First column compares IRT vs BiIRT models; second column compares all BiNN models.

estimate stabilizes the model training process and leads to better model fit. Moreover, data-driven question selection algorithms learned through bilevel optimization are much better than standard static CAT question selection algorithms and get better with more training data.

Study: Ability Estimation

The goal of real-world CAT systems is to accurately estimate the student ability parameter under IRT models, which is then used for scoring. Therefore, we conduct an additional experiment on the Eedi-2 dataset using the squared error between the current ability parameter estimate $\hat{\theta}_i^{(n)}$ and the true ability θ_i as the evaluation metric. Since the true student ability is unknown in real student response datasets, we use the ability value estimated from all questions each student responded to as a substitute. We compare two methods: IRT-Active, with the underlying 1PL IRT model trained on the data and BiIRT-Approx, where we only use the learned model-agnostic question selection algorithm for evaluation in the setting of existing CAT methods. Figure 8.3 (left) shows the ability estimation error (averaged over five folds) for different numbers of questions selected, n. We see that even though the goal of BiIRT-Approx is not ability parameter estimation, it is more effective than IRT-Active and can reach the same accuracy using up to 30% less questions, significantly reducing test length. Figure 8.3 (right) shows the same comparison for models trained on 25% and 50% of the training data. We see that BOBCAT improves significantly with more training data while existing CAT methods do not.

Study: C-BOBCAT

To validate C-BOBCAT, we also use two datasets collected from the Massachusetts Adult Proficiency Test (MAPT), the reading comprehension test (MAPT-Read), and the math test (MAPT-Math), to validate C-BOBCAT. In

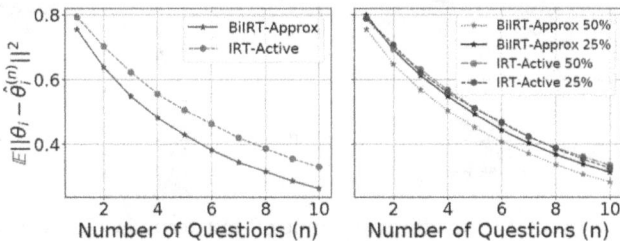

Figure 8.3 Ability estimation accuracy on the Eedi-2 dataset.

both MAPT datasets, there are a total of more than 90K students, 1.7K questions, and 4M question responses Sireci et al. (2008). We use the Scaled Chi-square Statistics of the question exposure rate (EXPOSE-CHI) and the average value of test overlap rate between every two students (OVERLAP-MU) to measure question exposure and test overlap rates (Ozturk & Dogan, 2015). Here, we label all methods with a prefix C-, indicating their modified optimization objectives with the additional entropy regularization term.

In Figure 8.4, we use a series of plots to demonstrate how C-BOBCAT trades off test accuracy (AUC on held-out meta data) versus test security (EXPOSE-PHI and OVERLAP-MU). For both C-BINN-Approx and C-BI-IRT-Approx, each point on the curve corresponds to a specific value of the hyperparameter λ. The baselines correspond to single points since they do not support this tradeoff. We observe that AUC and EXPOSE-PHI are positively correlated in the first column of the graph. Both metrics reach the minimum as λ approaches infinity, i.e., when the categorical question selection distribution's entropy is maximized. In this scenario, the question selection algorithm selects each question with equal probability, which decreases both the question exposure rate and test accuracy. Both metrics reach the maximum as λ approaches zero, i.e., when the categorical question selection distribution's entropy is minimized. In this scenario, the question selection algorithm greedily selects the question that leads

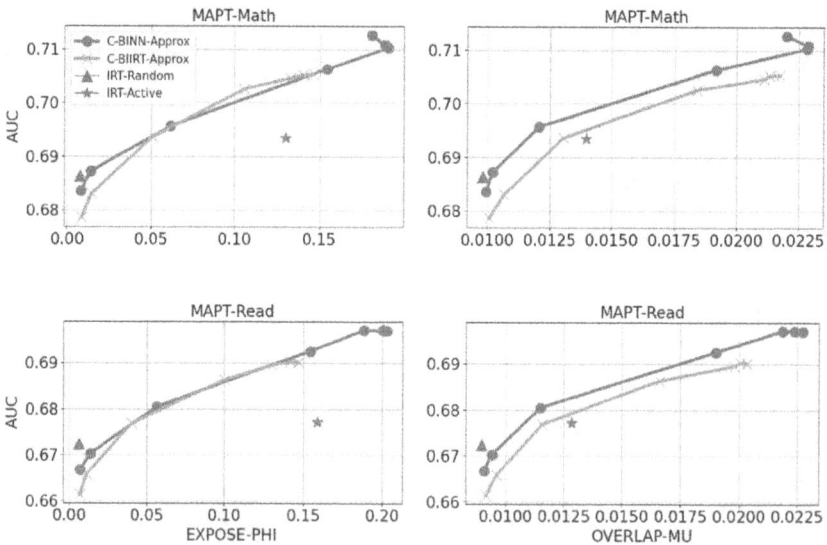

Figure 8.4 C-BOBCAT can effectively trade off test accuracy (*y*-axis, AUC on held-out meta data) for test security (*x*-axes, **EXPOSE-PHI** and **OVERLAP-MU**) on both datasets.

to the highest test accuracy, which also results in a high question exposure rate. A similar relationship can also be found between OVERLAP-MU and AUC in the second column of the graph. More importantly, with the same EXPOSE-PHI and OVERLAP-MU values, both C-BINN-Approx and C-BIIRT-Approx achieve higher AUC values than the IRT-Active baseline. This observation implies C-BOBCAT is agnostic of the underlying response model and always achieves a better balance between test accuracy and question exposure and test overlap rates than the IRT-Active baseline.

CONCLUSIONS AND FUTURE WORK

In this work, we proposed BOBCAT, a bilevel optimization framework for CAT, which is agnostic of the underlying student response model and learns a question selection algorithm from training data. Through extensive experiments on five real-world student response datasets, we demonstrated that BOBCAT can significantly outperform existing CAT methods at reducing test length. We also used a constrained version of BOBCAT to effectively balance test accuracy and security. Avenues of future work include i) studying the fairness aspects of BOBCAT due to potential biases in training data and ii) studying the impact of using the question and response content in CAT settings, driven by recent development on large language model-based student models (Liu, Wang, Baraniuk, & Lan, 2022).

ACKNOWLEDGEMENTS

The authors thank the NSF (under grants 1917713, 2118706, 2202506, 2215193) for partially supporting this work.

NOTES

1. Our implementation is publicly available at https://github.com/arghosh/BOBCAT and https://github.com/umass-ml4ed/C-BOBCAT.
2. https://github.com/riiid/ednet
3. https://www.kaggle.com/junyiacademy/learning-activity-public-dataset-by-junyi-academy
4. https://eedi.com/projects/neurips-education-challenge
5. https://sites.google.com/site/assistmentsdata/home/assistment-2009-2010-data

REFERENCES

Cheng, S., Liu, Q., Chen, E., Huang, Z., Huang, Z., Chen, Y., ... Hu, G. (2019). Dirt: Deep learning enhanced item response theory for cognitive diagnosis. In *International conference on information and knowledge management* (pp. 2397–2400).

Choi, Y., Lee, Y., Shin, D., Cho, J., Park, S., Lee, S., ... Heo, J. (2020). Ednet: A large-scale hierarchical dataset in education. In *International conference on artificial intelligence in education* (pp. 69–73).

Feng, W., Ghosh, A., Sireci, S., & Lan, A. (2023). Balancing test accuracy and security in computerized adaptive testing. In *Proceedings of the international conference on artificial intelligence in education.*

Finn, C., Abbeel, P., & Levine, S. (2017). Model-agnostic meta-learning for fast adaptation of deep networks. In *International conference on machine learning* (Vol. 70, pp. 1126–1135).

Franceschi, L., Frasconi, P., Salzo, S., Grazzi, R., & Pontil, M. (2018). Bilevel programming for hyperparameter optimization and meta-learning. In *International conference on machine learning* (pp. 1568–1577).

Ghosh, A., & Lan, A. (2021). Bobcat: Bilevel optimization-based computerized adaptive testing. In *Proceedings of the thirtieth international joint conference on artificial intelligence (ijcai;* pp. 2410–2417).

Goodfellow, I., Bengio, Y., & Courville, A. (2016). *Deep learning.* MIT Press.

Han, K. C. T. (2018). Components of the item selection algorithm in computerized adaptive testing. *Journal of Educational Evaluation for Health Professions, 15.*

Jang, E., Gu, S., & Poole, B. (2017). Categorical reparameterization with gumbel-softmax. *ICLR.*

Kingma, D. P., & Ba, J. (2015, May). Adam: A method for stochastic optimization. In *Proceedings international conference on learning representations.*

Koh, P. W., & Liang, P. (2017). Understanding black-box predictions via influence functions. In *International conference on machine learning* (pp. 1885–1894).

Lee, K., Maji, S., Ravichandran, A., & Soatto, S. (2019). Meta-learning with differentiable convex optimization. In *IEEE conference on computer vision and pattern recognition* (pp. 10657–10665).

Lewis, D. D., & Gale, W. A. (1994, July). A sequential algorithm for training text classifiers. In *Proc. acm sigir conference on research and development in information retrieval* (pp. 3–12).

Li, X., Xu, H., Zhang, J., & Chang, H.-h. (2020). *Deep reinforcement learning for adaptive learning systems.* arXiv preprint arXiv:2004.08410

Liu, N., Wang, Z., Baraniuk, R., & Lan, A. (2022). Open-ended knowledge tracing for computer science education. In *Proceedings of the 2022 conference on empirical methods in natural language processing* (pp. 3849–3862).

Lord, F. (1980). *Applications of item response theory to practical testing problems.* Erlbaum Associates.

Luecht, R. M., & Sireci, S. G. (2011). A review of models for computer-based testing. research report 2011–12. *College Board.*

Nurakhmetov, D. (2019). Reinforcement learning applied to adaptive classification testing. In *Theoretical and practical advances in computer-based educational measurement* (pp. 325–336). Springer.

Ozturk, N. B., & Dogan, N. (2015). *Investigating item exposure control methods in computerized adaptive testing.*

Rajeswaran, A., Finn, C., Kakade, S. M., & Levine, S. (2019). Meta-learning with implicit gradients. In *Advances in neural information processing systems* (pp. 113–124).

Rasch, G. (1993). *Probabilistic models for some intelligence and attainment tests.* MESA Press.

Reckase, M. D. (2009). *Multidimensional item response theory models.* Springer.

Settles, B. (2012, Nov.). Active learning. *Synthesis Lectures on Artificial Intelligence and Machine Learning, 6*(1), 1–114.

Settles, B., T. LaFlair, G., & Hagiwara, M. (2020). Machine learning-driven language assessment. *Transactions of the Association for Computational Linguistics, 8*, 247–263.

Sireci, S. G., Baldwin, P., Martone, A., Zenisky, A. L., Kaira, L., Lam, W.,... et al. (2008). Massachusetts adult proficiency tests technical manual, version 2. *Center for Educational Assessment Research Report No, 677.*

Ueno, M., & Miyazawa, Y. (2019). Uniform adaptive testing using maximum clique algorithm. In *Artificial intelligence in education: 20th International Conference, AIED 2019, Chicago, Il, June 25–29, 2019, Proceedings, part I 20* (pp. 482–493).

Ueno, M., & Miyazawa, Y. (2022). Two-stage uniform adaptive testing to balance measurement accuracy and item exposure. In *Artificial intelligence in education: 23rd international conference, AIED 2022, Durham, UK, July 27–31, 2022, Proceedings, part I* (pp. 626–632).

van der Linden, W. J., & Glas, C. A. (2000). *Computerized adaptive testing: Theory and practice.* Springer.

van der Linden, W. J., & Pashley, P. J. (2009). Item selection and ability estimation in adaptive testing. In *Elements of adaptive testing* (pp. 3–30). Springer.

Vats, D., Lan, A. S., Studer, C., & Baraniuk, R. G. (2016). Optimal ranking of test items using the rasch model. In *2016 54th annual Allerton conference on communication, control, and computing (Allerton;* pp. 467–473).

Vats, D., Studer, C., Lan, A. S., Carin, L., & Baraniuk, R. (2013). Test-size reduction for concept estimation. In *Educational data mining 2013.*

Wang, F., Liu, Q., Chen, E., Huang, Z., Chen, Y., Yin, Y.,... Wang, S. (2020). Neural cognitive diagnosis for intelligent education systems. In *Proceedings of the AAAI Conference on artificial intelligence* (Vol. 34, pp. 6153–6161).

Wang, Z., Lamb, A., Saveliev, E., Cameron, P., Zaykov, Y., Hernández-Lobato, J. M.,... et al. (2020). *Diagnostic questions: The neurips 2020 education challenge.* arXiv preprint arXiv:2007.12061 .

Williams, R. J. (1992). Simple statistical gradient-following algorithms for connectionist reinforcement learning. *Machine Learning, 8*(3–4), 229–256.

Zhuang, Y., Liu, Q., Huang, Z., Li, Z., Shen, S., & Ma, H. (2022). Fully adaptive framework: Neural computerized adaptive testing for online education. In *Proceedings of the AAAI Conference on artificial intelligence* (Vol. 36, pp. 4734–4742).

CHAPTER 9

FROM ADAPTIVE TESTING TO PERSONALIZED ADAPTIVE TESTING

Applications of Recommender Systems

Okan Bulut
University of Alberta

The assessment process is a continuous cycle of eliciting reliable and meaningful evidence that informs formative and summative interpretations based on a construct of interest (William & Black, 1996). Summative assessments are often used for making important decisions such as admission to a university, placement decisions for remedial programs, and certification decisions for a particular profession. In contrast, formative assessments (e.g., progress monitoring tests in K–12 schools) are typically designed to support student learning and inform data-based decision-making in the classroom (Van der Kleij et al., 2015). Both types of assessments aim to measure an individual's proficiency in the target construct as accurately and efficiently as possible. However, traditional forms of assessment (e.g., paper-and-pencil and computerized tests) often fail to accomplish this goal due to their inability to tailor the difficulty

Machine Learning, Natural Language Processing, and Psychometrics, pages 177–199
Copyright © 2024 by Information Age Publishing
www.infoagepub.com
177

level of the test to each examinee's ability level (Luecht & Sireci, 2011). Furthermore, using fixed forms with the same test items can lead to major test security concerns, such as examinees memorizing and sharing test items.

Researchers developed computerized adaptive testing (CAT) as a response to the limitations of traditional assessments. CAT can tailor itself to each examinee's ability level and thereby select the most optimal items from a large item bank. As a novel form of testing dating back to the early 1970s, CAT has revolutionized educational testing by allowing a more efficient and accurate evaluation of a wide range of constructs. Today, numerous assessment programs around the world, such as the Graduate Management Admission Council's Graduate Management Admission Test, Renaissance's Star Reading and Star Math assessments, and the National Council of State Boards of Nursing's National Council Licensure Examination, implement CAT for measuring various skills and abilities. In addition to large-scale assessment programs, CAT has also been used in other settings, such as formative assessments (Yang et al., 2022), diagnostic testing (Cheng, 2009), progress monitoring (Eggen, 2018), intelligent tutoring systems (Wauters et al., 2010), and self-assessment (Guzmán, & Conejo, 2005).

Typically, CAT is implemented based on the item parameters calibrated with a particular item response theory (IRT) model, such as the two-parameter logistic (2PL) model. As the examinee answers the items, a provisional estimate of ability is obtained after each item based on the examinee's responses (e.g., either correct or incorrect answers in a multiple-choice item) and item paraemeters (e.g., difficulty and discrimination). Then, the next item is selected from the item bank by finding the item that provides the most information at the current ability level. In other words, CAT optimizes the measurement process for each examinee through a personalized test tailored to their ability levels. Yet, there are also some limitations to CAT. For example, CAT assumes that the examinee puts forth their best effort throughout the test. If, however, the examinee starts showing aberrant response behaviors (e.g., rapid guessing), the sequential selection of most informative items can be jeopardized significantly, leading to biased ability estimates. Also, as the primary goal of CAT is to maximize the accuracy and efficiency of the measurement process, the potential impact of examinee characteristics (e.g., learning preferences or style) and item attributes (e.g., content, item type, and cognitive complexity) are often disregarded in the item selection process, limiting the personalization of examinees' learning experiences.

BEYOND ADAPTIVE TESTING

Over the last decade, the definitions of adaptivity and personalization in education have undergone significant changes (Ayoub, 2020). With artificial intelligence (AI) becoming increasingly integrated into our lives, researchers have been able to create adaptive learning systems that use AI-powered technologies to enhance personalization in education (Gupta et al., 2022). Although personalized learning is viewed as the most effective way to transform education for the future, some researchers argue that current educational systems still need to evolve further to meet the unique needs of today's learners (Furini et al., 2022). Therefore, additional research is necessary to determine how digital learner data can be used to personalize learning experiences.

To address this substantial gap, it is necessary to develop more comprehensive learning models that can be tailored to individual needs. This can be achieved by using recommendation algorithms that rely on big data analytics and AI techniques (Furini et al., 2022). While customers of online platforms like Netflix and Amazon are already familiar with receiving personalized content recommendations based on various parameters (e.g., age, location, and user preferences), the use of recommender systems in education has been limited so far. An example of recommender systems in education is personalized learning paths created for learners enrolled in online learning platforms, such as Coursera, edX, and Udemy, as well as those who use intelligent tutoring systems. As each learner focuses on a particular skill or content area, the system can provide personalized feedback and content recommendations that address their weaknesses while offering more opportunities to build on their strengths (Wongvorachan et al., 2022; Yasmin & Mazhar, 2022).

In 2016, Essa proposed a framework for personalized and adaptive learning. This framework consists of five models that interact with each other: domain model (what the learner needs to know), learner model (what the learner currently knows), assessment model (how one can infer a learner's knowledge state), pedagogical model (what activities are needed for the learner to move the next knowledge state), and transition model (what the learner is ready to learn next). While all of these models are essential for achieving personalized learning, this chapter focuses on the assessment model and how it can be enhanced by using recommender systems. Specifically, we explain how recommender systems can choose the most suitable items or tasks for learners based on their current state of learning and acquired knowledge. In the next section, we will provide a detailed discussion of how recommender systems work and describe different types of algorithms used by modern recommender systems.

RECOMMENDER SYSTEMS

A recommender (or recommendation) system is a type of machine learning that uses data from items and/or users to assist users in finding the most appropriate item from a large number of options, such as a movie to watch or a book to buy. These systems are "personalized information agents that provide recommendations: suggestions for items likely to be of use to a user." Burke (2007, p. 377). Over the last two decades, recommender systems have been an essential part of modern life, helping individuals in a wide range of areas, from e-commerce (suggesting suitable products to online shoppers) to online streaming services (suggesting songs or movies tailored to users based on their preferences or interests). Many popular companies such as Netflix, YouTube, and Amazon use recommender systems to suggest relevant items to their customers quickly and avoid overwhelming them with too many options. This approach not only helps users avoid information overload but also enhances the user experience. The 2016 Netflix Prize competition offered a grand prize of $1 million to participants who were tasked to find the best algorithm for predicting user ratings for movies on Netflix, providing strong evidence of the importance of recommender systems.

According to Adomavicius and Tuzhilin (2005), there are three primary methods for building a recommender system: (a) content-based methods, (b) collaborative filtering (CF), and (c) hybrid methods (see Figure 9.1). Content-based methods build a latent interaction model based on item and/or user attributes that explain the observed user-item interactions and then use this model to make recommendations. The CF method relies on previously observed interactions between users and items to produce new

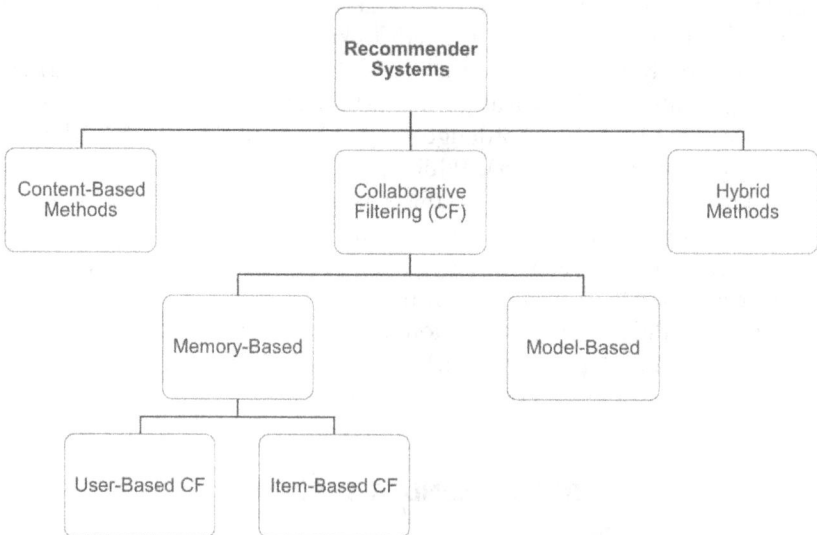

Figure 9.1 A summary of the different types of recommender systems.

recommendations. This is typically accomplished by using memory-based (also known as neighborhood-based) and model-based approaches. Memory-based CF approaches work with the values of previously recorded interactions to look for the nearest neighbors and make recommendations (e.g., recommending the most popular items among the closest neighbors of a target user). Model-based CF approaches assume a generative model underlying the user-item interactions and use this model to make new predictions (i.e., recommendations) for users. The hybrid CF methods aim to combine CF and content-based methods to produce more robust recommendations. In the following sections, we will describe these approaches in more detail.

CONTENT-BASED FILTERING

Content-based filtering makes explicit use of domain knowledge about users and/or items to produce meaningful recommendations for users. Domain knowledge refers to the extraction of item profiles (i.e., item attributes) through a content analyzer and user profiles based on data representative of the user's preferences. For example, the domain knowledge can be generated from various user characteristics such as age, gender, or location and item attributes such as genre, director, main actors, or duration in the context of movie recommendations. Similarly, an online learning platform utilizing content-based filtering can ask its users upfront about what content or skills they want to learn (or improve) and exploit this information to recommend different learning modules matching the users' preferences. In the final step, content-based filtering uses various similarity metrics (e.g., cosine similarity, Euclidean distance, and Pearson correlation) to find and recommend the items most similar to what the user profile suggests that the user would prefer. The success of content-based filtering relies on having complete and accurate information about the attributes of items, rather than relying on input from other users.

COLLABORATIVE FILTERING

CF is a popular method utilized by recommendation systems to anticipate a user's preferences by considering the preferences of other users with similar interests. The CF methods have proven to be a successful approach in different fields, including e-commerce (Linden, Smith, & York, 2003), movie and music recommendation (Jacobson et al., 2016; Koren, 2008), and identifying spam comments (Raghavan et al., 2012). This type of information filtering leverages the past interactions of a group of users to suggest items to other users. That is, the CF methods rely on the collaborative power of observed ratings provided by multiple users to make recommendations (Aggarwal, 2016). These ratings can be in the form of either explicit feedback (e.g., assigning a numerical rating to a product on a scale from one star to five stars, using Likert-scale options to indicate user appreciation, and thumb up/down given after watching a video) or implicit feedback inferred from user actions (e.g., a customer's purchase history or the list of previously played songs). High inter-item or inter-user correlations between ratings inform the prediction of unspecified ratings (i.e., ratings for unseen items). Unlike content-based filtering, the CF methods do not require additional knowledge (i.e., metadata) about user characteristics or item attributes beyond the observed ratings. As more user-item interactions are recorded over time, the additional information gained through these interactions makes the CF methods produce more accurate recommendations.

As explained earlier, there are two types of CF algorithms: memory-based and model-based. The memory-based CF methods directly work with user-item interactions and item-item similarities. The former predicts a user's rating of an item based on their past ratings and those of other users who have rated the same item. On the other hand, the latter predicts a user's rating of an item based on similarities between the item and other items that the user has rated. The model-based CF methods rely on a latent interaction model that can reconstruct the observed user-item interactions as accurately as possible. Then, this mathematical model trained on past item-user interactions can be used to make predictions about new users. In the following sections, we will describe the memory-based and model-based CF methods in more detail.

User-Based Collaborative Filtering

As a user-centered approach, user-based CF aims to identify users with the most similar profiles based on their distances from the target user (i.e., nearest neighbors) to recommend the most popular items among these neighbors. Assume that the user–item interaction matrix ($\mathbf{R}$) consists of ratings (r_{uj}) from m users ($u = 1, 2, \ldots, m$) on n items ($j = 1, 2, \ldots, n$). In the first step, the neighbors of the target user u are identified based on the target user's similarity to the remaining users on mutually observed (i.e., common) ratings denoted as I_{uv}. For example, the similarity between the target user u and another user v can be calculated based on Pearson correlation as follows:

$$Sim(u,v) = cor(u,v) = \frac{\sum_{i \in I_{uv}} (r_{ui} - \mu_u)(r_{vi} - \mu_v)}{\sqrt{\sum_{i \in I_{uv}} (r_{ui} - \mu_u)^2 \sum_{i \in I_{uv}} (r_{vi} - \mu_v)^2}}, \quad (9.1)$$

where μ_u and μ_v are the mean ratings for users u and v. Alternatively, cosine similarity can be computed as a similarity index between the two users:

$$Sim(u,v) = \cos(u,v) = \frac{\sum_{i \in I_{uv}} r_{ui} r_{vi}}{\sqrt{\sum_{i \in I_{uv}} (r_{ui})^2 \sum_{i \in I_{uv}} (r_{vi})^2}} \tag{9.2}$$

Once the similarity values between the target user and all the other users are computed, the nearest neighbors of the target user can be located using the k-nearest neighbors (KNN) algorithm, which searches for the top k nearest neighbors based on their distance (i.e., similarity) to the target user. Instead of keeping a fixed number of nearest neighbors, threshold filtering can also be applied by keeping all the neighbors whose similarity values are greater than a given threshold (Nikolakopoulos et al., 2021).

In the final step, a neighborhood-based prediction function is used to predict target user u's ratings for unseen items and make a recommendation. This function computes the weighted average rating of each unseen item j among the top-k nearest neighbors of target user u. Assuming $P_u(j)$ represents k closest users to target user u who have ratings for item j, the prediction function can be written as follows:

$$\hat{r}_{uj} = \frac{\sum_{v \in P_u(j)} Sim(u,v) r_{vj}}{\sum_{v \in P_u(j)} |Sim(u,v)|}. \tag{9.3}$$

Equation 9.3 can be further enhanced to provide by using mean-centered ratings instead of the raw ratings, which yields a mean-centered prediction (Nikolakopoulos et al., 2021):

$$\hat{r}_{uj} = \mu_u + \frac{\sum_{v \in P_u(j)} Sim(u,v)(r_{vj} - \mu_v)}{\sum_{v \in P_u(j)} |Sim(u,v)|}. \tag{9.4}$$

The mean-centering process in Equation 9.4 yields a better relative prediction with respect to the ratings already observed in the user-interaction matrix (Aggarwal, 2016). Based on the predicted ratings from the above equations, a recommendation process is initiated to create a top-N list that includes N items with the highest predicted ratings for user u. Figure 9.2 illustrates the recommendation process based on the user-based CF filtering method.

Item-Based Collaborative Filtering

The underlying assumption of item-based CF is that users are likely to prefer items similar to those they rated highly in the past (Sarwar et al., 2001). Thus, ratings for the new (i.e., unseen) items are predicted using the target user's own ratings on neighboring (closely related) items. That is, neighborhoods are defined by similarities among the items (see Figure 9.3). The item-based similarity is often a common choice in recommender systems

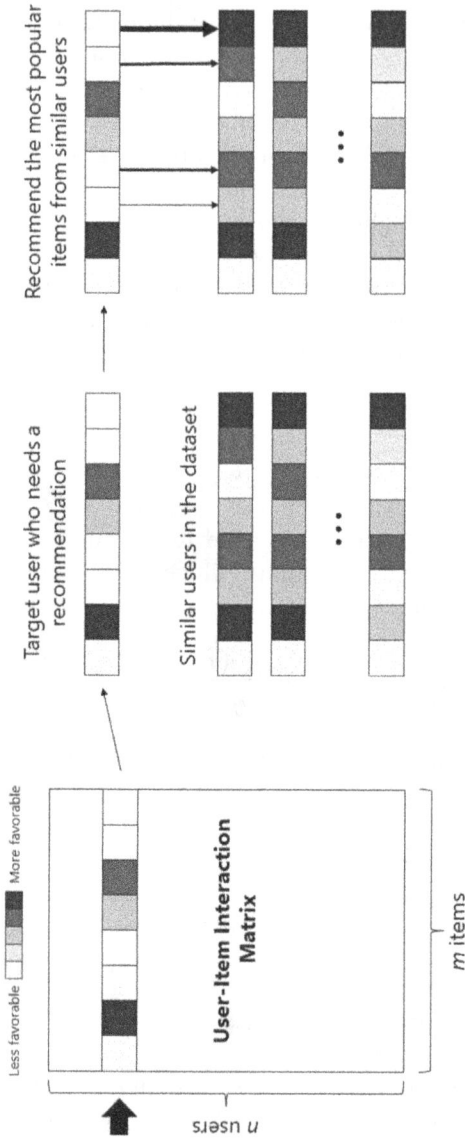

Figure 9.2   An example of user-based collaborative filtering.

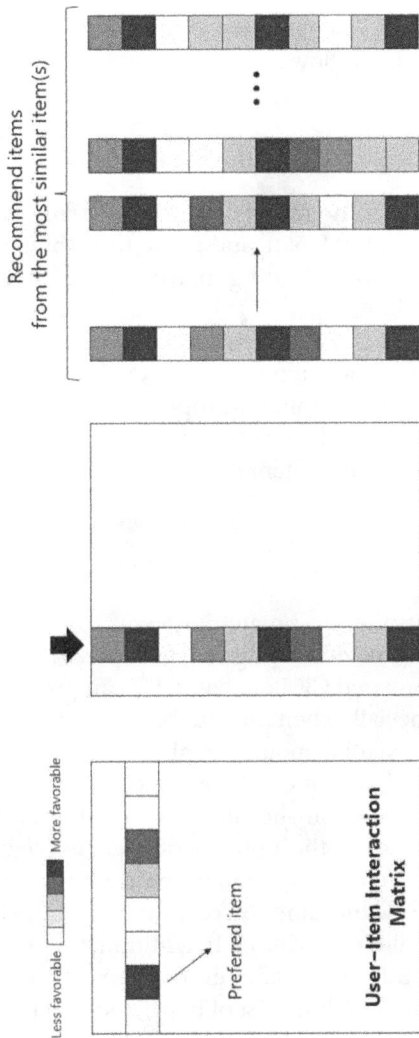

Figure 9.3 An example of item-based collaborative filtering.

because the item's neighborhood changes more slowly than the target user's neighborhood.

Unlike the user-based CF methods using the Pearson correlation as a similarity measure, the item-based CF methods typically employ the adjusted cosine similarity between the items as it generally yields better results (Aggarwal, 2016). Assume that U_{ij} represents the common users who rated both items i and j. Then, the adjusted cosine similarity between the two items can be computed as follows:

$$\text{Adjusted } \cos(i, j) = \frac{\Sigma_{u \in U_{ij}} (r_{ui} - \mu_i)(r_{uj} - \mu_j)}{\sqrt{\Sigma_{u \in U_{ij}} (r_{ui} - \mu_i)^2 \Sigma_{u \in U_{ij}} (r_{uj} - \mu_j)^2}}, \tag{9.5}$$

where r_{ui} and r_{uj} represent the ratings assigned to items i and j by the common users (U_{ij}). In Equation 9.5, μ_i and μ_j are the average ratings for each item, creating a mean-centered rating matrix to compute the adjusted cosine similarity.

After the similarity values are obtained for target item t and the remaining items in the user-item interaction matrix, the KNN algorithm (or a similarity threshold) can be used to determine the top-k most similar items to the target item. In the final step, a prediction function is applied to obtain the predicted rating of user u for target item $t(\hat{r}_{ut})$ based on the rating of item $j(r_{uj})$:

$$\hat{r}_{ut} = \frac{\Sigma_{u \in U_{ij}} \text{Adjusted } \cos(j, t) r_{uj}}{\Sigma_{u \in U_{ij}} |\text{Adjusted } \cos(j, t)|}, \tag{9.6}$$

where $Q_t(u)$ represents the top-k matching items to target item t for which the user u has already provided ratings (Aggarwal, 2016).

Compared with user-based CF, item-based CF can produce more accurate recommendations, especially when the number of users is much greater than the number of items (Nikolakopoulos et al., 2021; Sarwar et al., 2001). In contrast, a user-based CF system can be more desirable for scenarios where the number of users is much smaller than the number of items (Herlocker et al., 2004). However, when the number of users exceeds the number of items, item-based CF methods can be more efficient and scalable as they require much less memory and time to compute the similarity values among the items (Nikolakopoulos et al., 2021). In addition, the choice of item-based or user-based CF depends on the amount of change in the users and items (e.g., selecting item-based CF if the list of items does not change frequently).

Model-Based Collaborative Filtering

Unlike the memory-based CF methods, the model-based CF methods do not directly look for similarities among users or items based on the observed user-item interaction matrix. Instead, these methods assume that there is a generative latent model (also known as latent factor models) that can explain how each user interacts with each item. Under this assumption, the observed user-item interaction matrix is decomposed into a product of two smaller and dense matrices: a user-factor matrix ($\mathbf{X}$) containing user representations (or embeddings) and an item-factor matrix ($\mathbf{Y}$) containing item representations (or embeddings). Figure 9.4 illustrates how a high-dimensional interaction matrix ($\mathbf{R}$) can be decomposed into a K–dimensional space with $\mathbf{X}$ and $\mathbf{Y}$ representing the user and item matrices, respectively. Computing the dot product of these dense vectors yields the reconstructed interaction matrix, $\hat{\mathbf{R}}$, with a certain degree of accuracy.

Model-based CF methods generally involve a form of matrix factorization, such as singular value decomposition (SVD) and non-negative matrix factorization (NMF), to transform the items and users to a joint latent factor (i.e., embedding) space. In addition to the user-item interaction matrix, matrix factorization can be applied to the similarity matrix (for users or items). A matrix of similarity values computed based on a similarity measure such as the Pearson correlation and cosine similarity can be densified by computing a low-rank approximation of the matrix using a matrix factorization method (Nikolakopoulos et al., 2021). Regardless of which matrix (i.e., the similarity matrix or the user-item interaction matrix) is selected, the use of matrix factorization methods can alleviate practical issues such as the cold-start problem and sparsity in the data (for a detailed discussion of popular matrix factorization methods, see Aggarwal [2016] and Koren et al. [2009]).

Model-based CF methods have several advantages over memory-based CF methods (Aggarwal, 2016). First, model-based methods using latent factor models are generally more accurate than memory-based methods. Second, the model-based methods are computationally more efficient because the size of the learned model with item and user embeddings is much smaller than the original user-item interaction matrix. Third, model-based systems work faster in the pre-processing phase of the model training, producing recommendations more efficiently. Lastly, the summarization approach of the model-based methods with regularization adjustments can help prevent overfitting, leading to less biased recommender systems.

HYBRID METHODS

Hybrid systems combine multiple recommendation techniques or algorithms to provide more accurate and effective recommendations. By integrating multiple methods, such as CF methods and content filtering, hybrid

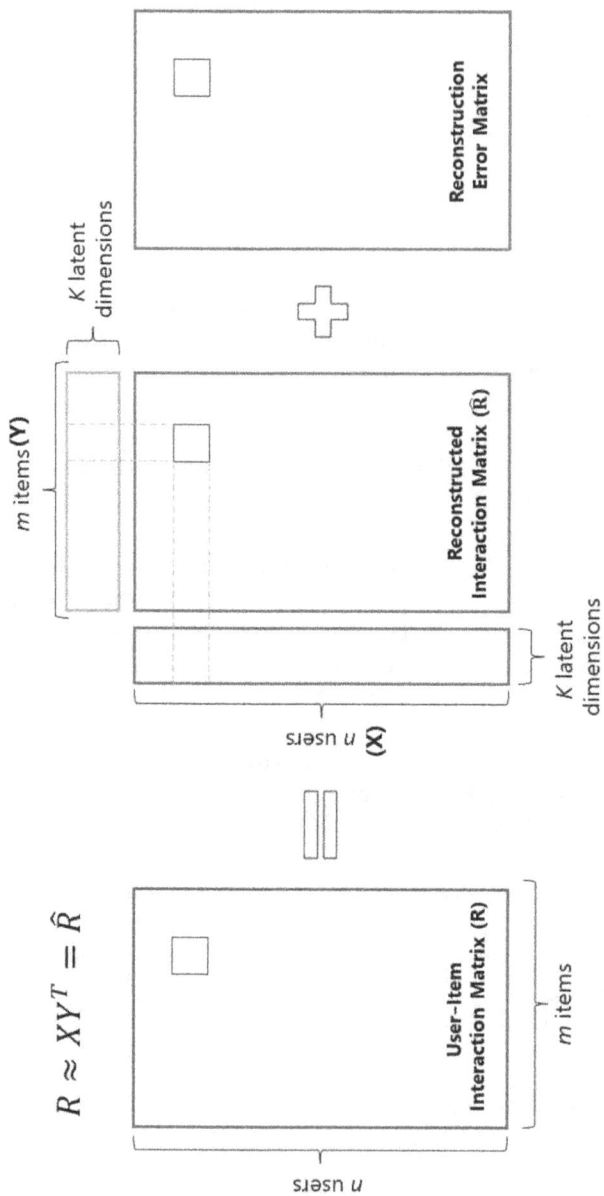

Figure 9.4 An example of model-based collaborative filtering.

systems can leverage heterogeneous data sources, capture different aspects of user preferences and item characteristics, and provide more accurate and personalized recommendations (Elahi et al., 2023). The main idea behind hybrid systems is to exploit the strengths of different approaches and overcome their limitations (Çano & Morisio, 2017). For example, within an educational context, the content-based component of a hybrid system may consider different attributes of the educational resources (e.g., topic, keywords, and difficulty level), while the user-based CF component of the system can examine the preferences or behaviors of similar learners to generate more personalized recommendations.

Hybrid systems can also use one technique to enhance the results of the other, such as using content-based filtering to improve recommendations generated by collaborative filtering. This can help hybrid systems mitigate issues like the cold-start problem (i.e., not having sufficient observed data about users or items) and improve recommendation accuracy by considering user behavior and item attributes. Additionally, an ensemble design can combine predicted ratings from off-the-shelf algorithms into a single and more robust output through parallel and sequential ensembles (Aggarwal, 2016; Burke, 2002). Figure 9.5 demonstrates an example of a hybrid recommender system that combines the features based on user characteristics and item attributes with the observed ratings (i.e., user and item embeddings) in predicting a target user's ratings for unseen items.

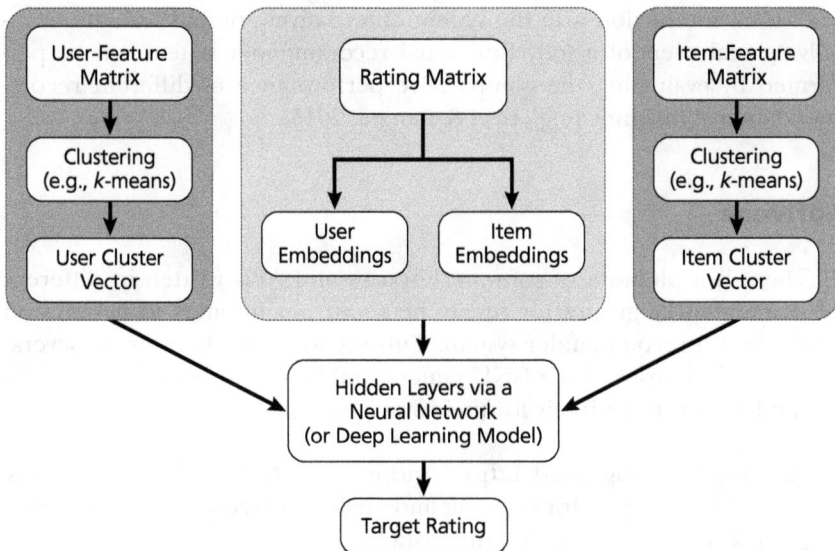

Figure 9.5 An example of a hybrid recommender system.

Evaluating Recommender Systems

The performance of a recommender system can be evaluated through offline evaluation methods, such as by accuracy metrics computed based on historical data (e.g., ratings from previous users). Various accuracy metrics, such as mean squared error (MSE), root mean squared error (RMSE), and mean absolute error (MAE), can be computed based on the difference between the predicted and observed ratings in a historical data set. Coverage is another important evaluation criterion for recommender systems (Aggarwal, 2016). This measure quantifies the proportion of items recommended by the system (item-space coverage) and the proportion of users who can receive a meaningful recommendation (user-space coverage). There is often a trade-off between accuracy and coverage because the accuracy of a recommender system is likely to decrease as it begins to cover a larger number of users with less meaningful recommendations (i.e., less desirable items).

Novelty (i.e., how different a recommended item is with respect to what has been previously seen by the user), diversity (the average pairwise dissimilarity between recommended items), and serendipity (i.e., the level of surprise in successful recommendations) are the other key qualities beyond accuracy that enable a thorough evaluation of recommender systems (McNee et al., 2006; Vargas & Castells, 2011). In addition to offline evaluations, user studies can also be implemented by recruiting a sample of participants to test the recommender system and collecting their feedback before and after their interaction with the system. Alternatively, online evaluations involving real users of a fully functional recommender system can be performed by evaluating the comparative performance of different recommendation algorithms (e.g., Beel & Langer, 2015).

Software

There is a plethora of software libraries and APIs written in different programming languages for researchers and practitioners to design and implement a recommender system. This section provides a list of several well-known libraries with a GNU general public license, enabling users to use and modify them freely for their own projects.

1. **Surprise** (Hug, 2020; https://github.com/NicolasHug/Surprise) is a Python library for building and analyzing recommender systems that deal with explicit rating data.
2. **LightFM** (Kula, 2015; https://github.com/lyst/lightfm) is a well-known Python library including a number of popular recommen-

dation algorithms. This library allows item and user metadata to be incorporated into the matrix factorization algorithms to deal with practical issues such as the cold-start problem.

3. **TensorFlow Recommenders** (https://github.com/tensorflow/recommenders) is another Python library for building recommender systems. The library relies on Google's TensorFlow and Keras (providing an interface for TensorFlow), which can significantly accelerate the model training and evaluation processes when building a recommender system.

4. **recommenderlab** (Hahsler, 2022; https://github.com/mhahsler/recommenderlab) is a library written in R that provides a research infrastructure to develop and evaluate recommender systems using various CF algorithms (e.g., user-based and item-based CF, SVD, and alternating least squares).

5. **LibRec** (Guo et al., 2015; https://guoguibing.github.io/librec/) is a Java library with more than seventy state-of-the-art recommendation algorithms capable of both rating prediction and item ranking.

6. **Gorse** (https://github.com/gorse-io/gorse) is an open-source library written in Go. The library comes with several useful functions, such as an AutoML tool for searching the best recommendation model automatically and a dashboard with a graphical user interface (GUI) for data management and system monitoring.

ADAPTIVE TESTING WITH RECOMMENDER SYSTEMS

In the sections above, we provided a brief overview of the algorithms used for building recommender systems, various methods for evaluating the performance of recommender systems, and popular software libraries for designing, implementing, and evaluating these systems. The final section of this chapter will discuss the utility of recommender systems as an engine for adaptive testing. Specifically, we will describe how to build an IRT-powered recommender system capable of producing effective recommendations for item selection in adaptive testing. The framework described in this section can be applied to CAT where individual items are administered sequentially and on-the-fly assembled multistage adaptive testing (OMST; Zheng & Chang, 2015) where a set of items (i.e., modules) are administered in a group-sequential design.

The success of an adaptive testing application depends highly on the use of an appropriate item selection method. In CAT and MST without non-statistical constraints (e.g., content coverage), item selection (or module assembly in MST) is made based on the maximum Fisher information (MFI) method (Thissen & Mislevy,1990; Weiss, 1982). This MFI method maximizes

Fisher's information at the provisional ability estimate after each item in CAT (or each stage in OMST) by selecting highly discriminating items with difficulty levels closer to the provisional ability estimate. However, this method has been criticized by several researchers in terms of measurement accuracy (Chang & Ying, 1996), unbalanced item exposure rates (Li & Schafer, 2005), and high overlap rates among examinees (Chen et al., 2003).

Previous studies showed that the CF methods could be adopted to solve various psychometric issues, including item selection for adaptive testing (e.g., Bulut, 2022). Although the CF methods are widely used in previous studies focused on recommender systems, these methods have rarely been utilized in the literature on educational measurement and psychometrics. In one of the earlier studies, Töscher and Jahrer (2010) used the CF algorithms to predict students' abilities to respond to items correctly, similar to how IRT models can estimate the probability of a correct answer for a given item. Bergner et al. (2012) formalized unidimensional and multidimensional IRT models as a special case of the model-based CF. Their approach produced "difficulty-like" and "discrimination-like" parameters for the items and an ability parameter for the examinees using regularized logistic regression. There are also a few studies where researchers used polytomous IRT models to enhance (or correct) the accuracy of the observed ratings in the user-item interaction matrix when generating recommendations with the used-based CF methods (Hu et al., 2009).

Recently, researchers also demonstrated how the memory-based CF methods could be harnessed as an item selection method for CAT and OMST to address the limitations of the MFI method described above (Bulut, 2022; Xiao & Bulut, 2022). This approach assumes that there is a historical data set in the form of an $N \times J$ examinee–item interaction matrix in which each row ($n = 1, 2, 3, \ldots, N$) corresponds to an examinee with known ability levels and each column ($j = 1, 2, 3, \ldots, J$) corresponds to an item from the item bank with known item parameters. Cell values of this matrix contain the Fisher information values calculated based on the examinees' ability levels and the item parameters. This approach yields a full examinee–item interaction matrix with zero sparsity because Fisher information can be calculated for each item–examinee pair with known item and ability parameters. A recommender system based on this matrix could recommend the items with the highest information to each examinee. Alternatively, the cell values of the examinee-interaction matrix may consist of the probability of correct answer for each item and examinee combination. A recommender system based on this matrix could recommend the items with probability values close to 0.5 or another pre-determined threshold. Figure 9.6 demonstrates the examinee-item interaction matrices based on these two approaches.

Xiao and Bulut (2022) implemented user-based and item-based CF methods for adaptive item recommendation within the OMST framework.

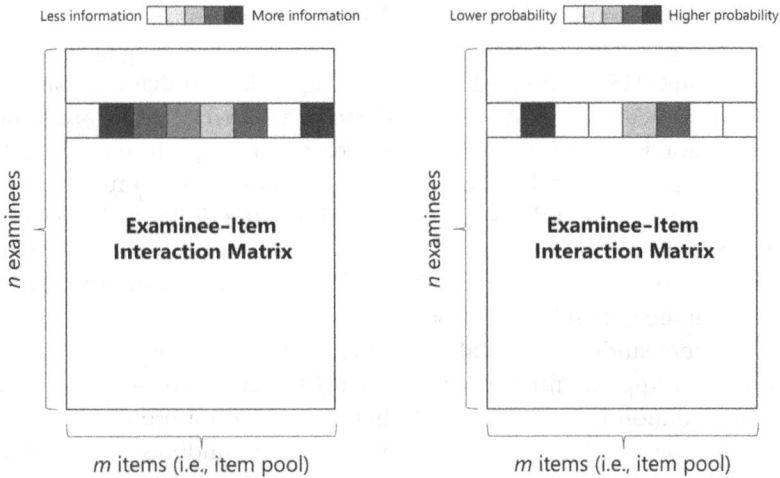

Figure 9.6 Examinee–item interaction matrices based on Fisher information (left) and the probability of correct answer (right)

In this approach, OMST begins with a pre-assembled module, and thus there is no adaptive item selection until the examinee completes the first stage. Then, information obtained from the first stage is incorporated into the CF methods for creating on-the-fly assembled modules in the second and subsequent stages. Using the information obtained from earlier stages (i.e., Fisher information values for the administered items), the user-based CF method recommends top-N items based on the target examinee's nearest neighbors with similar Fisher information values. In contrast to the user-based CF method, the item-based CF method looks for the top-N nearest neighbors of the target examinee's administered items and recommends the items that yield similar or higher information. For user- and item-based CF methods, N represents the length of the module being assembled. Alternatively, a larger number of items can be identified, and a random set of items can be selected for each examinee (e.g., identifying the top 20 items and selecting 10 items from this group randomly for a 10-item module) to increase the diversity in item selection.

Xiao and Bulut's (2022) approach eliminates the cold-start problem—not having any prior information about new users (e.g., Zhao, 2016), as the first stage of OMST informs the subsequent stages. In addition, calculating the expected Fisher information for the entire item bank yields a training dataset without missing values, eliminating the sparsity problem due to insufficient data for identifying similar examinees or items (Papagelis et al., 2005). Therefore, memory-based CF methods (i.e., item-based and user-based CF) appear to work effectively for adaptive item recommendations. Xiao and Bulut used a Monte Carlo simulation study to evaluate the performance of the user-based and item-based CF methods based on the accuracy of final ability estimates in the OMST framework. Their findings indicated that user-based CF yielded more accurate ability estimates than item-based CF and conventional item selection with MFI. In contrast, item-based CF outperformed the other methods regarding item bank utilization (i.e., lower rates of unused items in the item bank). The authors also cautioned that the similarity between the examinees in the training dataset and new examinees (i.e., target examinees) might have a large impact on the performance of the memory-based CF methods in the item selection process.

In a recent study, Bulut et al. (2023) extended Xiao and Bulut's (2022) approach by implementing the user-based CF method for sequential item recommendation in CAT. Although their study did not use the MFI-based item selection as a baseline for comparison, their findings indicated that the user-based CF method could also be used for accurate item selection in CAT. Furthermore, this study incorporated process data (e.g., examinees' action sequences in interactive problem-solving tasks) into adaptive testing based on Zhang et al.'s (2023) process-based ability estimation method. Bulut et al. (2023) also argued that process data could be directly utilized as user characteristics for making item recommendations within a hybrid recommender system. These findings suggest that memory-based CF methods can be helpful for item recommendation in CAT applications while allowing researchers to consider ancillary information (e.g., action sequences, response time, and clickstream data) to produce more personalized recommendations.

SUMMARY

In this chapter, we discussed how AI-powered recommender systems could be harnessed to enhance the assessment component of personalized learning. These systems use recommendation algorithms based on machine learning techniques to analyze a student's responses in real time and suggest appropriate items or tasks to accurately evaluate their current knowledge level. In addition to adaptive item selection, recommender systems can also be used for other tasks associated with assessment outcomes, such as personalizing the assessment schedule to each learner's pace and readiness to demonstrate growth (Bulut et al., 2020, 2022; Shin & Bulut, 2022). We encourage educators to consider incorporating such systems into their instructional practices, as they have shown promising results in enhancing personalized learning experiences. As we conclude this chapter, we want to reiterate that there is still a need for further research on the use of recommender systems at all levels of education to determine their effectiveness and long-term impact on various learning outcomes.

REFERENCES

Adomavicius, G., & Tuzhilin, A. (2005). Toward the next generation of recommender systems: A survey of the state-of-the-art and possible extensions. *IEEE Transactions on Knowledge and Data Engineering, 17*(6), 734–749. https://doi.org/10.1109/TKDE.2005.99

Aggarwal, C. C. (2016). *Recommender systems.* Springer International Publishing.

Ayoub, D. (2020). *Unleashing the power of AI for education | MIT technology review.* Retrieved May 20, 2023 from https://www.technologyreview.com/2020/03/04/905535/unleashing-the-power-of-ai-for-education

Beel, J., & Langer, S. (2015). A comparison of offline evaluations, online evaluations, and user studies in the context of research-paper recommender systems. In S. Kapidakis, C. Mazurek, & M. Werla, (Eds.), *TPDL 2015: Research and advanced technology for digital libraries* (pp. 153–168). Springer. https://doi.org/10.1007/978-3-319-24592-8_12

Beel, J., & Langer, S. (2015). A comparison of offline evaluations, online evaluations, and user studies in the context of research-paper recommender systems. In *Research and Advanced Technology for Digital Libraries: 19th International Conference on Theory and Practice of Digital Libraries, TPDL 2015, Poznań, Poland, September 14–18, 2015, Proceedings 19* (pp. 153–168). Springer International Publishing.

Bergner, Y., Droschler, S., Kortemeyer, G., Rayyan, S., Seaton D., & Pritchard, D. E. (2012). *Model-based collaborative filtering analysis of student response data: Machine-learning item response theory.* Paper presented at the International Conference on Educational Data Mining, Chania, Greece. Retrieved from http://files.eric.ed.gov/fulltext/ED537194.pdf

Bulut, O. (2022, November). *From adaptive testing to personalized adaptive testing: Applications of machine learning algorithms.* Paper presented at the 2022 Maryland Assessment Research Center Virtual Conference. https://doi.org/10.7939/r3-hmwm-yv98

Bulut, O., Cormier, D. C., & Shin, J. (2020). An intelligent recommender system for personalized test administration scheduling with computerized formative assessments. *Frontiers in Education, 5,* 1–11. https://doi.org/10.3389/feduc.2020.572612

Bulut, O., Shin, J., & Cormier, D. C. (2022). Learning analytics and computerized formative assessments: An application of Dijkstra's shortest path algorithm for personalized test scheduling. *Mathematics, 10*(13), 2230. https://doi.org/10.3390/math10132230

Bulut, O., Yildirim-Erbasli, S. N., He, S., Tan, B., & Gao, Y. (2023, April). Adaptive item recommendation using process data and examinee background characteristics. In Q. He & O. Bulut (Chairs), *Empowering process data for data-informed decision-making in measurement.* Paper presented at the annual meeting of the National Council on Measurement in Education, Chicago, IL.

Burke, R. (2002). Hybrid recommender systems: Survey and experiments. *User Modeling and User-Adapted Interaction, 12*, 331–370. https://doi.org/10.1023/A:1021240730564

Burke, R. (2007). Hybrid web recommender systems. The adaptive web: Methods and strategies of web personalization. In P. Brusilovsky, A. Kobsa, & W. Nejdl (Eds.), *The adaptive web* (pp. 377–408). Lecture Notes in Computer Science, vol 4321. Springer. https://doi.org/10.1007/978-3-540-72079-9_12

Chang, H. H., & Ying, Z. (1996). A global information approach to computerized adaptive testing. *Applied Psychological Measurement, 20*(3), 213–229. https://doi.org/10.1177/014662169602000303

Chen, S. Y., Ankenmann, R. D., & Spray, J. A. (2003). The relationship between item exposure and test overlap in computerized adaptive testing. *Journal of Educational Measurement, 40*(2), 129–145. https://doi.org/10.1111/j.1745-3984.2003.tb01100.x

Cheng, Y. (2009). When cognitive diagnosis meets computerized adaptive testing: CD-CAT. *Psychometrika, 74*, 619–632. https://doi.org/10.1007/s11336-009-9123-2

Çano, E., & Morisio, M. (2017). Hybrid recommender systems: A systematic literature review. *Intelligent Data Analysis, 21*(6), 1487–1524. https://doi.org/10.3233/IDA-163209

Eggen, T. J. (2018). Multi-segment computerized adaptive testing for educational testing purposes. *Frontiers in Education, 3*. https://doi.org/10.3389/feduc.2018.00111

Elahi, M., Kholgh, D. K., Kiarostami, M. S., Oussalah, M., & Saghari, S. (2023). Hybrid recommendation by incorporating the sentiment of product reviews. *Information Sciences, 625*, 738–756. https://doi.org/10.1016/j.ins.2023.01.051

Furini, M., Gaggi, O., Mirri, S., Montangero, M., Pelle, E., Poggi, F., & Prandi, C. (2022). Digital twins and artificial intelligence: As pillars of personalized learning models. *Communications of the ACM, 65*(4), 98–104. https://doi.org/10.1145/3478281

Guo, G., Zhang, J., Sun, Z., & Yorke-Smith, N. (2015, June). Librec: A Java library for recommender systems. In *UMAP workshops* (Vol. 4, pp. 38–45). Retrieved from https://citeseerx.ist.psu.edu/document?repid=rep1&type=pdf&doi=823888e601885ea5339ffb1d1898015e67e2d1f6

Gupta, P., Kulkarni, T., & Toksha, B. (2022). AI-based predictive models for adaptive learning systems. In P. P. Churi, S. Joshi, M. Elhoseny, & A. Omrane (Eds.), *Artificial intelligence in higher education* (pp. 113–136). CRC Press.

Guzmán, E., & Conejo, R. (2005). Self-assessment in a feasible, adaptive web-based testing system. *IEEE Transactions on Education, 48*(4), 688–695. https://doi.org/10.1109/TE.2005.854571

Hahsler, M. (2022). recommenderlab: An R framework for developing and testing recommendation algorithms. *ArXiv.* /abs/2205.12371 https://doi.org/10.48550/arXiv.2205.12371

Herlocker, J. L., Konstan, J. A., Terveen, L. G., & Riedl, J. T. (2004). Evaluating collaborative filtering recommender systems. *ACM Transactions on Information Systems (TOIS), 22*(1), 5–53. https://doi.org/10.1145/963770.963772

Hu, B., Zhou, Y., Wang, J., Li, L., & Shen, L. (2009). Application of item response theory to collaborative filtering. In W. Yu, H. He & N. Zhang (eds), *Advances in neural networks–ISNN 2009* (pp. 766–773). Berlin, Heidelberg: Springer.

Hug, N. (2020). Surprise: A Python library for recommender systems. *Journal of Open Source Software, 5*(52), 2174. https://doi.org/10.21105/joss.02174

Jacobson, K., Murali, V., Newett, E., Whitman, B., & Yon, R. (2016, September). Music personalization at Spotify. In *Proceedings of the 10th ACM Conference on Recommender Systems* (pp. 373–373). https://doi.org/10.1145/2959100.2959120

Koren, Y. (2008, August). Factorization meets the neighborhood: A multifaceted collaborative filtering model. In *Proceedings of the 14th ACM SIGKDD international conference on knowledge discovery and data mining* (pp. 426–434). https://doi.org/10.1145/1401890.1401944

Koren, Y., Bell, R., & Volinsky, C. (2009). Matrix factorization techniques for recommender systems. *Computer, 42*(8), 30–37. https://doi.org/10.1109/MC.2009.263

Kula, M. (2015). Metadata embeddings for user and item cold-start recommendations. In T. Bogers & M. Koolen (Eds.), *Proceedings of the 2nd Workshop on New Trends on Content-Based Recommender Systems co-located with 9th ACM Conference on Recommender Systems (RecSys 2015)*, Vienna, Austria, September 16–20, 2015. (pp. 14–21). Retrieved from http://ceur-ws.org/Vol-1448/paper4.pdf

Li, Y. H., & Schafer, W. D. (2005). Increasing the homogeneity of CAT's item-exposure rates by minimizing or maximizing varied target functions while assembling shadow tests. *Journal of Educational Measurement, 42*(3), 245–269. https://doi.org/10.1111/j.1745-3984.2005.00013.x

Linden, G., Smith, B., & York, J. (2003). Amazon.com recommendations: Item-to-item collaborative filtering. *IEEE Internet Computing, 7*(1), 76–80. https://doi.org/10.1109/MIC.2003.1167344

Luecht, R. M., & Sireci, S. G. (2011). A review of models for computer-based testing. (Research Report no 2011-12). College Board, New York.

McNee, S. M., Riedl, J., & Konstan, J. A. (2006, April). Being accurate is not enough: how accuracy metrics have hurt recommender systems. In *CHI'06 extended abstracts on human factors in computing systems* (pp. 1097–1101). https://doi.org/10.1145/1125451.1125659

Nikolakopoulos, A. N., Ning, X., Desrosiers, C., & Karypis, G. (2021). Trust your neighbors: A comprehensive survey of neighborhood-based methods for recommender systems. In Ricci, F., Rokach, L., Shapira, B. (Eds), *Recommender systems handbook* (pp. 39–89). Springer. https://doi.org/10.1007/978-1-0716-2197-4_2

Papagelis, M., Plexousakis, D., & Kutsuras, T. (2005). Alleviating the sparsity problem of collaborative filtering using trust inferences. In P. Herrmann, V. Issarny, & S. Shiu (Eds.), *Trust management. iTrust 2005.* Lecture Notes in Computer Science, vol 3477. Springer. https://doi.org/10.1007/11429760_16

Pujahari, A., & Sisodia, D. S. (2020, January). Model-based collaborative filtering for recommender systems: An empirical survey. In *2020 First International Conference on Power, Control and Computing Technologies (ICPC2T)* (pp. 443–447). IEEE. Raipur, India. https://doi.org/10.1109/ICPC2T48082.2020.9071454

Raghavan, S., Gunasekar, S., & Ghosh, J. (2012, September). Review quality aware collaborative filtering. In *Proceedings of the sixth ACM conference on Recommender systems* (pp. 123–130). https://doi.org/10.1145/2365952.2365978

Sarwar, B., Karypis, G., Konstan, J., & Riedl, J. (2001, April). Item-based collaborative filtering recommendation algorithms. In *Proceedings of the 10th international conference on World Wide Web* (pp. 285–295). Association for Computing Machinery. https://doi.org/10.1145/371920.372071

Shin, J., & Bulut, O. (2022). Building an intelligent recommendation system for personalized test scheduling: A reinforcement learning approach. *Behavior Research Methods, 54*, 216–232. https://doi.org/10.3758/s13428-021-01602-9

Thissen, D., & Mislevy, R. J. (1990). Testing algorithms. In H. Wainer (Ed.), *Computerized adaptive testing: A primer* (pp. 101–134). Erlbaum.

Töscher, A., & Jahrer, M. (2010). Collaborative filtering applied to educational data mining. *In KDD cup 2010: Improving cognitive models with educational data mining.* Retrieved from https://pslcdatashop.web.cmu.edu/KDDCup/workshop/papers/KDDCup2010_Toescher_Jahrer.pdf

Van der Kleij, F. M., Vermeulen, J. A., Schildkamp, K., & Eggen, T. J. (2015). Integrating data-based decision making, assessment for learning and diagnostic testing in formative assessment. *Assessment in Education: Principles, Policy & Practice, 22*(3), 324–343. https://doi.org/10.1080/0969594X.2014.999024

Vargas, S., & Castells, P. (2011, October). Rank and relevance in novelty and diversity metrics for recommender systems. In *Proceedings of the fifth ACM conference on Recommender systems* (pp. 109–116). https://doi.org/10.1145/2043932.2043955

Wauters, K., Desmet, P., & Van Den Noortgate, W. (2010). Adaptive item-based learning environments based on the item response theory: Possibilities and challenges. *Journal of Computer Assisted Learning, 26*(6), 549–562. https://doi.org/10.1111/j.1365-2729.2010.00368.x

Weiss, D. J. (1982). Improving measurement quality and efficiency with adaptive testing. *Applied Psychological Measurement, 6*(4), 473–492. https://doi.org/10.1177/014662168200600408

Wiliam, D., & Black, P. (1996). Meanings and consequences: A basis for distinguishing formative and summative functions of assessment? *British Educational Research Journal, 22*(5), 537–548. https://doi.org/10.1080/0141192960220502

Wongvorachan, T., Lai, K. W., Bulut, O., Tsai, Y.-S., & Chen, G. (2022). Artificial intelligence: Transforming the future of feedback in education. *Journal of Applied Testing Technology, 23*(Special Issue 1), 95–116.

Xiao, J., & Bulut, O. (2022). Item selection with collaborative filtering in on-the-fly multistage adaptive testing. *Applied Psychological Measurement, 46*(8), 690–704. https://doi.org/10.1177/01466216221124089

Yang, A. C., Flanagan, B., & Ogata, H. (2022). Adaptive formative assessment system based on computerized adaptive testing and the learning memory cycle for personalized learning. *Computers and Education: Artificial Intelligence, 3*, 100104. https://doi.org/10.1016/j.caeai.2022.100104

Yasmin, H., & Mazhar, R. (2022). AI in education: A few decades from now. In P. P. Churi, S. Joshi, M. Elhoseny, & A. Omrane (Eds.), *Artificial intelligence in higher education* (pp. 2–30). CRC Press.

Zhang, S., Wang, Z., Qi, J., Liu, J., & Ying, Z. (2023). Accurate assessment via process data. *Psychometrika, 88*(1), 76–97. https://doi.org/10.1007/s11336-022-09880-8

Zhao, X. (2016). *Cold-start collaborative filtering* [Doctoral dissertation, University College London]. https://discovery.ucl.ac.uk/id/eprint/1474118/

Zheng, Y., & Chang, H. H. (2015). On-the-fly assembled multistage adaptive testing. *Applied Psychological Measurement, 39*(2), 104–118. https://doi.org/10.1177/0146621614544519

CHAPTER 10

AI AND MACHINE LEARNING FOR NEXT GENERATION SCIENCE ASSESSMENTS

Xiaoming Zhai
University of Georgia

The rapid advancement of artificial intelligence (AI) in recent years has brought about transformative changes in various domains, including science assessment. Conventional methods of assessment in science education, particularly in classroom settings, often rely on multiple-choice questions (Zhai & Li, 2021), which may not fully capture students' understanding and engagement with scientific practices. This problem is even pronounced with the realization of three-dimensional learning in science—integrating science and engineering practices, disciplinary core ideas, and crosscutting concepts—a new vision set forth in the *Framework for K–12 Science Education* (National Research Council, 2012). This vision presents challenges for Next Generation Science Assessments because traditional assessments often fall short of capturing the complexities of scientific thinking during science and engineering practices. However, with the advent of machine learning (ML) techniques—an advanced artificial intelligence (AI), there

Machine Learning, Natural Language Processing, and Psychometrics, pages 201–219
Copyright © 2024 by Information Age Publishing
www.infoagepub.com
201

is a growing opportunity to revolutionize the assessment practices in the science learning (Zhai, Haudek, Shi, et al., 2020).

To assess Next Generation Science Learning and foster critical thinking and problem-solving skills, efforts have been put into developing ML- and performance-based assessments, which can engage students in science and engineering practices. Performance-based assessments usually require students to observe phenomena and develop explanations, arguments, or solutions (Harris et al., 2019). These assessment tasks require students to represent their thinking using multimodalities, such as writing or drawing (Zhai & Nehm, 2023). However, writing and drawing are challenging to score in a timely fashion. For classroom assessment practices, without timely feedback, the promise of such assessments might be significantly compromised. That is, one of the primary reasons that teachers use assessments is to solicit information about students' learning and, based on which, adjust instruction and make instructional decisions. It can be expected that teachers might be reluctant to use these complex assessment tasks if scores are not available in a timely fashion. In this case, technologies are desired. ML, due to its ability to automatically score written responses and drawn models, is promising, with which vast efforts in assessment development thus can be beneficial to millions of students (Jiao & Lissitz, 2020; Zhai, Krajcik, et al., 2021). Moreover, with the increasing adoption of online learning platforms and the availability of vast amounts of educational data, the changing landscape of education creates an opportune moment for leveraging ML algorithms to improve science assessment practices (Linn et al., 2023; Zhai et al., 2023). By harnessing the power of ML, we can develop more personalized and adaptive assessments that provide students with timely feedback and promote deeper learning experiences.

This chapter aims to explore the potential of ML-based assessments in shaping the next generation science education. This chapter has three major goals. Firstly, we aim to review the evolution and current state of ML-based assessments in science education, identifying the challenges and opportunities they present. To achieve this, we will synthesize the existing research and highlight the various ML approaches and techniques used in this field. Secondly, we intend to introduce a framework accounting for ML-based assessments scoring accuracy in science learning environments. This framework will provide guidelines for educators and researchers to develop effective and accurate assessment tools that integrate ML algorithms. At last, we will discuss the most pressing issues of ML-based assessments in science education and the future directions. By achieving these goals, we hope to contribute to the ongoing efforts in advancing science education and paving the way for the ML-based Next Generation Science Assessments that better align with the vision of science learning set forth in the *Framework*.

NEXT GENERATION SCIENCE ASSESSMENTS: A SHIFT FROM CONCEPTUAL CHANGE TO KNOWLEDGE-IN-USE

The *Framework for K–12 Science Education* (NRC, 2012) introduced significant reforms in science education by outlining a set of science and engineering practices, disciplinary core ideas, and crosscutting concepts to guide science instruction in K–12 classrooms. These reforms represent a major shift away from conceptual change to knowledge-in-use learning, advertising that scientific knowledge is meaningful for students only if students can apply the knowledge in designing solutions, constructing explanations, and solving problems. Rote memorization of science concepts or principles contributes limited to students' science learning and the consequential success in their lives and careers. Therefore, Next Generation Science Learning should aim to enhance students' scientific competencies and foster deeper thinking through practice-based learning.

Achieving Next Generation Science Learning presents several challenges for classroom assessment practices. According to students' grade levels and learning progression, the Next Generation Science Standards ([NGSS]; NGSS Lead States, 2013) specify a series of performance expectations, which provide benchmarks for learning. These performance expectations are three-dimensional, integrating science and engineering practices, crosscutting concepts, and disciplinary core ideas. Assessing such performance expectations thus becomes critical to facilitate classroom learning. However, traditional forms of assessments, such as multiple-choice exams, are no longer sufficient to evaluate students' uses of scientific knowledge and their ability to engage in scientific practices. The *NGSS* call for more authentic assessments that reflect real-world scientific inquiry and the application of scientific knowledge. This shift towards authentic assessment poses challenges in terms of designing and administering assessments that accurately measure students' abilities—thinking critically, solving problems, and engaging in scientific practices.

Assessments that need to align with the three dimensions outlined in the *Framework* and the performance expectations in the *NGSS* require the development of performance-based tasks, open-ended questions, and hands-on experiments. Researchers, such as Harris et al. (2019), developed evidence-centered approaches to crafting assessment tasks that are usually performance-based constructed responses. To assess students' three-dimensional performance, they designed two- or three-level analytic rubrics specifically tailored to each item. These rubrics were created based on evidence-based guiding principles, aiming to evaluate student performance at the beginning, developing, and proficient levels. The determination of the number of rubric levels was influenced by the complexity of the aspects being evaluated.

To illustrate this challenge, we cite an example assessment task (i.e., Red dye diffusion) developed to assess Next Generation Science Learning (see Figure 10.1). This task targets one performance expectation from the NGSS (NGSS Lead States, 2013) at the middle school level: MS-PS1-4. *Develop a model that predicts and describes changes in particle motion, temperature, and state of a pure substance when thermal energy is added or removed.* The performance expectation requires students to be able to develop models that can predict and describe changes in particle motion, temperature, and state of a pure substance when thermal energy is added or removed. This task thus focuses on red dye particles' motion in the water. To engage students in scientific practice, this task first provides students with a video that demonstrates dye diffusion in water at three different temperatures. Students are then asked to construct models to explain their observations from the video and provide a written description of their models. A drawing pad with various drawing tools, three drawing boxes, and a text box for writing is provided to facilitate this task (see Figure 10.1 for the task, answer space, and student example responses).

Performance-based assessments, such as *Red dye diffusion,* are critical to assess and facilitate Next Generation Science Learning, but place additional burdens on teachers to score these assessments. Specifically, teachers are not able to assign scores, evaluations, or feedback to every student in ongoing classrooms. Even for after-class use of the assessments, it is costly and time-consuming for teachers to score student responses. For example, assigning scores to each student's drawn and written responses to the example item may averagely cost 1 minute. For a normal middle school science teacher who teaches 100 students (four classes and each with 25 students), it would cost 100 minutes to score this individual assessment task, which can be a factor in decreasing teachers' motivation to use the assessment tasks.

In summary, Next Generation Science Assessment practice is challenging not only in development and design but also scoring and use of the scores. The *Framework* brought about a shift in classroom assessment practices, necessitating authentic and automatically scored assessments aligned with the *Framework*'s three dimensions. New technologies that may enable the automatic scoring of complex assessments are desired.

EVOLUTION OF MACHINE LEARNING-BASED AUTOMATIC SCORING FOR SCIENCE ASSESSMENTS

Machine learning can address these challenges by entailing automatic scoring systems and providing timely and objective feedback to both students and teachers. ML algorithms can analyze students' responses and performance on various assessment tasks, including written responses, lab

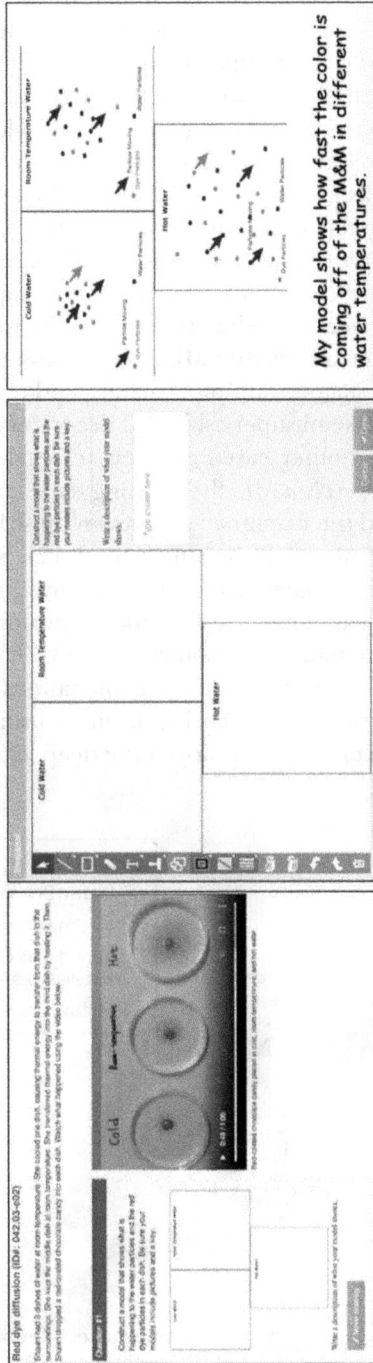

Figure 10.1 Assessment task: "Red dye diffusion" item screenshot (left), response interface (right), and a student response (bottom). Source: adapted from Zhai, He, & Krajcik, 2022)

reports, or project-based assignments. These algorithms can assist teachers in handling the time-consuming task of grading, assess the quality of students' performance and thinking, and provide immediate feedback on their strengths and areas for improvement. These systems can provide consistent and efficient scoring, reducing teachers' workload and allowing them to focus on providing personalized instruction and support.

The realm of science assessments has witnessed the application of five distinct types of ML applied in science assessments: *supervised, unsupervised, semi-supervised ML, pre-trained model,* and *zero-short.* All five types share a fundamental characteristic, which is the machine's capacity to "learn" from accumulated "experience" rather than adhering to explicit human instructions (Zhai, Yin, et al., 2020). ML-based assessment applications generally encompass two stages: training/learning and testing/predicting. Supervised, unsupervised, semi-supervised ML, pre-trained model, and zero-short differ from one another based on their respective approaches to training. In the case of *supervised ML*, the training data are initially labeled by human annotators, and the machine learns from these labeled instances (examples see Haudek et al., 2012; Nehm et al., 2012). Supervised ML is the most frequently used approach in automatic scoring given its high accuracy. For example, our research has assessed student performance when engaging in scientific argumentation (Wilson et al., 2023; Zhai, Haudek, et al., 2022), investigation (Maestrales et al., 2021), explanations (Zhai, He, et al., 2022), etc., and achieved satisfactory scoring accuracy using supervised ML (see Figure 10.2). Our recent work employed the deep learning algorithms

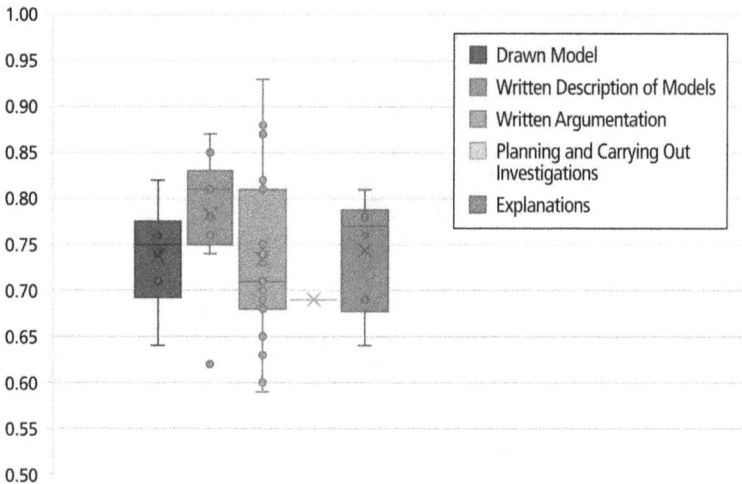

Figure 10.2 Automatic scoring accuracy for science assessments involving different scientific practices.

(e.g., neural networks) further extend the usability of this approach from language models to computer visions, and thus ML can automatically score student-drawn models (Wang et al., In press; Zhai, He, et al., 2022). In addition, my colleagues and I have applied supervised ML to assess teachers' pedagogical content knowledge (Zhai, Haudek, Stuhlsatz, et al., 2020).

Conversely, *unsupervised ML* relies on unlabeled data, requiring the machine to detect underlying patterns by analyzing the structural properties within the data corpus. Although unsupervised ML has the potential to reduce resource consumption and costs by eliminating the need for human labeling, it may lead to decreased accuracy in scoring students' responses, which can prove problematic for most forms of science assessments. In the earlier years, Urban-Lurain et al. (2013) have used unsupervised ML to assist in scoring rubric development, using the identified patterns from student responses. However, unsupervised ML is rarely used for scoring purposes by itself. Hybrid approaches, such as *semi-supervised ML,* have been developed to address challenges that need a large amount of labeled data, wherein humans employ a portion of labeled data to train the machine while also allowing it to learn the data structure from the unlabeled portions. Irrespective of the specific ML type employed, the development and validation of rigorous algorithms are standard practices before the algorithms can be deployed to predict/classify instances within new corpora.

Figure 10.3 provides a comprehensive outline of the general procedure employed for ML applications in science assessment. Commencing with science performance expectations, assessment tasks and rubrics are constructed by item developers. Subsequently, student responses to these tasks are collected. In cases where supervised or semi-supervised ML is utilized, human experts are enlisted to score student responses based on the

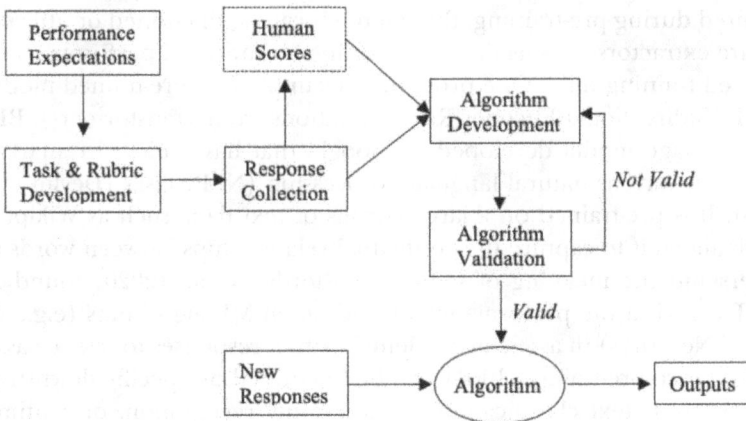

Figure 10.3 Machine learning-based assessment framework.

provided rubrics (Unsupervised ML usually omits the human scoring part). All information derived from student responses, including human scores, is then utilized to train the machine. The training process involves extracting a set of features or attributes from student responses and establishing their association with the provided labels through a specific algorithmic model chosen by researchers. Researchers have the flexibility to fine-tune the parameters of the algorithmic model to align with their research objectives. The outcome of the training process is an optimized algorithmic model that can be employed to identify patterns within new datasets or categorize responses accordingly. However, prior to making predictions on new corpora, it is customary to undertake a model validation procedure. Common validation methods include self-validation, data splitting, or cross-validation.

Among the various validation approaches employed in science assessment, cross-validation is the most prevalent (Zhai, Yin, et al., 2020). Cross-validation entails partitioning the data into n groups and employing (n-1) groups for training the machine, while the remaining group is utilized to evaluate the algorithm's performance. Specifically, the algorithm is employed to predict labels for the remaining group, and a comparison is made between the machine-assigned labels and the human-assigned labels to calculate a mean machine-human agreement (MHA). This process is repeated n times to ensure that each group has an opportunity to serve as the testing set. The average of the *n* MHAs serves as an indicator of the algorithm's capability. If the average MHA satisfies predefined success criteria, the algorithm can be applied to new datasets.

Pre-trained models in ML have emerged as powerful tools that offer significant advantages in various domains. These models are pre-trained on vast amounts of high-quality data and possess the ability to learn intricate patterns and representations. By leveraging the knowledge and expertise acquired during pre-training, these models can be fine-tuned or utilized as feature extractors for specific tasks, leading to improved performance and reduced training time. One prominent example of a pre-trained model is BERT (Bidirectional Encoder Representations from Transformers). BERT is a language model developed by Google that has achieved remarkable success in various natural language processing (NLP) tasks (Devlin et al., 2018). It is pre-trained on a large corpus of text data, such as Wikipedia, which allows it to capture the contextual relationships between words and understand the meaning of sentences. Riordan et al. (2020) found that BERT can rival the performance of traditional ML algorithms (e.g., SVR, Neural Networks) in assessing students' written responses to science assessments. Once pre-trained, BERT can be fine-tuned on specific downstream tasks, such as text classification, named entity recognition, or sentiment analysis. During fine-tuning, BERT's parameters are adjusted using task-specific data, enabling the model to specialize in a particular NLP task.

Liu et al. (2023) used more than 5,0000 student-written responses to fine-tune (unsupervised ML) a SciEdBERT and found that this fine-tuned BERT performed better than the general BERT in terms of developing scoring models. This is because, one of the key advantages of BERT is its ability to comprehend the context and meaning of words based on the surrounding words in a sentence, considering both the left and right contexts. This bidirectional understanding makes BERT particularly effective in tasks that require a deep understanding of language nuances. Liu et al. (2023) took advantage of BERT as a pre-trained model and further enhanced its ability to comprehend student writing in science education. Developers and researchers can benefit from its extensive language understanding capabilities without the need to train a model (supervised ML) from scratch. This not only saves significant computational resources and time but also allows for faster development and deployment of NLP applications across a wide range of domains, including information retrieval, question answering, and language translation. Their versatility and effectiveness make pre-trained models a valuable asset in accelerating and enhancing ML applications across a wide range of fields.

Zero-shot ML refers to a paradigm where a model is able to perform a task or make predictions on classes or concepts that are not seen during training. It involves transferring knowledge from seen classes to unseen classes by leveraging semantic relationships or embeddings. In zero-shot learning, the model is trained on a labeled dataset with a subset of classes, referred to as "seen classes." The model learns to understand the relationship between the input features and the class labels. During training, the model also learns to associate auxiliary information or semantic embeddings with each class, which captures the underlying semantic relationships between classes. Once trained, the zero-shot learning model can generalize to predict or classify instances from "unseen classes" that were not present in the training set. Wu et al. (2023) developed a zero-shot approach— matching exemplars as next sentence prediction (MeNSP), using pre-trained models. Without training data, MeNSP was able to score student written responses with Cohen's Kappa ranges between 0.30 to 0.57. This is achieved by utilizing the learned semantic embeddings or auxiliary information to reason about the unseen classes based on their relationships with the seen classes. With few-shot (i.e., a few training samples), MeNSP can increase the lower end of scoring accuracy of Cohen's Kappa from 0.30 to 0.38. This approach significantly reduced the machine training efforts and may be used for low-stakes settings.

The key distinction between *zero-shot* learning and *pre-trained models* lies in the nature of the transferred knowledge. Pre-trained models, such as those based on transfer learning, are initially trained on a large-scale dataset to learn general features and representations of the data. These models are then fine-tuned on a specific task using labeled or unlabeled data related to that task. The transferred knowledge in pre-trained models comes from the learned general representations. In contrast, zero-shot learning focuses on transferring knowledge about semantic relationships or embeddings between classes. The model learns to understand the underlying connections between classes during training, allowing it to generalize to unseen classes during inference. Both pre-trained models and zero-shot learning leverage prior knowledge, but they differ in the type of knowledge transferred. Pre-trained models transfer general feature representations, while zero-shot learning transfers knowledge about semantic relationships or embeddings. The choice between these approaches depends on the specific requirements and availability of labeled data for the task at hand.

Deploying ML and automatic scoring in the context of science assessments also presents its own set of challenges. One major challenge is ensuring the validity of automated scoring systems, particularly for complex and open-ended tasks (Zhai, Krajcik, et al., 2021). The algorithms need to be trained on large datasets of well-annotated responses to accurately assess students' work and provide meaningful feedback. Additionally, concerns regarding the fairness and bias of automated scoring systems need to be addressed. ML algorithms should be developed and tested to ensure they are not biased against certain groups of students based on their race, gender, or socioeconomic status. To achieve this goal, it is essential to study the potential factors holding accountable for machine scoring accuracy.

A FRAMEWORK ACCOUNTING
FOR AUTOMATIC SCORING ACCURACY

The most critical question for ML-based Next Generation Science Assessments is scoring accuracy, as it is the foundation to secure unbiased scores and fair uses of the scores. Machine scoring accuracy is usually measured by comparing machine scores with human consensus scores, indicated by Machine-Human Agreements (MHAs). In our prior work (Zhai, Shi, et al., 2021), we reviewed the literature and meta-analyzed the factors impacting machine scoring accuracy. In this study, we presented this extended framework that identifies five categories of factors moderating MHAs: (i) assessment external features, (ii) assessment internal features, (iii) examinee features (e.g., grade, school level, ELL), (iv) machine training and validation approaches (e.g., sample size, human rater reliability), and (v) technical features (e.g., algorithm, attribute abstraction).

Assessment external features, such as length of responses, rubrics, assessment scenarios, and type of assessment, have been proposed as factors moderating MHAs. Length of student responses is regarded as a critical factor that limits MHAs because longer responses tend to provide more information for ML so that ML scoring may be more accurate. Therefore, it is not surprising that Nehm et al. (2012) found that scoring models were most effective in scoring longer responses, though longer responses are typically more challenging to score for human raters given their high cognitive demand for scoring. Despite this, it is noted that Nehm et al. (2012) only reported a weak relationship between response length and MHA. Scenarios or prompts are also external features that might moderate machine performance. Clear scoring criteria are necessary to achieve high MHAs (Lottridge et al., 2018). Many of the assessment external features have been examined in the science education literature, including the subject domain which was found to significantly impact MHAs (Zhai, Shi, et al., 2021).

Assessment internal features, such as the number of concepts, complexity of construct, degree of overlap of concepts, and variation in concepts, have been shown to moderate MHAs. Some studies have explored the factors contributing to MHAs in text-based responses involving concepts. Williamson et al. (2010) proposed three key factors: the number of concepts elicited by an item, the variety of ways used to express these concepts, and the distinctness of the concept expressions. Leacock et al. (2013) suggested that a smaller number of well-defined concepts could contribute to MHAs, while Lottridge et al. (2018) identified the number, complexity, degree of overlap, and variation in concepts as moderators of MHAs. To specify the machine scoring ability, Lottridge et al. (2018) developed a comprehensive five-level framework for rating machine scoring ability. Item difficulty and complexity of constructs might also moderate MHAs, but few studies have provided empirical evidence to support this claim. McGraw-Hill Education (2014) discovered that machine performance decreased when scoring more difficult items, particularly those tapping into higher-order knowledge. Zhai, Haudek, Shi, et al. (2020) argued that the complexity of constructs may moderate MHAs, which was verified by Haudek and Zhai (2021) using empirical evidence.

Examinee features, such as grade, school level, and English language learners (ELLs), have been a topic of particular concern for machine scoring. However, not all studies have found that machine scoring is sensitive to examinee features. Examinee characteristics, including grade level and school level, have been the focus of machine scoring research in recent years (Zhai, Shi, et al., 2021). The impact of examinee diversity on machine scoring has been the subject of particular concern, with ELLs and lower-grade band students being especially vulnerable to scoring discrepancies (Wilson et al., 2023). Previous studies, such as Bridgeman et al. (2012), compared machine and human scores of Graduate Record Examinations (GRE) and the Test of English as a Foreign Language (TOEFL) assessments. These studies have reported varying scores for ELLs from different countries that were scored by machines and humans, with some languages being scored higher by machines than humans, and vice versa.

While some studies, such as Liu et al. (2016), have found the difference in machine scores between ELLs and non-ELLs to be negligible, Ha and Nehm (2016a; 2016b) have found that ELLs' constructed responses contain twice as many machine-scored words (MSW) than non-ELLs. However, MSW was found to be a relatively uncommon occurrence in student responses, comprising only 2% of the corpus, and therefore, had minimal impact on machine-scored assessments. A recent study shows that machine scoring has the potential to enlarge the gap in average scores between ELLs and other students on science assessments (Wilson et al., 2023). Again, this effect only happened at a very small number of assessment items. For other examinee factors such as gender, Mao et al. (2018) have found that machine scoring is not as sensitive to factors such as gender differences compared to human raters.

Machine training and validation approaches have been examined in previous studies and yielded inconsistent results. The techniques used to train and validate machine algorithms have been a subject of debate, with notable differences in the outcomes of different approaches. Specifically, Nehm et al. (2012) applied two training approaches to examine MHAs. With one set of items, they used the individual item responses to train the machine and then validated the algorithms using the same set of responses. In a second study, they used one set of responses to train the machine and then validated the algorithms using another set of responses. Although both approaches obtained satisfactory Cohen's κ, they found a decrease in MHAs from the latter approach. This finding suggests that the choice of the training and validation approach could significantly affect the accuracy of MHAs. Nehm and Haertig (2012) also suggested potential relationships between machine and human rater performance on scoring based on item types. Lottridge et al. (2018) argued that rater behavior in labeling training data is a critical factor accounting for machine capability. However, tests of this assumption have yielded inconsistent results. For example, Bridgeman et al. (2012) found that MHAs can be high even though the machine scoring accuracy was lower than the human–human agreement.

Given that more studies have employed cross-validation approaches, rather than self- and split-validation, a prior review study (Zhai, Yin, et al., 2020) compared the MHAs generated using these different validation approaches. Cross-validation was found to yield higher MHAs compared to both self- and split-validation approaches. Training size of the corpus is another factor that has been widely discussed as a contributor to MHA (e.g., Nehm et al., 2012). One approach to account for these differences in training sample size is to consider a weighted mean Cohen's κ. The use of a weighted mean Cohen's κ could address the challenges of varying training sample sizes and enhance the accuracy of MHAs.

Technical features, such as algorithm types or attribute abstraction approaches, are also regarded as crucial factors contributing to diverse MHAs. Algorithmic models, for instance, have been found to be most critical to machine scoring accuracy (Zhai, Shi, et al., 2021), suggesting that the assessment used and algorithm models developed in the study may limit the generalizability of findings. Attributes are those features inherent to student responses that may be used to link student performance and scores. These attributes are the foundation of machine algorithm development. Lintean et al. (2012) compared two attribute abstraction approaches using different grain sizes and found that algorithms developed using individual words as attributes over-performed those developed using a set of words as a unit. Additionally, increasing the number of features was found to positively impact machine-based assessment performance. Although several technical features have been examined by Zhai, Shi et al. (2021), the most updated ML, such as pre-trained or zero-shot approaches—have not been thoroughly investigated. As such, little is currently known about how the most updated ML algorithms moderate machine-based assessment performance.

The above review of the literature has revealed considerable inconsistencies regarding how various factors moderate MHAs. This is because most studies only employed a limited number of assessment tasks, and the tests themselves were developed and validated using different approaches. Identifying variables that different studies have in common and are suitable for review would help to advance work in this growing area. Our meta-analysis has contributed to synthesizing available evidence and examining claims about the factors that contribute to MHAs in science assessment, but more research is needed to include the most updated ML algorithms and study the factors accounting for the variable MHAs in future work.

ISSUES AND FUTURE DIRECTIONS

While AI and ML have significantly extended the functionality of science assessment, been able to assess complex constructs, and ease humans' efforts (Zhai, 2021), there are pressing issues both theoretically and practically that hinder the in-depth uses of ML-based science assessments. Addressing these issues is essential to move the field forward.

Model Generalizability

As ML techniques continue to advance, ensuring model generalizability becomes an important area of focus for Next Generation Science Assessments. In the current landscape, ML-based assessments largely rely on individual algorithmic models trained to assign scores for individual assessment tasks. Training individual algorithmic models is costly, and the problem needs to be addressed to make ML-based assessments available to a broader audience. While current models show promise in their ability to make accurate predictions on unseen data, there is still a need to improve their generalizability across different contexts, populations, and assessment tasks. Future research should explore strategies to enhance the transferability of ML models, such as incorporating more diverse and representative training data, leveraging domain adaptation techniques, and developing robust feature selection methods. Additionally, investigating the impact of model architecture and hyperparameter tuning on generalizability will be crucial in building more reliable and adaptable assessment models.

Moreover, advancements in federated learning can also contribute to model generalizability. Federated learning allows models to be trained collaboratively across multiple institutions or organizations without sharing raw data, thereby addressing issues related to data privacy and data distribution heterogeneity. Exploring federated learning approaches in the context of science assessments can lead to more robust models that can adapt to diverse educational settings while preserving data privacy.

Unbalanced Data

Addressing the issue of unbalanced data is another key direction for future advancements in ML-based science assessments. Many real-world assessment datasets suffer from class imbalance, where certain classes or categories of responses are significantly underrepresented (Jiao et al., 2023). This poses challenges for training accurate and unbiased models, as the learning algorithms may become biased towards the majority class without further examinations (Zhai & Nehm, 2023).

To overcome this, researchers should explore techniques like oversampling minority classes, undersampling majority classes, or using advanced sampling methods like SMOTE (Synthetic Minority Over-sampling Technique). Additionally, the development of novel loss functions that explicitly account for class imbalance can improve the model's ability to handle skewed datasets. Moreover, exploring ensemble learning methods that combine multiple models trained on balanced subsets of data can lead to improved performance and better handling of imbalanced classes.

Furthermore, as the field progresses, it will be essential to address intersectional biases that may arise from the combined effects of class imbalance and other demographic factors. Researchers should investigate techniques that consider the interplay between different demographic variables, such as gender, race, and socioeconomic status, to ensure that ML-based science assessments are fair and equitable for all students.

Machine Learning-Based Assessment User Guidelines

As ML-based assessments become more prevalent, it is crucial to develop user guidelines and best practices to ensure their effective and ethical use. Educators, administrators, and policymakers need guidance on how to integrate these assessments into existing educational frameworks, interpret their results, and make informed decisions based on the outcomes (Zhai & Krajcik, 2022). Future research should focus on creating comprehensive guidelines that address issues like test administration, data privacy, transparency in algorithmic decision-making, and potential biases and limitations of the models. These guidelines should also highlight the importance of human judgment and expertise in conjunction with ML-based assessments. Collaboration between researchers, educational practitioners, and policymakers will be vital in developing user-friendly tools and resources to support the successful implementation of ML-based science assessments in educational settings.

Additionally, as technology advances, it is crucial to continuously monitor and update guidelines to address emerging challenges and ethical considerations. For example, guidelines should adapt to advancements in explainable AI techniques, ensuring that users can understand how the ML models arrive at their predictions. The inclusion of guidelines for continuous model monitoring and evaluation will also enable educators and administrators to identify and address potential biases or limitations in real-time, fostering transparency and accountability in ML-based science assessments.

Interpretations and Uses of Scores

The interpretations and uses of scores obtained from ML-based science assessments require careful consideration to ensure their meaningful and responsible utilization in science education. As these assessments provide predictions or classifications based on complex algorithms, it is necessary to establish clear guidelines on how to interpret and communicate these scores effectively to stakeholders, such as students, teachers, parents, and policymakers. Future research should explore methods for generating interpretable explanations for the predictions made by ML models, allowing users to understand the underlying reasoning and factors contributing to the scores. Techniques such as attention mechanisms, saliency maps, and rule-based explanations can provide insights into the features or patterns that influenced the model's decision, enhancing the transparency and trustworthiness of the assessment process.

Furthermore, investigating how these scores can be effectively integrated into educational decision-making processes, such as personalized instruction, curriculum design, and student support systems, will be essential for maximizing the benefits of ML-based science assessments. By aligning the assessment results with specific instructional interventions, educators can provide targeted support to students, identify areas for improvement, and foster individualized learning experiences. However, it is crucial to balance the use of ML-based scores with holistic assessments that consider multiple dimensions of student performance, including non-cognitive skills and qualitative feedback, to ensure a comprehensive understanding of student abilities (Zhai & Nehm, 2023).

To support the responsible use of ML-based scores, the development of comprehensive data literacy programs for educators, students, and other stakeholders is necessary. These programs should focus on enhancing the understanding of the limitations and potential biases of ML models, promoting critical thinking about assessment results, and fostering informed decision-making based on multiple sources of evidence.

In conclusion, the future of ML for Next Generation Science Assessments lies in enhancing model generalizability, addressing unbalanced data challenges, developing user guidelines, and improving the interpretations and uses of scores. By tackling these key areas, researchers and practitioners can pave the way for more reliable, fair, and meaningful assessments that leverage the power of ML to enhance science education and foster deeper understanding and engagement among students.

ACKNOWLEDGMENTS

The author declares no conflict of interest. This material is based upon work supported by the National Science Foundation (NSF) under Grant No. 2101104, 2138854. Any opinions, findings, and conclusions or recommendations expressed in this material are those of the author(s) and do not necessarily reflect the views of the NSF.

REFERENCES

Bridgeman, B., Trapani, C., & Attali, Y. (2012). Comparison of human and machine scoring of essays: Differences by gender, ethnicity, and country. *Applied Measurement in Education, 25*(1), 27–40.

Devlin, J., Chang, M.-W., Lee, K., & Toutanova, K. (2018). *Bert: Pre-training of deep bidirectional transformers for language understanding.* arXiv preprint arXiv:1810 .04805

Ha, M., & Nehm, R. (2016a). Predicting the accuracy of computer scoring of text: Probabilistic, multi-model, and semantic similarity approaches. In *Proceedings of the National Association for Research in Science Teaching, Baltimore, MD, April,* 14–17.

Ha, M., & Nehm, R. H. (2016b). The impact of misspelled words on automated computer scoring: a case study of scientific explanations. *Journal of Science Education and Technology, 25*(3), 358–374. https://link-springer-com.proxy1 .cl.msu.edu/content/pdf/10.1007%2Fs10956-015-9598-9.pdf

Harris, C. J., Krajcik, J. S., Pellegrino, J. W., & DeBarger, A. H. (2019). Designing knowledge-in-use assessments to promote deeper learning. *Educational Measurement: Issues and Practice, 38*(2), 53–67. https://doi.org/10.1111/emip.12253

Haudek, K. C., Prevost, L. B., Moscarella, R. A., Merrill, J., & Urban-Lurain, M. (2012). What are they thinking? Automated analysis of student writing about acid–base chemistry in introductory biology. *CBE—Life Sciences Education, 11*(3), 283–293.

Haudek, K. C., & Zhai, X. (2021). *Exploring the effect of assessment construct complexity on machine learning scoring of argumentation.* National Association of Research in Science Teaching, Florida.

Jiao, H., & Lissitz, R. (2020). *Application of artificial intelligence to assessment.* Information Age Publishing.

Jiao, H., Yadav, C., & Li, G. (2023). *Integrating psychometric analysis and machine learning to augment data for cheating detection in large-scale assessment.*

Leacock, C., Messineo, D., & Zhang, X. (2013). *Issues in prompt selection for automated scoring of short answer questions.* Annual conference of the National Council on Measurement in Education, San Francisco, CA.

Linn, M. C., Donnelly-Hermosillo, D., & Gerard, L. (2023). Synergies between learning technologies and learning sciences: promoting equitable secondary school teaching. In *Handbook of research on science education* (pp. 447–498). Routledge.

Lintean, M., Rus, V., & Azevedo, R. (2012). Automatic detection of student mental models based on natural language student input during metacognitive skill training. *International Journal of Artificial Intelligence in Education, 21*(3), 169–190.

Liu, O. L., Rios, J. A., Heilman, M., Gerard, L., & Linn, M. C. (2016). Validation of automated scoring of science assessments. *Journal of Research in Science Teaching, 53*(2), 215–233.

Liu, Z., He, X., Liu, L., Liu, T., & Zhai, X. (2023). Context matters: A strategy to pre-train language model for science education. In N. Wang & e. al. (Eds.), *AI in education 2023* (Vol. CCIS 1831, pp. 1–9). Springer. https://doi.org/10 .1007/978-3-031-36336-8_103

Lottridge, S., Wood, S., & Shaw, D. (2018). The effectiveness of machine score-ability ratings in predicting automated scoring performance. *Applied Measurement in Education, 31*(3), 215–232.

Maestrales, S., Zhai, X., Touitou, I., Baker, Q., Krajcik, J., & Schneider, B. (2021). Using machine learning to score multi-dimensional assessments of chemistry and physics. *Journal of Science Education and Technology, 30*(2), 239–254. https://doi.org/10.1007/s10956-020-09895-9

Mao, L., Liu, O. L., Roohr, K., Belur, V., Mulholland, M., Lee, H.-S., & Pallant, A. (2018). Validation of automated scoring for a formative assessment that employs scientific argumentation. *Educational Assessment, 23*(2), 121–138.

McGraw-Hill Education, C. (2014). *Smarter balanced assessment consortium field test: Automated scoring research studies* https://www.smarterapp.org/documents/Field Test_AutomatedScoringResearchStudies.pdf

National Research Council. (2012). *A framework for K–12 science education: Practices, crosscutting concepts, and core ideas.* National Academies Press.

Nehm, R. H., Ha, M., & Mayfield, E. (2012). Transforming biology assessment with machine learning: automated scoring of written evolutionary explanations. *Journal of Science Education and Technology, 21*(1), 183–196. https://link-springer-com.proxy1.cl.msu.edu/content/pdf/10.1007%2Fs10956-011-9300-9.pdf

Nehm, R. H., & Haertig, H. (2012). Human vs. computer diagnosis of students' natural selection knowledge: testing the efficacy of text analytic software. *Journal of Science Education and Technology, 21*(1), 56–73. https://link-springer-com.proxy1.cl.msu.edu/content/pdf/10.1007%2Fs10956-011-9282-7.pdf

NGSS Lead States. (2013). *Next generation science standards: For states, by states.* National Academies Press.

Riordan, B., Bichler, S., Bradford, A., Chen, J. K., Wiley, K., Gerard, L., & Linn, M. C. (2020). *An empirical investigation of neural methods for content scoring of science explanations.* Proceedings of the Fifteenth Workshop on Innovative Use of NLP for Building Educational Applications.

Urban-Lurain, M., Prevost, L., Haudek, K. C., Henry, E. N., Berry, M., & Merrill, J. E. (2013). *Using computerized lexical analysis of student writing to support just-in-time teaching in large enrollment STEM courses.* 2013 IEEE Frontiers in education conference (FIE).

Wang, C., Zhai, X., & J., S. (in press). Applying machine learning to assess paper-pencil drawn models of optics. In X. Zhai & J. Krajcik (Eds.), *Uses of artificial intelligence in STEM education.* Oxford University Press.

Williamson, D. M., Bennett, R. E., Lazer, S., Bernstein, J., Foltz, P. W., Landauer, T. K., & Sweeney, K. (2010). *Automated scoring for the assessment of common core standards.* http://professionals.collegeboard.com/profdownload/Automated-Scoring-for-theAssessment-of- Common-Core-Standards.pdf

Wilson, C., Haudek, K., Osborne, J., Stuhlsatz, M., Cheuk, T., Donovan, B., Bracey, Z., Mercado, M., & Zhai, X. (2023). Using automated analysis to assess middle school students' competence with scientific argumentation. *Journal of Research in Science Teaching,* 1–32. https://doi.org/10.1002/tea.21864

Wu, X., He, X., Li, T., Liu, N., & Zhai, X. (2023). Matching Exemplar as Next Sentence Prediction (MeNSP): Zero-shot Prompt Learning for Automatic Scoring in Science Education. In N. Wang et al. (Eds.), *AI in education 2023* (Vol. LNAI 13916, pp. 1–13). Springer. https://doi.org/https://doi.org/10.1007/978-3-031-36272-9_33

Zhai, X. (2021). Practices and theories: How can machine learning assist in innovative assessment practices in science education. *Journal of Science Education and Technology, 30*(2), 139–149. https://link.springer.com/article/10.1007/s10956-021-09901-8

Zhai, X., Haudek, K., & Ma, W. (2022). Assessing argumentation using machine learning and cognitive diagnostic modeling. *Research in Science Education.* https://doi.org/https://doi.org/10.1007/s11165-022-10062-w

Zhai, X., Haudek, K. C., Shi, L., Nehm, R., & Urban-Lurain, M. (2020). From substitution to redefinition: A framework of machine learning-based science assessment. *Journal of Research in Science Teaching, 57*(9), 1430-1459. https://doi.org/10.1002/tea.21658

Zhai, X., Haudek, K. C., Stuhlsatz, M. A., & Wilson, C. (2020). Evaluation of construct-irrelevant variance yielded by machine and human scoring of a science teacher PCK constructed response assessment. *Studies in Educational Evaluation, 67,* 100916. https://doi.org/https://doi.org/10.1016/j.stueduc.2020.100916

Zhai, X., He, P., & Krajcik, J. (2022). Applying machine learning to automatically assess scientific models. *Journal of Research in Science Teaching, 59*(10), 1765–1794.

Zhai, X., & Krajcik, J. (2022). Pseudo AI bias. *arXiv preprint.* https://doi.org/10.48550/arXiv.2210.08141

Zhai, X., Krajcik, J., & Pellegrino, J. (2021). On the validity of machine learning-based Next Generation Science Assessments: A validity inferential network. *Journal of Science Education and Technology, 30*(2), 298–312. https://doi.org/10.1007/s10956-020-09879-9

Zhai, X., & Li, M. (2021). Validating a partial-credit scoring approach for multiple-choice science items: an application of fundamental ideas in science. *International Journal of Science Education, 43*(10), 1640–1666. https://doi.org/10.1080/09500693.2021.1923856

Zhai, X., & Nehm, R. (2023). AI and formative assessment: The train has left the station. *Journal of Research in Science Teaching.* https://doi.org/10.1002/tea.21885

Zhai, X., Neumann, K., & Krajcik, J. (2023). AI for tackling STEM education challenges. *Frontiers in Education, 8*(1183030). https://www.frontiersin.org/articles/10.3389/feduc.2023.1183030/full

Zhai, X., Shi, L., & Nehm, R. (2021). A meta-analysis of machine learning-based science assessments: Factors impacting machine-human score agreements. *Journal of Science Education and Technology, 30*(3), 361–379. https://doi.org/10.1007/s10956-020-09875-z

Zhai, X., Yin, Y., Pellegrino, J. W., Haudek, K. C., & Shi, L. (2020). Applying machine learning in science assessment: A systematic review. *Studies in Science Education, 56*(1), 111–151.

CHAPTER 11

AN AI-BASED PLATFORM FOR REAL TIME ASSESSMENT, SCAFFOLDING, AND ALERTING ON STUDENTS' SCIENCE PRACTICES

Janice D. Gobert
Rutgers Graduate School of Education

Inq-ITS Research & Development Team
Apprendis, LLC

INTRODUCTION TO THE PROBLEM

American students continue to fall behind on science. According to the most recent international data analyzed by the OECD's (Organisation for Economic Co-operation and Development) Programme for International Student Assessment (PISA; OECD, 2018), American students rank 18th on science, down from 13th in 2009 (OECD, 2010), and are outperformed by many other developed countries (Schleicher, 2019). Within the United

Machine Learning, Natural Language Processing, and Psychometrics, pages 221–235
Copyright © 2024 by Information Age Publishing
www.infoagepub.com

States, reform frameworks, such as the Next Generation Science Standards (NGSS, 2013) have been developed to guide instruction in science and measure achievement. NGSS requires that students learn a set of practices and that teachers provide evidence of students' competencies on each of these practices.

These practices or competencies,[1] however, are not easily mastered by students (Kuhn, 2005), nor are they easily or efficiently assessed by teachers. We interviewed approximately 1000 teachers to date about their needs for implementing the NGSS (cf. Sao Pedro, 2018), and found that meeting the requirements of the NGSS poses many challenges (Reiser, 2013). Specifically, teachers lack time, lab space, and materials for both *assessing* and *teaching* the practices, particularly when they have large class sizes (e.g., Oregon with up to 50 students per class).

For example, typical *multiple choice tests*, often used for assessment of students' science knowledge, are easy to grade but only capture factual knowledge, rather than the authentic practices of science as described in NGSS (2013) or 21st C. skills frameworks (www.P21.org). These types of assessments also put students into four bins typically, and thus do not reflect the full range of competencies exhibited by science learners across the various practices (Duncan & Chinn, 2021; Kuhn, 2005); nor is this level of granularity informative enough to guide teachers' instruction. *Summative science tests* are problematic because they, too, often rely on multiple-choice items; furthermore, these are given too late to allow for any data-driven instruction to improve students' competencies.

Hands-on experiments represent authentic science skills but require expensive and sometimes dangerous equipment, and require time to set up. These are also very difficult to grade rigorously. For example, in a typical class, students are all doing science experiments at their own pace, possibly even working on different experiments (see Figure 11.1). Lab reports, written in conjunction with hands-on experiments, take too long to grade (up to 20 minutes/lab report/student), and grading is subject to both bias and fatigue (Myford, & Wolfe, 2009). Furthermore, writing based tasks are not always an accurate reflection of what a student knows (Gobert, 2016; Li, Gobert, & Dickler, 2017a, 2018b). For example, Billy (see right, Figure 11.1) is a highly skilled science learner who is competent at the "doing" of inquiry practices, i.e., forming a question, collecting data, interpreting data, etc., but has trouble describing what he knows in writing, i.e., generating explanations, arguing from evidence, etc. John (see left, Figure 11.1), is a student who can parrot back what he has read or heard but does not deeply understand the content, nor can he actually conduct skilled inquiry as expected by the NGSS (2013). If a teacher is using students' written work, i.e., lab reports, for assessment, Billy represents a *false negative* (i.e., skilled at *doing* science but not good at writing about it); conversely, Johnny represents a *false positive*

Figure 11.1 A typical classroom in which students are all doing hands on science experiments.

(i.e., good at parroting but does not understand what he is writing about). In two separate classroom-based studies, we have shown that between 30–60% of students are mis-assessed if students' writing is used as the primary means to assess them (Li, Gobert, & Dickler, 2017a; Li et al., 2018b). This is demonstrable evidence that writing should not be used as the only form of assessment; nor should multiple choice items (as outlined above).

Bringing the issue of students who are "false negatives" and "false positives" to the forefront is important for a number of reasons. First, the field of science education has attributed our poor science performance to the latter "type" of student whose knowledge may be "a mile wide but an inch deep" (Rillero, 2016), but as shown above, there many students who are highly skilled and knowledgeable in science but the assessment being used is too coarse-grained to capture their competencies. Second, these highly skilled science learners may not gain entry to AP science classes in high school or STEM majors in college, despite their strengths. Additionally, students like Johnny (false positives) can be passed along year after year when they are not competent at doing science. This situation is problematic because there is a lack of skilled STEM workers to fill the many high tech jobs in the knowledge economy (Bereiter, 2002). Third, the NGSS requires that students be competent at a full range of science practices that include both *doing* science (form questions, collect data, interpret data, and mathematics associated with science, etc.), as well as *communicating about* science (i.e., generating explanations, arguing from evidence, etc.); however few assessments can measure the full range of competencies prescribed by the

NGSS (2013). Fourth, due to #3, there is virtually no rigorous and robust support for teachers' instruction and students' learning of NGSS practices. Thus, we need to move beyond the existing assessments used in classrooms and leverage new techniques to develop richer, more rigorous assessments for NGSS or the vision and potential for the NGSS (2013) cannot be realized. In short: students need competencies to be science-literate and fulfill STEM jobs, teachers need materials to support their assessment and instruction of science practices, and administrators and policy makers need students with better science competencies. In our work, we argue that performance assessment undergirded by AI (Gobert et al., 2016, 2017, 2019) can rigorously *assess* and *scaffold* students in real time on all the practices expected by the NGSS, and can also support teachers in the assessment and instruction of these practices in real time—all at scale! (Gobert et al., 2023a, b; Mislevy, Yan, Gobert, & Sao Pedro, 2020).

INQ-ITS GOALS, OVERVIEW, DESIGN SPECIFICATIONS, AND COMPONENTS

Goals

As previously stated, our goal with Inq-ITS is to *rigorously assess* and scaffold science practices for both the *doing* of and *communicating* about science, at scale. Specifically, we sought to better support students in their learning of science practices in real time, and we sought to better support teachers in both their assessment of science practices in real time and their instruction of science practices in real time.

Overview

Inq-ITS (www.inqits.com; Gobert et al., 2013, 2023a) is a science platform for the real time assessment, scaffolding, and instruction of science learning. As of this writing, Inq-ITS has 157 simulation-based assessments for science (grades 4–11) that include content variables based on students' alternative conceptions and students' difficulties with practices (Kuhn, 2005), including question formation, conducting controlled experiments, interpreting data, doing mathematics associated with science inquiry, and communicating findings. The development of activities was done by: reviewing the NRC (2012), NGSS frameworks (2013), and relevant research on students' difficulties with inquiry practices at the middle school and early high school levels, by interviewing teachers, conducting think-aloud studies with students using both hands-on and virtual materials (Gobert &

Sao Pedro, 2017), and by conducting classroom studies (see inqits.com/research for papers).

Inq-ITS provides benefits to both students and teachers. For students, the Inq-ITS platform provides authentic science inquiry with simulation-based activities (described in more detail later); with these students form a question, collect data to test it, interpret data, including the math associated with science, and then explain their findings with evidence. While students work, they are assessed on their competencies on NGSS practices in real time and get real time feedback, triggered by patented, AI-based algorithms (Gobert et al., 2016, 2017, 2019), which lead to robust learning of science practices that transfer across topics and over long periods of time (Li et al., 2019a, b, c; Gobert et al., 2023b). Lastly, students receive a report on their progress on each of the practices, and the system has Spanish glossaries and activities for ELLs.

For teachers, Inq-ITS has real time reports and real time, actionable alerts. Alerts are automatically sent to a teacher dashboard, Inq-Blotter, to support their real time instruction of science practices. The alerts identify which students are struggling on each of the NGSS practices and the specific ways in which they are struggling. The alerts in Inq-Blotter also contain TIPS (**T**eacher **I**nquiry **P**ractice **S**upports) to guide instruction as to how to help their students either in whole class mode (if many students are struggling with the same practice), in small groups for differentiated instruction of a specific practice, etc., or to an individual student. These TIPS lead to demonstrable improvement on students' learning (Dickler, 2021; Dickler, Gobert, & Sao Pedro, 2021; Adair & Dickler, 2020). Inq-ITS and Inq-Blotter are used in all 50 states and about 50 countries as of this writing. For more

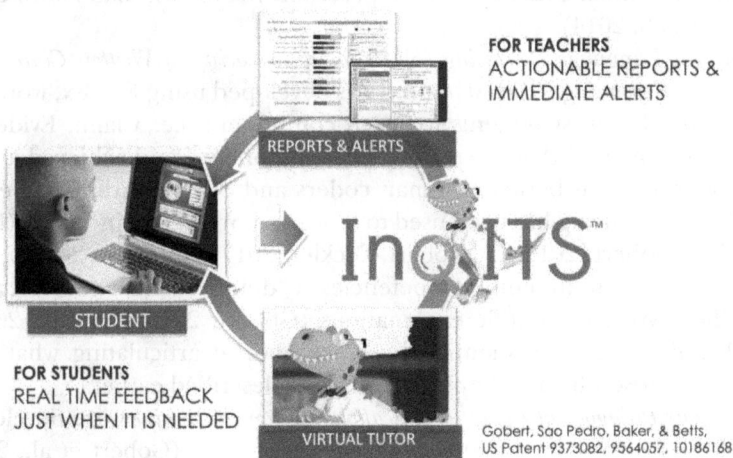

FOR TEACHERS
ACTIONABLE REPORTS &
IMMEDIATE ALERTS

REPORTS & ALERTS

Inq-ITS™

STUDENT

FOR STUDENTS
REAL TIME FEEDBACK
JUST WHEN IT IS NEEDED

VIRTUAL TUTOR

Gobert, Sao Pedro, Baker, & Betts,
US Patent 9373082, 9564057, 10186168

Figure 11.2   Overview of Inq-ITS core components.

details about Inq-Blotter, including initial studies leading to its development, see Gobert et al., 2023a; Adair et al., 2020, 2022).

INQ-ITS ACTIVITIES AND COMPONENTS

Inq-ITS includes a no-Install, cross-Platform web-based software that runs over the web, and a Lightweight learning Management System (LMS) that manages all materials. Inq-ITS also includes the following components.

Inquiry Activities and Robust Inquiry Activity Authoring Architecture: Inq-ITS has 157 simulation-based activities for NGSS standards for middle and high school Physical, Life, and Earth Science as of this writing.

Representational Tools: Each activity utilizes tools (e.g., question construction tool, graph tool, table tool) that elicit students' thinking and enable assessment of inquiry practices. Recently, we added a series of tools to support the assessment and scaffolding of student mathematical practices that are done in the context of science inquiry (Adair et al., 2023).

Inquiry Assessment Algorithms: We automatically score competencies and their respective sub-competencies for asking questions, planning and carrying out investigations, analyzing/interpreting data, mathematics associated with inquiry, and warranting claims. Sub-competencies for each practice was done by breaking down each NGSS practice into more concrete, appropriately sized sub-practices (also referred to as sub-components). Our algorithms were built and validated using middle school student data (Sao Pedro et al., 2010, 2012, 2013a,b, 2014; Gobert et al., 2012, 2013; Moussavi, 2018), and are robust across inquiry activities with diverse students and match human coders with high precision (84 to 99%; Sao Pedro et al., 2012, 2013ab, 2014).

Natural Language Processing (NLP) for auto-scoring of Written Claim, Evidence, and Reasoning (CER) statements was developed using Reg-Ex, word distance, and if-then statements for each component, i.e., Claim, Evidence, and Reasoning and their respective sub-components, and achieved a high level of agreement between human coders and our algorithms (Li et al., 2017b). This scoring has been used to score and predict their quality (Dickler, Li, & Gobert, 2019; Li, Gobert, Dickler, 2017b; Li et al., 2018c), and can identify when students' competencies at "doing" science does not align with their written scientific explanations (Gobert, 2016; Li et al., 2017a, 2018b), allowing us to identify those are poor at articulating what they know and those who are simply parroting, as described earlier.

Rex, our Pedagogical Agent, and Scaffold Authoring Engine were developed to deliver scaffolds to students when the algorithms (Gobert et al., 2016, 2017, 2019) detect that students are struggling on inquiry practices. In random controlled trials for each practice (i.e., data collection, data analysis, warranting claims), we showed that students who received scaffolding were better able to learn these practices than those who did not receive scaffolding. Findings were robust within the topic on which they were scaffolded and students transferred their competencies to new topics when scaffolding was removed even 170 days later (Li et al., 2019a, b, c; Sao Pedro et al., 2013b, 2014; Gobert, Moussavi, et al., 2018). For a fuller description of Rex and the scaffolds, see Gobert et al., 2023b). We recently showed robust transfer for our math scaffolds as well (Adair et al., 2023).

Teacher Reports that provide competency and sub-competency data on the practices *and On-Boarding Materials* **that** support teachers' pedagogical practices; we also have a Teachers' Manual, FAQ, Curriculum Integration Guides, Technical Brief, and Walk-through videos.

Inq-Blotter Components

Inq-Blotter's components are as follows.

Actionable alerts for inquiry practices across all 150+ Inq-ITS activities: Alerts are generated for NGSS practices assessed by all Inq-ITS online lab activities. Each alert provides a 'diagnosis' of how students are struggling, based on Inq-ITS automatic assessment algorithms. For example, a teacher may get a specific alert when a student is analyzing data and they do not have controlled data to match the independent variable in their claim. They will get a different alert when another student who is analyzing data has a claim that does not match the trends in their data. In addition, if students are moving too slowly through a certain part of the inquiry process (e.g., forming questions), a *slow progress* alert will notify the teacher that a particular student is not making progress. The amount of time to signal a slow alert is configurable by the teacher.

Alert contextual information: By clicking on an alert, teachers see information about students' challenges on a particular practice and its sub-components for the activity s/he is currently working on. Teachers can use to this to tailor the feedback for their students. This includes:

1. A "diagnosis" based on how the student's inquiry competencies were assessed.
2. Information about students' overall performance on inquiry practices; scores are computed based on students' use with Inq-ITS over a 24 hour period and is reset nightly.
3. Prior alerts the student has received that day. All alerts that were received over the past 24 hours are presented; these are reset nightly.

4. Progress through activities: We indicate students' progress through lab activities using a progress bar, which allows teachers a visual representation for quick reference.
5. Amount of Rex feedback given to students: An indicator under the progress bar shows how much help the student was given by Rex for that activity (if the teacher has decided to implement with Rex for that activity). With this, the teacher can quickly see if Rex has been helping students less over time, indicating learning. This is very useful for students on IEPs or who are in Special Education since their learning trajectories are typically longer. For more information on our virtual tutor, see Gobert et al., 2023b; Li et al., 2019a, b, c).

Class-wide alerts: These alerts fire when a majority of students are having difficulty with a particular practice of inquiry (i.e., questions, collecting data, or analyzing data, etc.). The frequency of these alerts can be configured by the teacher from a settings menu. Once such an alert is fired, a detailed alert screen is presented to the teacher that contains: (a) a visualization and text description of how many students are struggling, and (b) a sorted list of students having the most difficulty.

Configurable Settings: Inq-Blotter has settings that are configurable by the teacher. These control how long alerts are visible and active, when slow progress alerts should be fired, and thresholds for generating class-wide alerts. These settings allow the teacher to custom tailor Inq-Blotter to their specific classroom needs at any point in the school year.

INQ-ITS DESIGN SPECIFICATIONS

As has been noted in work by Pellegrino et al. (2001) and others (Gotwals & Songer, 2010), the main goal of assessment is to provide robust evidence of students' competencies and/or knowledge. For our goals for Inq-ITS, namely, assessment, scaffolding, and instruction, using a framework with rigorous and explicit design principles was necessary in order to obtain valid assessment data about students' competencies; this is especially true in complex or ill-defined domains like science inquiry (Kuhn, 2005).

Inq-ITS design follows the specifications of the assessment triangle (Pellegrino et al., 2001) and of Evidence-Centered Design (Mislevy et al., 2012; Mislevy et al., 2020), the latter of which has been applied to inquiry, simulations, intelligent tutoring systems, and games (e.g., Clarke-Midura, et al., 2012; Shute, 2011; Mislevy et al., 2003, 2020). The assessment triangle outlines three corners, including cognition, observation, and interpretation (described in more detail below). Evidence-centered design builds off of

Pellegrino's assessment triangle by specifying the evidence needed to support the intended inferences including data aggregation and data interpretation (Mislevy et al., 2020). Each will be described in turn with regard to Inq-ITS design.

The first corner of the assessment triangle, *cognition*, involves making explicit the conceptions of how people learn and the knowledge and skills that are associated with the targeted knowledge or competencies. Since all assessments are based on an underlying theoretical framework about how people learn (Gotwals & Songer, 2010; Scardamalia & Bereiter, 2008), when designing assessment, it is important (we argue, necessary) to specify or operationalize the knowledge and/or cognitive processes underlying the targeted performance, skill, or conceptual knowledge within its respective domain. This includes both observable cognitive processes and those that are proposed as underlying cognitive activities associated with those processes.

Observation, the second corner of the assessment triangle (Pellegrino et al., 2001), concerns the way(s) by which a student's knowledge or competencies are observed for a target conception or skill/practice. The key to eliciting observations is designing an assessment item or task that will give students opportunities to demonstrate their knowledge and/or competencies. The tasks must also elicit a broad range of competencies, which is important for assessing partial and developing competencies (Gotwals & Songer, 2010). In Inq-ITS, students engage with simulations to conduct inquiry; these permit authentic science inquiry learning and assessment because they share many features with real apparatus, leveraging perceptual affordances (Norman, 1988; Gobert, 2005; Gobert, 2015). With simulations students are able to develop a hypothesis or ask questions, use models to plan and carry out investigations, analyze data (with or without mathematics), warrant claims, construct explanations, and argue from evidence. Further, Inq-ITS simulations, widgets, and tools capture students' interactions from which performance assessments are generated (see the interpretation corner of the triangle). This required operationalizing each inquiry practice into its respective sub-components (see Gobert et al., 2012; Mislevy et al., 2020).

The third corner, *interpretation*, refers to how people, i.e., researchers, *infer* students' internal knowledge, cognitive processes, and mental states (i.e., representations) from their observable behavior(s) or actions. The knowledge, processes, and mental states to be interpreted are those that have been made explicit in the cognition corner of the assessment triangle. These are elicited by the tasks the student engages in. As regards interpretation, the Inq-ITS infrastructure collects all mouse clicks, selections, and changes to the simulations, etc. and findings on how people learn in science were used to both distill and aggregate data (Gobert et al., 2013), and to design categories a priori, both of which are critical to interpretation, so that results are pedagogically meaningful to key stakeholders, i.e., teachers, parents, students, and policy-makers. In Inq-ITS, all students' data are distilled and aggregated, and machine learning, knowledge engineering, and natural language processing (NLP) algorithms are used: for performance assessment of students' competencies, to drive scaffolds to students as they work, and to drive alerts and TIPS to teachers. Computational techniques, and machine learning in particular, are used in Inq-ITS, to provids rigorous data on students' inquiry competencies. Machine learning, was used in Inq-ITS for a variety of reasons. As previously stated, it is well-suited to ill-defined problems, like science inquiry, and further, machine learning can handle the 4 V's (Laney, 2001) of log data, namely, the volume of log data, the veracity of log data, the velocity at which log data are generated, and the variability in data, given students' multi-faceted competencies across the science practices (Kuhn, 2005). It is critical that researchers attend to how the data will be analyzed as part of the early part of the assessment design, otherwise, one runs the risk of not being able make strong claims about students' knowledge and competencies (Mislevy et al., 2020).

In summary, Inq-ITS, whose design aligns with the assessment triangle (Pellegrino et al., 2001) and evidence-centered design (Mislevy et al., 2020) offers several benefits to students and teachers. Firstly, there are affordances of authenticity in conducting inquiry with simulations (Norman, 1988; Gobert, 2005, 2015), and simulation-based assessments offer greater validity than multiple choice tests. Additionally, Inq-ITS generates rich, high fidelity log files that are used for performance assessment, rather than product-only assessments of rote knowledge, and of students'. Providing performance assessment data on the full range of NGSS competencies is critical, especially since we have shown that students' writing is not always a good reflection of what they have learned (Gobert, 2016; Li et al., 2017a, 2018 a, b). Lastly, the innovative computational techniques undergirding Inq-ITS (Gobert et al., 2016, 2017, 2019) are transformative for scalable, stealth assessment and scalable real time scaffolding, which are critical to democratizing learning and to Science Education reform (NGAA, 2013). For research studies on Inq-ITS, see inqits.com/research.

NOTE

1. I use the terms competencies and practices (NGSS, 2013) interchangeably.

ACKNOWLEDGMENTS

This research was funded by the National Science Foundation (NSF-IIS -1629045, NSF-DRL-1252477, NSF-IIS-1902647) and the U.S. Department of Education (R305A210432, R305A120778, ED-IES-15-C-0018, ED-IES-16-C-0014). Any opinions, findings, etc., expressed are those of the authors and do not necessarily reflect those of the funding agencies.

REFERENCES

Adair, A., & Dickler, R. (2020). Supporting teachers supporting students: evidence-based TIPS in a dashboard to guide inquiry scaffolding. In *Proceedings of the International Conference of the Learning Sciences* (pp. 1769–1770).

Adair, A., Owens, J. A., & Gobert, J. (2022). Using epistemic network analysis to explore discourse patterns across design iterations of a teacher dashboard. In C. Chinn, E. Tan, C. Chan, & Y. Kali (Eds.), *16th International Conference of the Learning Sciences* (pp. 297–304). International Society of the Learning Sciences.

Adair, A., Sao Pedro, M., Gobert, J., & Segan, E. (2023). Real time AI-driven assessment and scaffolding that improves students' mathematical modeling during science investigations. In N. Wang, G. Rebolledo-Mendez, N. Matsuda, O. C. Santos, & V. Dimitrova (Eds.), *International Conference on Artificial Intelligence in Education* (pp. 202–216). Springer. https://doi.org/10.1007/978-3-031-36272-9_17

Bereiter, C. (2002). *Education and mind in the knowledge age.* Lawrence Erlbaum Associates.

Clarke-Midura, J., Code, J., Dede, C., Mayrath, M., & Zap, N. (2012). Thinking outside the bubble: Virtual performance assessments for measuring complex learning. In *Technology-based assessments for 21st century skills: Theoretical and practical implications from modern research* (pp. 125–148). Information Age Publishers.

Dickler, R. (2021). *An intelligent tutoring system and teacher dashboard to support students on mathematics in science inquiry* (Doctoral dissertation, Rutgers The State University of New Jersey, School of Graduate Studies).

Dickler, R., Gobert, J., & Sao Pedro, M. (2021). Using innovative methods to explore the potential of an alerting dashboard for science inquiry. *Journal of Learning Analytics, 8*(2), 105–122. https://doi.org/10.18608/jla.2021.7153

Dickler, R., Li, H., & Gobert, J. (2019, April). *Examining the generalizability of an automated scoring method and identifying student difficulties with scientific explanations.* Presented at American Educational Research Association (AERA): Learning and Instruction, Toronto, Canada.

Duncan, R. G., & Chinn, C. A. (2021). *International handbook of inquiry and learning.* Taylor and Francis. https://doi.org/10.4324/9781315685779

Gobert, J. (2005). Leveraging technology and cognitive theory on visualization to promote students' science learning and literacy. In J. Gilbert (Ed.), *Visualization in science education* (pp. 73–90). Springer-Verlag Publishers.

Gobert, J. (2015). Microworlds. *Encyclopedia of science education,* 638–639.

Gobert, J. (2016, May 13). http://www.usnews.com/news/articles/2016-05-13/op-ed-educational-data-mining-can-enhance-science-education

Gobert, J. D., Baker, R. S., & Sao Pedro, M. A. (June, 2016). *Inquiry skills tutoring system.* US Patent no. 9,373,082 (issued).

Gobert, J. D., Sao Pedro, M., Raziuddin, J., & Baker, R. S. (2013). From log files to assessment metrics: Measuring students' science inquiry skills using educational data mining. *Journal of the Learning Sciences, 22(4),* 521–563.

Gobert, J., Moussavi, R., Li, H., Sao Pedro, M., & Dickler, R. (2018). Real time Scaffolding of Students' Online Data Interpretation During Inquiry with Inq-ITS Using Educational Data Mining. In Abul K.M. Azad, Michael Auer, Arthur Edwards, and Ton de Jong (Eds), *Cyber-physical laboratories in engineering and science education.* Springer. https://doi.org/0.1007/978-3-319-76935-6_8

Gobert, J.D., & Sao Pedro, M. (2017). Inq-ITS: Design decisions used for an inquiry intelligent system that both assesses and scaffolds students as they learn. In A. A. Rupp & J. Leighton (Eds.). *Handbook of cognition and assessment.* Wiley/Blackwell.

Gobert, J., Sao Pedro, M., Baker, R.S., Toto, E., & Montalvo, O. (2012). Leveraging educational data mining for real time performance assessment of scientific inquiry skills within microworlds, *Journal of Educational Data Mining, 15*(4), 153–185.

Gobert, J. D., Sao Pedro, M. A., Betts, C. G. (2023a). An AI-based teacher dashboard to support students' inquiry: Design principles, features, and technological specifications. In N. Lederman, D. Zeidler, & J. Lederman (Eds.), *Handbook of research on science education,* (Vol. 3, pp. 1011–1044). Routledge. https://doi.org/10.4324/9780367855758

Gobert, J., Sao Pedro, M., Betts, C., & Baker, R.S. (February, 2017). *Inquiry skills tutoring system (child patent for alerting system).* US Patent no. 9,564,057 (issued).

Gobert, J., Sao Pedro, M., Betts, C., & Baker, R.S. (January, 2019). *Inquiry skills tutoring system (child patent for additional claims to Inq-ITS).* US Patent no. 10,186,168 (issued).

Gobert, J. D., Sao Pedro, M. A., Li, H., & Lott, C. (2023b). Intelligent tutoring systems: A history and an example of an ITS for science. In R. Tierney, F. Rizvi, K. Ercikan, & G. Smith, (Eds.), *International encyclopaedia of education* (Vol. 4, pp. 460–470) Elsevier. https://doi.org/10.1016/B978-0-12-818630-5.10058-2

Gotwals, A. W., & Songer, N. B. (2010). Reasoning up and down a food chain: Using an assessment framework to investigate students' middle knowledge. *Science Education, 94*(2), 259–281.

Inq-ITS. (n.d.) https://www.inqits.com

Kuhn, D. (2005). *Education for thinking.* Harvard University Press.

Laney, D. (2001). 3D data management: Controlling data volume, velocity and variety. *META Group Research Note, 6,* 70–73.

Li, H., Adair, A., Li, G., Dickler, R. F., & Gobert, J. (2023, April). *Evaluation of automated scoring methods for students' claim, evidence, reasoning responses in science.* Presented at the American Educational Research Association (AERA) Annual Meeting.

Li, H., Gobert, J., & Dickler, R. (2017a). Dusting off the messy middle: Assessing students' inquiry skills through doing and writing. In E. André, R. Baker, X. Hu, M. Rodrigo, & B. du Boulay (Eds.), *Artificial Intelligence in Education.*

AIED 2017. *Lecture Notes in Computer Science, Vol. 10331*, pp. 175–187. Cham: Springer. https://doi.org/10.1007/978-3-319-61425-0_15

Li, H., Gobert, J., & Dickler, R. (2017b). Automated assessment for scientific explanations in on-line science inquiry. A. Hershkovitz & L. Paquette (Eds.), *Proceedings of the 10th International Conference on Educational Data Mining* (pp. 214–219). Wuhan, China: EDM Society.

Li, H., Gobert, J., & Dickler, R. (2018a). The relationship between scientific explanations and the proficiencies of content, inquiry, and writing. In *Proceedings of the Fifth Annual ACM Conference on Learning at Scale* (p. 12–22). ACM. https://doi.org/10.1145/3231644.3231660

Li, H., Gobert, J., & Dickler, R. (2018b). Unpacking why student writing does not match their science inquiry experimentation in Inq-ITS. In J. Kay & R. Luckin (Eds.), *Rethinking learning in the digital age: Making the learning sciences count, 13th International Conference of the Learning Sciences (ICLS) 2018:* (Vol. 3, pp. 1465–1466). International Society of the Learning Sciences. https://repository.isls.org//handle/1/681

Li, H., Gobert, J., & Dickler, R. (2018c). *Automatically assessing scientific explanations in online inquiry.* Paper presented at EARLI (European Association for Research on Learning and Instruction): SIG 20 and 26 Conference, Jerusalem, Israel.

Li, H., Gobert, J., & Dickler, R. (2019a). Testing the robustness of inquiry practices once scaffolding is removed. In A. Coy, Y. Hayashi, & M. Chang (Eds.), *Proceedings of the Fifteenth International Conference on Intelligent Tutoring Systems* (pp. 204–213). Springer. https://doi.org/10.1007/978-3-030-22244-4_25

Li, H., Gobert, J., & Dickler, R. (2019b). Evaluating the transfer of scaffolded inquiry: What sticks and does it last? In S. Isotani, E. Millán, A. Ogan, P. Hastings, B. McLaren, & R. Luckin (Eds.), *Artificial intelligence in education* (pp. 163–168). Springer. https://doi.org/10.1007/978-3-030-23207-8_31

Li, H., Gobert, J., & Dickler, R. (2019c). Scaffolding during science inquiry. In J. C. Mitchell, K. Porayska-Pomsta, & D. Joyner (Eds.), *Proceedings of the Sixth Annual ACM Conference on Learning at Scale* (pp. 1–10). ACM. https://doi.org/10.1145/3330430.3333628

Mislevy, R. J., Behrens, J. T., DiCerbo, K. E., & Levy, R. (2012). Design and discovery in educational assessment: Evidence centered design, psychometrics, and data mining. *Journal of Educational Data Mining, 4*(1), 11–48.

Mislevy, R., Chudowsky, N., Draney, K., Fried, R., Gaffney, T., & Haertel, G. (2003). *Design patterns for assessing science inquiry*, SRI International, Menlo Park, CA.

Mislevy, R. J., Riconscente, M. M., & Rutstein, D. W. (2009). *Design patterns for assessing model-based reasoning (Large-Scale Assessment Technical Report 6).* Menlo Park, CA: SRI International. Retrieved May 31, 2011, from http://ecd.sri.com/downloads/ECD_TR6_Model-Based_Reasoning.pdf.

Mislevy, R., Yan, D., Gobert, J., & Sao Pedro, M. (2020). Automated Scoring with Intelligent Tutoring Systems. In D. Yan, A. Rupp, & P. Foltz (Eds.), *Handbook of automated scoring: Theory into practice.* Chapman and Hall.

Moussavi, R. (2018). *Design, development, and evaluation of scaffolds for data interpretation practices during inquiry.* Doctoral Dissertation, Worcester Polytechnic Institute.

Myford, C. M., & Wolfe, E. W. (2009). Monitoring rater performance over time: A framework for detecting differential accuracy and differential scale category use. *Journal of Educational Measurement, 46*(4), 371–389.

National Research Council. (2012). *A framework for K–12 science education: Practices, crosscutting concepts, and core ideas.* The National Academies Press. https://doi.org/10.17226/13165.

NGSS Lead States. (2013). *Next generation science standards: For states, by states.* The National Academies Press.

Norman, D. (1988). *The design of everyday things.* Basic Books.

OECD. (2010). *PISA 2009 results: What students know and can do—Student performance in reading, mathematics, and science (Volume I).* OECD Publishing.

OECD. (2018). *Education at a glance 2018: OECD indicators,* OECD Publishing. https://doi.org/10.1787/eag-2018-en

Pellegrino, J., Chudowsky, N., & Glaser, R. (2001). *Knowing what students know: The science and design of educational assessment.* National Academy Press.

Reiser, B. J. (2013). *What professional development strategies are needed for successful implementation of the Next Generation Science Standards?* http://www.k12center.org/rsc/pdf/b1_reiser.pdf

Rillero, P. (2016). Deep conceptual learning in science and mathematics: Perspectives of teachers and administrators. *Electronic Journal of Science Education, 20*(2), 1–18.

Sao Pedro, M. A. (2018). Real time formative assessment of NGSS mathematics practices for high school physical science. Awarded by US DoE Institute of Education Sciences (ED-IES-16-C-0022).

Sao Pedro, M. A., Baker, R. S., Montalvo, O., Nakama, A., & Gobert, J. D. (2010). Using text replay tagging to produce detectors of systematic experimentation behavior patterns. In R. Baker, A. Merceron, & P. Pavlik (Ed.), *Proceedings of the 3rd International Conference on Educational Data Mining* (pp. 181–190). Pittsburgh, PA.

Sao Pedro, M. A., Gobert, J. D., & Betts, C. G. (2014). Towards scalable assessment of performance-based skills: Generalizing a detector of systematic science inquiry to a simulation with a complex structure. In *Intelligent tutoring systems* (pp. 591–600). Springer International Publishing.

Sao Pedro, M., Baker, R., & Gobert, J. (2012). Improving construct validity yields better models of systematic inquiry, even with less information. *Proc. of the 20th Conference on User Modeling, Adaptation, and Personalization* (pp. 249–260). Montreal, QC.

Sao Pedro, M., Baker, R., & Gobert, J. (2013b). What different kinds of stratification can reveal about the generalizability of data-mined skill assessment models. *Proceedings of the 3rd Conference on Learning Analytics and Knowledge.* Leuven, Belgium.

Sao Pedro, M., Baker, R., Gobert, J., Montalvo, O., & Nakama, A. (2013a). Leveraging machine-learned detectors of systematic inquiry behavior to estimate and predict transfer of inquiry skill. *User Modeling and User-Adapted Interaction, 23*(1), 1–39.

Scardamalia, M., & Bereiter, C. (2008). Pedagogical biases in educational technologies. *Educational Technology, 48*(3), 3–11.

Schleicher, A. (2019). *PISA 2018: Insights and interpretations.* OECD Publishing.

Shute, V. J. (2011). *Stealth assessment in computer-based games to support learning.* In S. Tobias & J. D. Fletcher (Eds.), *Computer games and instruction* (pp. 503–524). Information Age Publishers.